"Frank Capra said, 'Film is a disease.' I caught the disease early on."

TOM SHONE

MARTIN SCORSESE

For my mother
TS

This revised edition first published in 2022 by
Palazzo Editions Ltd
15 Church Road
London, SW13 9HE
www.palazzoeditions.com

Hardback ISBN 9781786750372

Bound and printed in China

10 9 8 7 6 5 4 3 2 1

Front cover: Ferdinado Scianna/Magnum Photos
Back cover: top: Warner Bros./Pictorial Press; middle left: United Artists;
middle right top: Columbia; middle right bottom: United Artists; bottom: Red Granite
Page 1: In the frame. Portrait by Lynn Goldsmith, 1995.
Page 2: On the set of *Casino* (1995).

Contents

"So many directors have inspired me over the years. I wouldn't know how to start mentioning their names. We are indebted to them as we are to any original filmmaker who manages to survive and impose his or her vision in a very competitive profession.

When we talk about personal expression I am often reminded of Elia Kazan's film, *America, America*, the story of his uncle's journey from Anatolia to America—the story of so many immigrants that came to this country from a very, very foreign land. I kind of identified with it and was very moved by it. Actually I could see myself making this same journey but not from Anatolia, rather from my own neighborhood in New York, which was, in a sense, a very foreign land. I made the journey from that land to moviemaking, which was something unimaginable.

Actually when I was younger there was another journey I wanted to make. It was a religious one—I wanted to be a priest. However I soon realized that my real vocation, my real calling, was movies. I didn't really see a conflict between the Church and movies, the sacred and the profane. Obviously there are major differences but I can also see great similarities between a church and a movie house. Both are places for people to come together and share a common experience and I believe there is spirituality in films, even if it is not one that can supplant faith. I have found that over the years many films address themselves to the spiritual side of man's nature, from D. W. Griffith's film *Intolerance* to John Ford's *The Grapes of Wrath* to Alfred Hitchcock's *Vertigo* to Stanley Kubrick's *2001*, and so many more. It is as if movies answer an ancient quest for the common unconscious. They fulfill a spiritual need that people have to share a common memory."

Martin Scorsese, from *A Personal Journey Through American Movies*, 1995

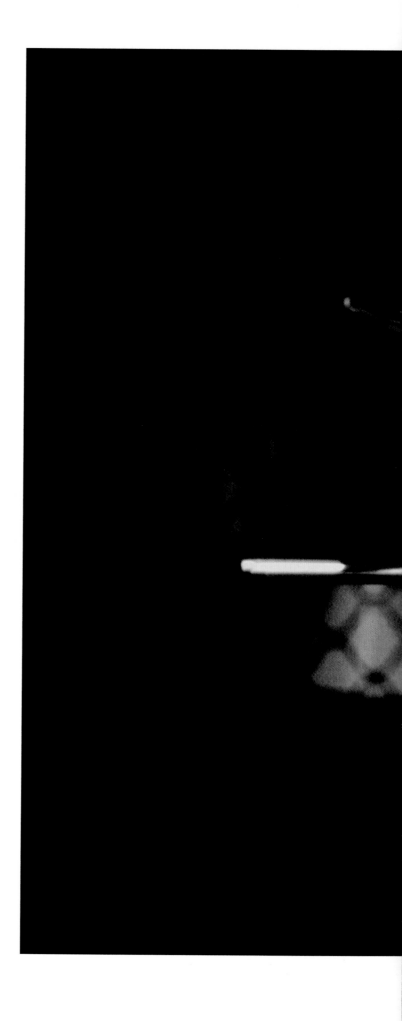

Pages 6–7: Filming *The Age of Innocence* (1993).

Opposite: Portrait by Marcel Hartmann, 2005.

Introduction

His hair is snowy white now, lending him the sleek gravitas of someone lit from above by a higher calling—maybe the priesthood, which he once thought of joining, before cinema became his religion. Alongside Woody Allen and Steven Spielberg, he is one of the handful of movie directors who are not just household names, but household faces, his quick grin, caterpillar eyebrows, and horn-rims signifying "film director" as surely as Hitchcock's rotund silhouette once did.

Now seventy-one, Martin Scorsese brims with undiminished vigor. He speaks fast, with a jackhammer rhythm once memorably compared by *New Yorker* film critic Anthony Lane to that of "a preacher caught between the pulpit and the gents," embarking on energetic, winding riffs that mix cinema history and personal reminiscence—from the look on the dog's face at the climax of Vittorio De Sica's *Umberto D.* ("one of the truly great performances") to the killing of the dog in *Of Mice and Men* ("devastating") to the Bichon Frisé puppy bought for him by his fourth wife, Barbara De Fina, while he was directing

"Films are like having a person around. And to have films be so much a part of your life that you can't live without them is kind of nice, and I thought that's what I wanted to achieve for other people."

9

Above: Boom time—on location for *Taxi Driver* (1976).

Opposite: Demoralized, with *New York, New York* (1977) his star lost some of its shine.

Goodfellas ("poor dog became a nervous wreck because of all the gunshots"). He ends with an explosive bolt of laughter, like an exclamation mark, that fills the room and rocks him back in his seat. He laughs a lot, he says, because as a child afflicted with asthma, he found it hard to laugh at all. These days, any hint of childhood shyness is limited to the fight-or-flight reflex you sometimes catch in his eyes and his position when hearing your questions: head down, staring into his lap, as if your words are missiles—*incoming fire.*

Of all his contemporaries, Scorsese's career is the most emblematic of the tectonic shifts that have transformed the medium in the last fifty years. Are the movies art or business? Can personal filmmaking sustain a full-length career? How long can a European-style auteur last in Hollywood? Thanks to Scorsese, we now know the answer to that last one: nine years. That's the length of the director's stay in Hollywood, measured from the moment when he arrived in Los Angeles in January 1971 and pinned the poster of the Vincente Minnelli film *Two Weeks in Another Town* above his bed, to the winter of 1979, when he returned

to New York, his stock in Hollywood ruined after the failure of *New York, New York*, his health wrecked by cocaine. And in between he made a bunch of movies—including *Mean Streets*, *Taxi Driver*, *Raging Bull*—explosive, hair-trigger works that are among the most personal the American cinema has seen, full of violence and jittery humor, rage and rock 'n' roll. "*Mean Streets* was a fragment of myself," he told an interviewer in 1981. When he read Paul Schrader's script for *Taxi Driver* he thought he had dreamed it. *Raging Bull* was "kamikaze filmmaking," a film he had to make even if it turned out to be his last.

Scorsese didn't make these movies so much as get them off his chest, or give you a piece of his mind. *Taxi Driver* and *Raging Bull* are, among other things, masterpieces of expressionism, the school of cinema pioneered by filmmakers in Weimar Germany and that was later filtered through the looming shadows and velvet dread of American film noir, which sought to use every trick at the directors' disposal— sets, costumes, camera angle, editing—to find a jagged visual poetry for the mental states of its protagonists. Scorsese's camera is umbilically

Robert De Niro as Jake LaMotta alone with his demons: the majestic opening credits of *Raging Bull* (1980), set to the intermezzo from Pietro Mascagni's *Cavalleria rusticana*.

tied to Travis Bickle throughout *Taxi Driver*—when Travis sits down in a diner, the camera sits down with him—and when Jake LaMotta faces off against Sugar Ray Robinson in the climactic fight of *Raging Bull*, Robinson appears backlit, a demonic silhouette, the audience forgotten while the camera tracks and zooms furiously to convey a single fact: Jake is fighting a demon, his own. He could as easily be fighting himself.

The only problem with filmmaking this personal, which bears its connection to its maker like shared breath, is that you can tell instantly when that connection is lost. Reviewing *Shine a Light* for the *New Yorker*, Anthony Lane "got the distinct impression of a style in search of a subject. The same thing happened with *The Aviator* and *The Departed*,

films that felt driven by their own fluency and facility but by no more pressing desires. What Scorsese adores in the Italian cinema that flared up at the end of the Second World War and burned through the next twenty years, and what he himself sought to rekindle in his early New York movies and in *Raging Bull*, was a sense of tales crying out to be told, and of directors being forced into new and incendiary ways of telling. I would trade the whole of *Shine a Light* for the pre-credit sequence in *Mean Streets*, when Harvey Keitel's head hits the pillow and the Ronettes burst and clatter onto the soundtrack with 'Be My Baby.'"

It is a common refrain among Scorsese's critics, particularly those who hold him in highest esteem or put any store by the notion that he

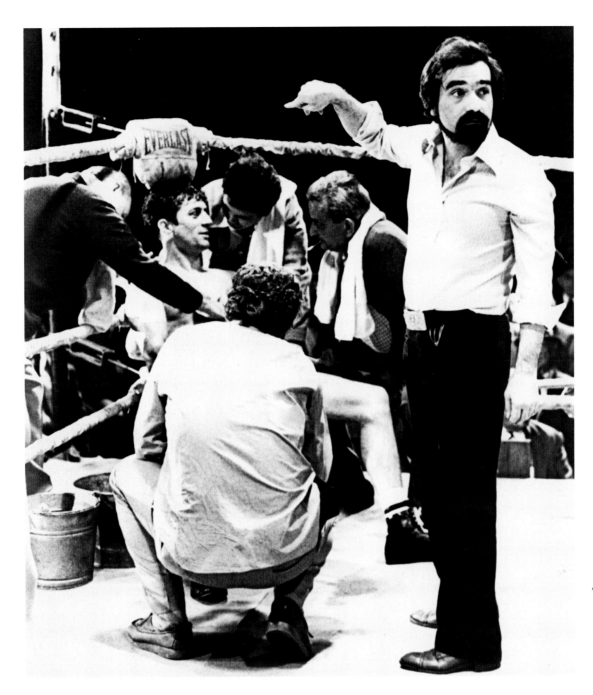

"You make movies, you're in the ring each time." Having been on the ropes in the late seventies, Scorsese came out swinging with *Raging Bull*.

is "America's greatest living director": that nothing in his filmography will ever quite beat the impassioned fluency of his work in the seventies. The questing intensity of his earlier films has given way to a maestro's proficiency. "Scorsese's may be the greatest biography in American film since that of Welles," writes David Thomson in *The New Biographical Dictionary of Film*, "and the most painful."

In the eighties Scorsese returned to New York, a chastened figure taking on smaller, leaner projects like *The King of Comedy, After Hours, The Color of Money*—a period of creative rehab and repair—and yet if there is any single period of Scorsese's career that is most underrated by critics it is this one.

If *Raging Bull* had shown how actors could hold their own in the era of special-effects spectacle—setting the mold for every transformative Oscar-winning performance, from Charlize Theron's in *Monster* to Christian Bale's in *The Fighter*—*After Hours* prefigures the crazy-camera-angled comedy of the Coens, *The King of Comedy* anticipates the dead zones and charisma bypasses of reality TV, while *The Color of Money* is the model for every down-and-dirty comeback vehicle with which movie stars now seek to reboot their careers, from *The Wrestler* to *Dallas Buyers Club*. Scorsese wasn't just surviving, he was single-handedly mapping out the independent-film landscape of the nineties and beyond.

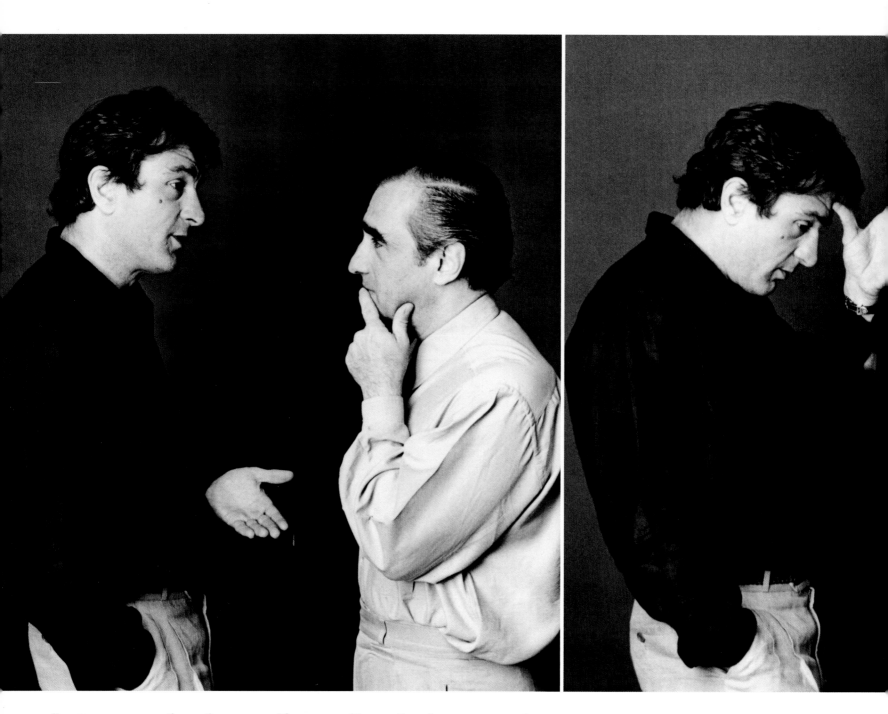

"We seemed to hit it off so well with choosing the same material. Not that we could articulate it. We kind of started to trust each other very strongly."

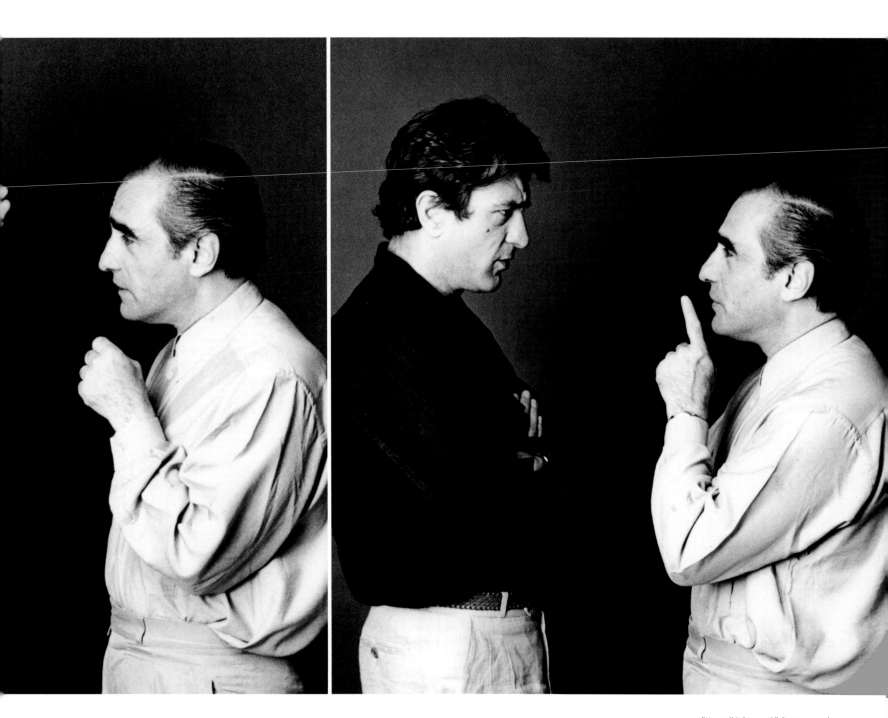

"You talkin' to me?" Scorsese and
Robert De Niro photographed in
1985 by Didier Olivré.

"Religion and the whole concept of the actual practice of Christian ethics in modern society is a theme that I'm always attracted to and is something that goes through my mind and my heart every day. It's a constant part of my life. But you know it's also a way of simplifying things because one does not always want to talk about your personal life to journalists or television, so it's also a way deflecting things. That's all it is, kid, movies and religion, thank you!"

Above: An uncredited cameo as a wealthy homeowner in *Gangs of New York* (2002).

Opposite: Portrait by Ken Schles, 1999.

Then there is *Goodfellas*, one of the greatest second-act comebacks in the history of movies, not least because it replicates the rollercoaster rise and cocaine-fueled fall of Scorsese's first act: The careers of film director and criminal have never felt so entwined. As much as his exposure to organized crime on the streets of Little Italy, Scorsese's experience in Hollywood, burned into him on an almost cellular level, was to prove such a vivid sense memory that any time he told a story that approximated to that meteoric arc—in *Goodfellas*, but also *Casino* and most recently *The Wolf of Wall Street*—his filmmaking would come suddenly, electrifyingly alive. In many ways, the twin themes unifying his later works have been success and failure, and in particular that American breed of success, first explored by Orson Welles in *Citizen Kane*, which is indistinguishable from failure—whether it be the hubris-filled free-for-all of *Goodfellas*, the inverted celebrity of Rupert Pupkin in *The King of Comedy*, the gleaming death runs of Howard Hughes in *The Aviator*, or the ashes and remembrance

of the aged Georges Méliès, brought back to life like a still-hot coal, in *Hugo*.

And Scorsese *has* found success, both at the box office—more than half of his biggest hits have been in the last decade—and at the Academy Awards, finally, with *The Departed*. (The movie won four Oscars in 2007, including for Best Picture and Best Director.) The artist has learned how to make money and win awards. If he bears the adulation and accolades that have followed a little uncomfortably, it may be because he is, in his eighth decade, as painfully aware of his duty to his own talent as the young man who set out in the early sixties, his head full of movies, his heart jumping at the thought of all that he wanted to say. "Whether it's *Shutter Island* or *Hugo* or *Public Speaking* or *Living in the Material World*," he explains, "in the end they're all responses to Hollywood narrative cinema, the kind that I grew up on. So I'll always be drawn there but I don't have the time any more. I try. I try to find that something that I'm burning to say."

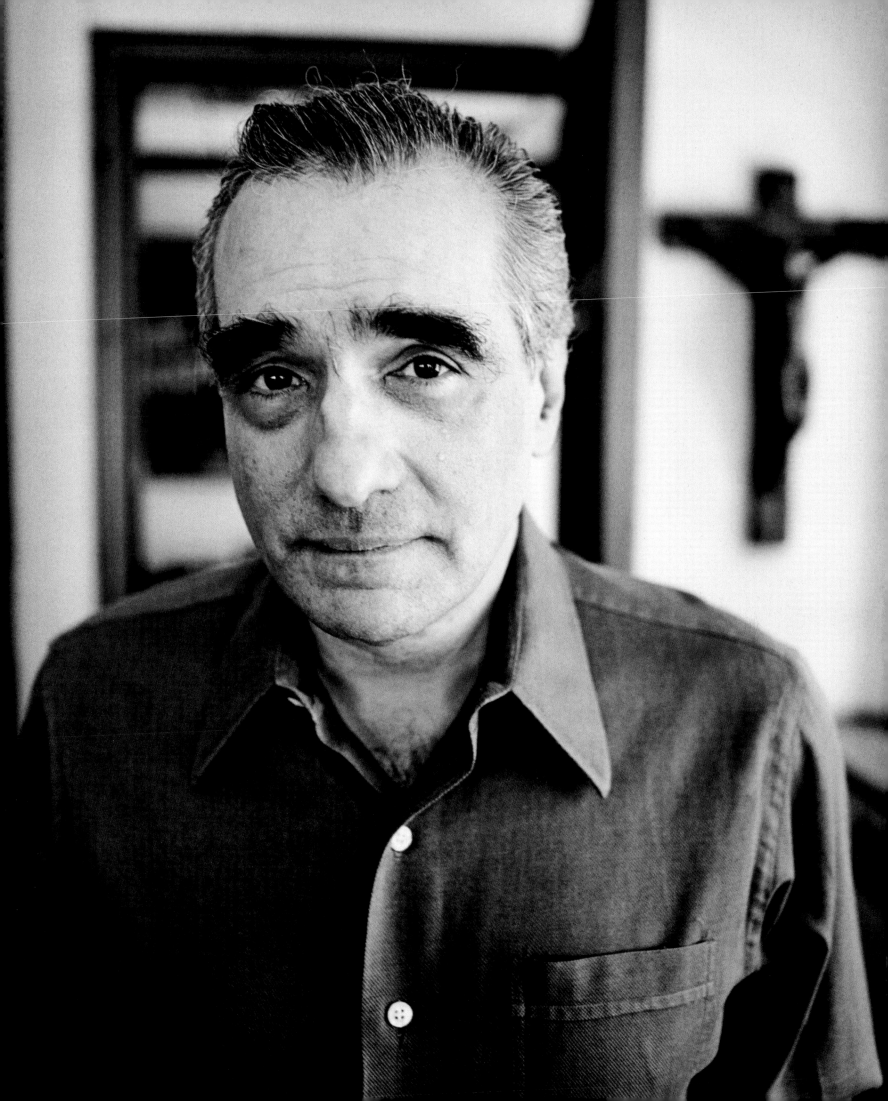

The Early Years

"During the first five or six years of my life I was mainly in the movie theater. I wasn't able to participate in sports or games so it became a place to dream, to fantasize, to feel at home."

Martin Scorsese first felt the power of the streets when he was eight. Up until that point the family had lived in Corona, Queens, in a big two-family house, with a little yard in the back, a tree out front, a park nearby, dogs. His parents, Charles and Catherine, worked in the Garment District as a clothes presser and a seamstress; they were both second-generation Sicilian immigrants who had worked hard to get out of Manhattan to Queens. "For them, it was like moving to the country," Scorsese said. "Really moving up." Then in 1950, for reasons the young Scorsese never properly understood, his father had some trouble with the landlord. There was a confrontation and fistfight which ended with the landlord picking up an ax. The next thing the boy knew, they had to move back to Manhattan, and back in with his grandparents, in the same tenement building on Elizabeth Street in Little Italy where his father had been born—six people in three rooms, a "humiliation." The first night there, Scorsese remembers going to the fire escape, looking down and taking in all the chaos below: "all this life, the

Taking the rooftop air, Scorsese, aged seven months, with his mother (left) and Aunt Lena and her son, Anthony (right).

Happy in Queens playing Cowboys and Indians; he wanted to be an actor.

noise, the kids running up and down the street, winos falling down. It was just a nightmare. I'll never forget that image."

Eventually, the family moved into their own apartment, a little way down the block at 253, with cream-colored brickwork. They were on the third floor, their Uncle Joey right beneath them. Sometimes, when it was hot, Marty and his brother, Frank, would sleep out on the fire escape, soaking up the sights and sounds of the street below, all the windows and doors open, *Aida* blaring from one apartment, rock 'n' roll from another. Little Italy in the 1950s was like a large Sicilian village smack bang in the middle of downtown Manhattan—a self-enclosed world, running by its own rules, most of its residents from Polizzi Generosa or Ciminna, two hillside villages in north-central Sicily. Guns were an everyday fact of life. Kids would bribe cops so they could play stickball in the street. You kept your head down and mouth shut. It was, said one of Scorsese's friends later, like being in occupied France.

Every morning, Marty would walk to school at Saint Patrick's Old Cathedral, the first Catholic cathedral in New York, on the southwest corner of Prince and Mott, carrying his little briefcase, stepping over the glass and blood on the street from where the drunks had attacked each other with bottles. Short, frail, and sickly, Scorsese was a momma's boy. At two weeks, he had coughed himself blue and almost died of whooping cough. At age three the doctors put him in a room and diagnosed a case of chronic asthma. He was always getting beat up by Frank, six years older than him and jealous of all the attention Marty's sickness got him. If it wasn't him and his brother fighting, it was his father and *his* brother, Uncle Joey, a colorful loudmouth who would talk back to whatever movie was playing on TV: *He'll do this and she'll leave him and the guy will kill the other guy.* His commentary was often more entertaining than the movie.

Joey was always in trouble of some sort, always in debt to some mobster he had borrowed money from. Scorsese remembers a lot of family sit-downs to make sure Joey wasn't killed by the Mob, which always ended with his father lending him money and his mother pleading with her husband: *Don't do it, don't lend him the money!*

> "I come from a world which is almost medieval in terms of morality. My father was very strict about that kind of thing. About certain things that are done and certain things that are not done. About trust and betrayal. And that has colored my life all along, and the movies that I've made."

A Scorsese family portrait, late 1940s: elder brother, Frank; parents, Charles and Catherine; and Martin.

How many times do I have to tell you? "Every night I'd hear the drama," he said. "For twenty, twenty-five years that's all I heard. About what's right and what's wrong and you're in a jungle. It had to do with the dignity of the name and respect—walking a tightrope of respect." Marty would sit there, taking it all in, getting steamed himself, unable to say a thing: absorbing, absorbing, absorbing. It wasn't until after his father died in 1993 that Scorsese realized how much *Mean Streets* was all about Charles and that brother of his. Same with *Raging Bull.* "The problem there in the house was something I've been dealing with ever since," he said.

Movie theaters were initially just a place to stash the kid. His father didn't know what the hell else to do with him, so he took him to the movies—to Loew's Commodore, the Yiddish theater on Second Avenue, or the Academy of Music on East Fourteenth Street. They always seemed to arrive in the middle of the movie, and stayed for the second showing until they'd caught up with the point where they walked in. The trailers made a big impression on the boy—Roy Rogers, in his fringed jacket, jumping from a tree onto his horse:

"That's Trigger," his father told him. "Do you know who Trigger is?"

"Yeah, it's something on a gun."

"No, it's a horse. Wanna come back next week and see?"

"Yeah."

It was the fantasy element that snared him at first: Westerns, musicals, science-fiction flicks like Robert Wise's *The Day the Earth Stood Still* or Howard Hawks's *The Thing*, though the director's name didn't mean much to him back then. He wanted to be an actor, a cowboy on a horse like the Red Stallion. He would act out his heroes in the bedroom mirror—Alan Ladd in *Shane*, Victor Mature in *My Darling Clementine*, Gary Cooper in *High Noon*—just as Travis Bickle and Jake LaMotta would act out *their* fantasies in front of a mirror. It used to drive his mother nuts how many times he would watch the same movie: *Is that film on again? Turn it off.* They were one of the first families on their block to get a TV set, a sixteen-inch RCA Victor. He was in the backyard when his cousin Peter rushed out shouting, "come and see a television set that's bigger than the whole house!"

"Watching men and women destroy themselves, ending their lives, dying right in front of you, and then going to church and hearing the priest talk about compassion, that stays with you."

Left: With Frank and Catherine, in Sunday best.

Opposite: As a teenager, Scorsese took photographs of the streets near his home in Little Italy.

Marty was glued. He would come home from school at three, before his parents got back from work, and turn on the TV, or else sit at the kitchen table drawing sketches of what he had seen, perfect little storyboards in 1:1.33 aspect ratio—the standard dimensions for black-and-white movies. He drew war films usually, made by United Artists, with Harold Hecht and Burt Lancaster in the credits. After seeing *High Noon* he drew the sheriff's badge that Gary Cooper threw on the ground next to his boot, just that, and went back again to see the movie again to find out more. He planned a gigantic Roman epic called "The Eternal City," but got bogged down in a gladiatorial fight at the beginning to mark the Emperor's return home from war. He went to 75 mm format for that—wider than widescreen.

He didn't show anyone, fearing ridicule. What did he think he was going to be when he grew up? A cowboy? The career options for asthmatic eight-year-olds in Little Italy in the 1950s seemed to him as follows: gangster or priest. His future as a gangster didn't look too good: getting beat up by his brother all the time, unable even to play stickball on the street. Every day he would see them, the men on the street with the haunted look in their eyes, good men unable to take the pressure any more. Maybe they were in the rackets, in with the wiseguys, but "when the time came for them to do what they had to do, they couldn't do it," so they just imploded. "They were humiliated constantly," Scorsese recalled.

That left the priests. Even the wiseguys would tip their hats to the priest at Mass on Sundays, getting their cars and their pets blessed. The first Mass Scorsese attended, just after entering Catholic school, made a big impression with its pageantry and theater and all the old Italians singing hymns in Latin. He took it all to heart: the guilt, the threat of eternal damnation. He believed he would go to hell if he missed Mass on Sunday or touched meat on Friday. His friends would tease him: *Jeez, Marty, do you really believe all that stuff the priest tells you?* He began to observe private rituals, avoiding certain numbers at all costs, obsessively hoarding lucky objects. For two or three years he was an altar boy, until he was thrown out for not making it to 7 a.m. Mass on

"I wanted to be a priest for a long time, and then I realized I would be a terrible priest."

Out with the gang on Houston Street (Scorsese is third from the right).

time. At the age of fourteen, he enrolled at Cathedral College, a junior seminary in Brooklyn, but fell in love with a girl, grew distracted from his studies, and was finally expelled after a year for roughhousing during prayers. He went instead to Cardinal Hayes High School up in the Bronx, riding on the subway every day to get there and back, the first time he had ventured so far out of Little Italy for any length of time.

Dressed in a leather jacket, listening to Little Richard and Elvis, Marty had found his shtick by now: making everyone laugh by talking very fast, loosing wild riffs and rants, turning his nerves into comedy. "[I wasn't] able to be physical on the same level as the other kids … So I went off in the other direction, as chronicler of the group, trying to be a nice guy to have around." By the age of thirteen or fourteen he had his own gang. They would hang out on weekends in bars or at after-hours clubs, trying to pick up girls, drinking hard liquor but never taking drugs. Whenever there was a fight, someone would yell, "c'mon, quick," and they would all rush over, but somehow—sometimes by accident, sometimes by design—it would all be over by the time they got there.

They were constantly on the lookout for trouble, antennae twitching. "They say my films are about paranoia," Scorsese would later observe, "but to me it's pure survival."

One time they were sitting in the back of a convertible at two in the morning; the owner of the car was a part-time cop, he was giving them a ride, but mouthing off a little too loudly for their liking so Marty and his friends got out to go home. Only one kid stays. The driver pulls off only to get stuck behind a car at the next intersection. The light is green. The guy honks his horn, walks around, finally he gets out his gun: *I'm a cop, move this car.* The other driver does what he's told. The next morning Scorsese hears that a half hour later the guy was driving down Astor Place when he looked over at the car next to his and saw a gun pointed back. He was shot to death, as was the kid. "We could have been killed," said Scorsese. "*Mean Streets* had to be made because I was in the car that night. I went backwards from that. How the hell did he get into a situation like that. We didn't even know the guys. And I said to myself: *That's* the story to tell."

In 1962 Scorsese embarked on a film course at New York University.

His own moviegoing quickly matured. At first he focused on the actors. He and his friends would watch *The Searchers* endlessly, learning the dialogue by heart, acting out the roles, particularly the John Wayne character, as Harvey Keitel would do in *Who's That Knocking at My Door?* Either that or they'd rip some poor movie to shreds. "The way I learned how to make movies was by being a wise guy in the theater," he said. "We were merciless."

But as time went on, he started noticing the same names cropping up again and again in the credits: That guy has a lot of horses in his movies, that one likes tough-guy dialogue. He caught *The Third Man* on TV, with all its canted camera angles. He saw *The Tales of Hoffmann*, and noticed the way the music related to the camerawork. Watching *High Noon*, he noticed the wide-angle shot isolating Cooper from the rest of the community. Why was it so effective to have Cooper so small in the frame like that? Who cut Coop down to size? It was the same line he had traced between the gangsters and the priests: *Who's in charge here?*

The director. The same job Douglas Fowley had in *Singin' in the Rain*, explaining to Jean Hagen what a microphone was; or the father of Kirk Douglas's character in *The Bad and the Beautiful*, so hounded by Hollywood that no one comes to his funeral. They were magnificent figures, full of contradictions—visionaries, rogues, martyrs, who appeared to hail from another world. There seemed no connection to Scorsese's own. Then in 1962 he happened upon a catalogue for New York University, whose Television, Motion Pictures, and Radio Department offered undergraduates one of the few film-history courses with actual hands-on filmmaking opportunities. Scorsese's father helped organize a student loan, and Marty turned up on orientation day to hear a member from each department speak. Someone from the English department got up, then the French department. Finally, the representative from the film department took his turn, a professor by the name of Haig Manoogian, who seemed lit up with the same fervor that had once attracted Marty to the seminary. Scorsese was bitten.

"We were open to so many different ways of making movies that we broke all the rules. That doesn't mean that we did films without learning the rules first. We knew the concept of master and medium shot and close-up and tracking and panning, but I was able to draw on many new films and create a vocabulary for myself with camera movement and cutting. And *What's a Nice Girl Like You* reflects that sort of freedom— kind of young, kind of silly, but …"

Charismatic and fiery, a passionate believer in cinema as a personal art form, Manoogian brought an almost religious zeal to his classes, talking for an hour and a half, fast, even faster than Scorsese. Once, he showed his students Erich von Stroheim's silent masterpiece *Greed* and when one of them asked, "where's the music?" Manoogian was furious. "Do you think this is a show?" he shouted. "Get the hell out." He would weed people out, semester by semester. It was all about making films about what you knew: fly-on-the wall documentaries like those by the Maysles brothers, Richard Leacock, and D. A. Pennebaker. "Suppose what you know is eating an apple," he would tell them. "Try to make a five- to six-minute picture on that. Very hard to do."

The first half of the 1960s was an exciting time to be at film school, just as the French New Wave was breaking. Scorsese marveled at the first two minutes of *Jules et Jim*, the way François Truffaut used voiceover to weave and hop around his story; or the way Jean-Luc Godard alternated jump cuts with adoring long shots of Anna Karina in *Vivre Sa Vie*. No establishing shots. No masters. No coverage.

He saw John Cassavetes's first film, *Shadows*, made with a lightweight 16 mm camera, and was blown away: "It made me realize that I could make a movie." At the local fleapit, he took in Roger Corman's biker-exploitation flick *The Wild Angels* and his Edgar Allan Poe adaptation *House of Usher*, Mario Bava's gothic horror *Black Sunday*, and Kenneth Anger's *Scorpio Rising* and was taken aback, not so much by the Hell's Angels as by the music. He'd always been told you couldn't use rock 'n' roll music because the licensing was too expensive, but here was Elvis, Ricky Nelson, music he knew, blasting from the screen.

The hands-on filmmaking instruction at NYU was limited, as was the equipment—just a 16 mm Arriflex camera and a Cine-Special— but at the end of the first year, Manoogian gave a summer workshop: thirty-six kids, six weeks to write, direct, edit, and print your own movie. They broke into six groups, the professor giving roles to each member: director, cameraman, grip, and so on. Scorsese saw that the ones who had written screenplays got to be director, so he whipped up a script, got it okayed, and was put in charge of a crew—his first.

Opposite: At the center of the action on the *Nice Girl* set.

Right: Scorsese's next student film was the zany crime caper *It's Not Just You, Murray!* (1964).

"Of all my films, *Murray* is the one that shows the old neighborhood, the way it looked in the sixties, right before it began to die out."

He set the film up in five days, and shot it in six: a short skit called *What's a Nice Girl Like You Doing in a Place Like This?* inspired by the new style of Yiddish surrealism being practiced on TV by Mel Brooks and Carl Reiner. It consisted of a fast-paced montage about a guy called Algernon who becomes so obsessed with a picture of a boat on a lake that he can't function socially. After overcoming his phobia for long enough to get married, he relapses and disappears into the picture.

It wasn't much, a tale of "pure paranoia," said Scorsese, "quite silly and childish all about the idea of clichés," but he crammed it with crazy camera angles and jokey in-camera effects—fast motion, slow motion, still photographs alternated with bursts of live action—all strung together with a voiceover narration à la *Jules et Jim*. It won him a scholarship, which his father was able to use to pay for his second-year tuition and led to another short film, *It's Not Just You, Murray!*, made in 1964 during the second semester of his junior year. Viewed today, these early short films remind you of the antic, neurotic humor wriggling through Scorsese's later work. *Goodfellas*, in particular, is foreshadowed

by *It's Not Just You, Murray!*, a larky *jeu d'esprit* about two incompetent small-time crooks named Joe and Murray running bootleg gin out of their backyard until they get busted by the cops. Scorsese's inhalations of Truffaut had paid off. Full of quick-fire dialogue and playful editing, the film has a puckish buoyancy, and an instinctive understanding of how to use voiceover—not to underline the image but play off it, with Joe attempting to explain away how he wound up behind bars ("I was misunderstood … and due to this misunderstanding … I didn't exactly have a great amount of free time to go many places for a while …") as the police raid plays out in one long, continuous take. The film won Scorsese the Jesse L. Lasky Intercollegiate Award at the 1965 Screen Producers Guild Awards, and led to the twenty-three-year-old being invited to Los Angeles for a week to work on an episode of *The Monkees*. "He was the star," classmate Jim McBride said later. "He was on a whole other level from the rest of us. He could quote films at you, describe them shot by shot. While we were humping around trying to find the right exposure, he was making these little gems."

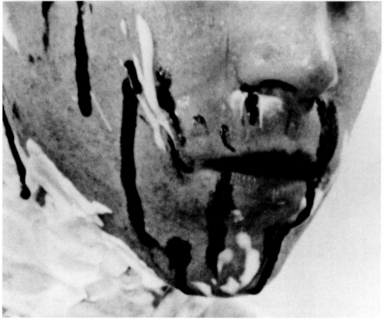

"Consciously [*The Big Shave*] was an angry outcry against the war. But in reality, something else was going on inside of me, I think, which really had nothing to do with the war."

Left: After graduating from NYU Scorsese made *The Big Shave* (1968), another amateur short which operated on one level as an allegory of US involvement in the Vietnam War.

Opposite: Scorsese (bottom left) responds in kind to Max Yasgur, organizer of the 1969 Woodstock Festival. Editing the 1970 documentary of the festival led to Scorsese's entry into Hollywood.

He was also making contact with collaborators who would prove vital to his career, including Thelma Schoonmaker, who helped him pull *What's a Nice Girl Like You Doing in a Place Like This?* back into shape after the negative was cut wrong; and Mardik Martin, his co-writer on *Murray*, an Armenian brought up in Iraq who had fled the country to avoid the draft and could barely speak English. Scorsese was the only one who could talk to him, and bonded instantly with this nervy, diminutive outsider. With *Murray* such a success, they decided to collaborate on something even more autobiographical, drawing on Scorsese's upbringing on the streets; it was initially called "Season of the Witch," but eventually became *Mean Streets*.

His first feature film was another project, shot ostensibly under the auspices of NYU—the first 35 mm film to be made at a university.

Although there was no graduate program at that time, Haig Manoogian helped produce it, with $6,000 from a student loan raised by Scorsese's father. Marty put an ad in *Show Business Weekly* for actors to audition, and had a comedian friend sit behind a desk on the eighth floor of the university's Greene Street building to interview them. One young actor, with narrow shoulders, a mop of hair, and a sweet, insinuating manner, took his seat.

"What are you doing here?" they demanded.

"I came to answer an ad."

"What ad? We didn't take out any ad. Who the hell are you?"

They then got into a terrific argument that went on for several minutes before Scorsese broke character. "You're wonderful," he said. The actor was furious.

"Why didn't you tell me it was an improv?"

"I just never thought about it."

The young actor's name was Harvey Keitel. Scorsese had his lead for *Who's That Knocking at My Door*.

THE DIRECTOR

"I want to communicate on the basic human level—sad, funny, violent, peaceful. I don't want to do movies unless they further me not only as a filmmaker but as a person, unless I can say what I want to say with them."

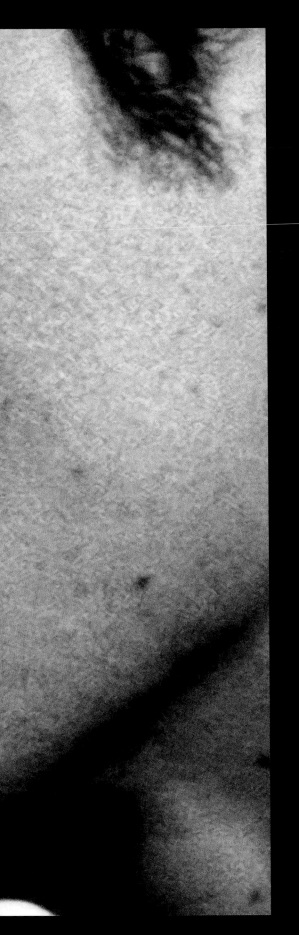

Who's That Knocking at My Door
1967

"In some ways I don't particularly like my first feature, *Who's That Knocking at My Door*, because of all the problems we had making it. I know what I wanted to do when I started the film, but I couldn't do it with the amount of money I had."

Appearing in off-Broadway plays while eking out a living as a court stenographer, Harvey Keitel had been about to give up on acting when he answered Scorsese's ad. The opposite of the volatile director, he had an emotional suppleness which Scorsese found appealing. "I tended to pull back, but he would be much more comfortable around new people, or new women. He was a little more fearless." The two men became fast friends, almost like brothers, during the shooting of *Who's That Knocking at My Door*, with Keitel sleeping in a cot at the director's apartment. They would spend the next two years making the film, off and on, trying to scrape together the money to complete it. "It was a nightmare," said Keitel. "You started shooting a scene, then two months later when you wanted to reshoot, the actors had cut their hair, or had another job and couldn't work."

An early version of the film, shown in Chicago, featuring just Keitel's character and his friends, minus the romance, was a disaster. There was just a lot of drinking and driving around New York without much happening. Everyone hated it. The theater it screened in, the

Biograph, was the one where John Dillinger got shot. "That makes two things that died on that block," joked one of Scorsese's uncles.

Meanwhile, the director's first marriage was falling apart, almost as quickly as it had come together. While still an undergraduate, Scorsese had met and fallen in love with fellow NYU student Laraine Marie Brennan. They were married on May 15, 1965. Upon graduation they moved into her tiny apartment in Jersey City, where they had a baby daughter, Catherine, in the first week of December. Marty would get up in the middle of the night to rock his infant to sleep while catching a late-night showing of *Psycho*, sometimes sneaking out to work on "Season of the Witch" with Mardik Martin. The two men would sit shivering in Martin's car in the dead of winter, their breath steaming up the windows, writing about their New York, their streets, their stories—all the while wondering if they were crazy. "Our wives hated us," recalled Martin. "'Why don't you guys give up and get a decent job? What are you talking about, films?' We couldn't go home because they would pick on us." They thought of calling the movie "This Film Could

Pages 34–5 and above: The lead roles in Scorsese's first full-length movie were played by Harvey Keitel and Zina Bethune.

Save Your Marriage" and filling it with bad advice. Scorsese's short film *The Big Shave*, about a guy who cuts his own throat shaving and bleeds out, came from this time. "A wager pushed to absurd consequences," he called it. "That's how I was feeling at the time."

Finally, a lifeline came his way, from Manoogian and another of his students who had somehow managed to come up with the $37,000 Scorsese needed to finish *Knocking*. They'd found a horror-movie distributor, Joseph Brenner, the man behind the release of such exploitation films as *Violent Women* and *The Sin Syndicate*, who told them he could get it into theaters if they put a nude scene into it. Scorsese was in Amsterdam at the time, so he found a place that looked like a Bowery loft, flew Keitel over, and shot a sex scene which he dropped right into the middle of some dialogue about good and bad girls—virgins and "broads"—and slapped some Doors music on it, smuggling the edited film back through customs.

Eventually completed in 1967, with Scorsese's father paying the lab bill, *Who's That Knocking at My Door* made its premiere at that

year's Chicago Film Festival. A loosely autobiographical sketch, a Portrait of the Artist as a Young Romeo, about a young Italian-American man called J.R. (Keitel), caught between his girl and his friends, between youth and adulthood, between sex and the Church. "I'm sort of in between positions as they say," J.R. tells a blonde (Zina Bethune) he meets on the Staten Island Ferry. He tries to impress her with a ten-minute spiel about John Wayne and *The Searchers*. "I haven't seen that many John Wayne pictures," she says. "Wuz you born in America?" he only half-jokes. Their encounter, it transpires, is being recalled by J.R. while bored during a card game with his friends. Much of the film plays out like that: ribbons of infatuated daydream unspooling in the mind of a young man newly in love. Scorsese captures the Walter Mitty–like schism of infatuation beautifully. Horsing around with his friends, getting drunk, driving around in their Thunderbird to the sound of the Bell Notes, J.R. finds his mind forever wandering—back to a rooftop with Bethune, where he talks and talks endlessly about Lee Marvin ("he kills people, he breaks

Starting here, motifs of the Crucifixion would occur frequently in Scorsese's work.

"We were overambitious until we found that we couldn't move the camera to get the angles we wanted. However, it was accurate about the way we were when nothing was going on, just sitting or driving around. On one level that's what the film was about; on another it was about sexual hang-ups and the Church."

furniture"), or to his room, where they make out beneath the watchful eye of his Mary Magdalene figurines—a remarkable sequence of close-ups, the two figures limned by the sinuous curve of cheek, lips, and eyelashes, the black-and-white photography anticipating the similarly tender love scene in *Raging Bull*.

The film also features a glorious slo-mo sequence of J.R. and his friends fooling around with a gun, everyone ducking as it swings their way; a bravura shoot-out (imaginary) constructed entirely from stills of movie posters; and a hike up a mountain in the Catskills, with J.R. and his friends kvetching all the way ("It isn't bad enough I have to spend the day in a bar with a bunch of hillbillies, drinking …"). Everyone seems to be doing their best Scorsese impression, including Keitel, whose moon-faced features and mischievous grin summon all the yearning Scorsese put into his pictures before he fell in with that saturnine genius Robert De Niro. The last third of the picture is more indicative of what was to come, with Keitel recoiling from Bethune upon learning that she has

been raped, then making a loftily condescending attempt to "forgive" her. Scorsese's Catholicism fumigates the film's climax as overpoweringly as a thurible. He would find a much better way of interleaving similar material in *Mean Streets*, although *Who's That Knocking at My Door* remains an astonishing debut, fluid and vital and heartfelt. A young Roger Ebert caught it in Chicago and called it "artistically satisfying and technically comparable to the best films being made anywhere." The film subsequently opened in 1970 at the Carnegie Hall cinema in New York, where Roger Corman got John Cassavetes in to see it. "This movie is as good as *Citizen Kane*," said Cassavetes. "No, it's better than *Citizen Kane*. It's got more heart." Scorsese was walking on air.

More good news: An agent, Harry Ufland, had seen his short films, and signed him up, immediately getting him a job directing *The Honeymoon Killers*. Scorsese didn't like the script but he agreed anyway, and set about shooting the two-hundred-page screenplay entirely in master shots, imposing himself as a virtuoso of the camera,

trying to turn a simple low-budget noir into a Carl Dreyer film. He wasn't trying to make the movie, he was trying to make his reputation. He was fired after one week—"and rightly so." Finally, after co-editing the 1970 documentary *Woodstock*, he got a call from Fred Weintraub, a vice president at Warner Brothers, who asked him to edit another rock documentary, called *Medicine Ball Caravan*. "Why don't you come out to LA?" said Weintraub. "Come out for two weeks and see what you can do with the picture. I won't screw you too bad. And you'll have a nice time. See what happens."

The offer seemed too good to pass up. There was no other way to get into Hollywood at that time. So in January of 1971 he moved out to Los Angeles, by himself, renting an apartment and pinning the poster of the 1962 Vincente Minnelli film *Two Weeks in Another Town* above his bed to remind him of all the directors he had worshipped as a young boy: Minnelli, Ford, Ray, Hawks. His marriage was over. Time to direct movies.

Boxcar Bertha

1972

"Mostly I attempted to show the characters as people acting like children, playing with violence until they start getting killed."

"Roger gives you great freedom as long as you stay within the 'Corman genre'. *Boxcar Bertha* had guns and costumes, so I accepted."

In his first two weeks in Hollywood, Scorsese met Francis Ford Coppola, Steven Spielberg, and George Lucas. A William Morris agent put him in contact with Roger Corman, who asked him if he was interested in doing a sequel to his 1970 gangster movie *Bloody Mama*. Brian De Palma also introduced him to a writer named Paul Schrader who had a script in his back pocket called *Taxi Driver*. It was a glorious time. "We were just so excited," Scorsese would say later. "The period from '71 to '76 was the best period, because we were just starting out. We couldn't wait for our friends' next pictures, Brian's next picture, Francis's next picture, to see what they were doing."

After his experience on *The Honeymoon Killers*, Scorsese was nervous about doing Corman's film, a Depression-era drama called *Boxcar Bertha*, essentially a Bonnie and Clyde knock-off about a persecuted union organizer, "Big" Bill Shelly (David Carradine), and his hobo girl, Bertha Thompson (Barbara Hershey), who go on the run, riding boxcars, after Bertha is caught up in the murder of a wealthy gambler. The script ran to two hundred pages and was very dense.

"Rewrite as much as you want," Corman told him, "but remember, Marty, that you must have some nudity at least every fifteen pages"— an instruction that Scorsese managed to follow, shooting some quite unexpectedly tender scenes between Hershey and Carradine, who were lovers at the time. This time, he storyboarded the entire movie. Each character was going to die in his own way, with different camera angles. He rewrote the script, enlarging Barry Primus's character, a cowardly Yankee gambler who became almost Scorsese's alter ego, and loaded the film with references to *The Wizard of Oz*, including the line "Don't pay attention to the man behind the curtain." There would be a Scarecrow, Lion, and Tin Man (Carradine, Primus, and Bernie Casey). He even had Hershey's hair styled into Dorothy-like pigtails.

It was a perfect example of what Scorsese would later call a "smuggler's film," meaning a work for a studio layered with auteur's references that only some people would pick up on, like a dog whistle. Such facetiousness shows how queasy he was at the prospect of being leashed in the first place. Shot on location down in Arkansas in just

Pages 40–41: Barbara Hershey in the title role of Bertha Thompson.

Opposite: Hershey and David Carradine were so in love they didn't have to act.

Above: Scorsese with Barry Primus, whose part the director enlarged in his rewrite of the script.

Right: Cast and crew on location in Arkansas.

twenty-four days, with his first full cast and crew and a budget of $600,000, this was to be his first experience of working for a studio, even a small one like Roger Corman's American International Pictures. Corman had a reputation for being pretty hands-off, but even so he came down to the set to see how everything was going, and later visited Scorsese in his motel room.

"Do you have any preparation?" he asked him.

"I'll show you," said Scorsese, bringing out his storyboards, three or four hundred of them. "This cuts to this and this goes that way, and this is just normal coverage but then there's a move this way …"

"Wait a minute. Do you have this for the whole picture?"

"Yes."

"I don't have to see any more."

Corman took to walking around the set scowling, to put the fear of God into the crew and hurry them up. As they neared the end of the shoot, he took Scorsese aside and told him he needed a chase scene. Scorsese asked for another day's shooting. Corman refused, but Scorsese somehow shoehorned it into his already bulging schedule. With Corman still hovering over him in the editing room, Scorsese finished the film on time, coming in at a tidy ninety minutes.

The head of AIP, Samuel Arkoff, hated the film—the digressions, the private jokes, the New Wave artsiness, all the details Scorsese loved. "The improvised interview in the brothel, the old man eating glass, the whore at the back of the room who is actually a man in drag, the gag with the doors, I stole it, and the interview too, from *Vivre Sa Vie*— and the mood of fantasy that pervades the whole episode. Everything in the film is so weird. And Barbara Hershey and David Carradine had such fun. They were so madly in love that they didn't need to act."

The film remains an endearing oddity, an early bit of creative slumming which suffers from the tonal drift that would come to characterize Scorsese's work for hire. He keeps the action coming—there's a plane crash, a riot, a jail break, a chase, a train heist, all strung together with a breezy harmonica score, the plot seemingly summoned into existence solely to put a grin on the face of Barbara Hershey, skipping boxcars with Carradine and his gang. Hershey was twenty-four at the time, and the movie luxuriates in her flushed, hayseed

beauty from its first shot: Bertha hoisting up her dress to scratch her thigh while Carradine gazes on her lustfully from a railroad line. It's an exploitation picture, unquestionably, with Hershey in the loosest-fitting wardrobe in every scene, but the frankness with which Bertha's own sexuality is addressed, plus Scorsese's fluency with the camera, wipes any leer from the film. It has a genuine erotic charge.

His editing too is already showing great sophistication, squeezing every drop from his low-budget setups. There is a shotgun shoot-out

"I used the element of surprise violence to emphasize that when you least expect it, things are destroyed, people are killed."

Left: Bertha with Von Morton (Bernie Casey), one of the other members of her boxcar-hopping gang.

Above, right: The gang pulls off a daring train robbery.

Right: The shocking and incongruous crucifixion scene at the end of the movie.

at the end, with people blown back out of their boots, the camera following them as they fly through the air, that is a small marvel of setup, choreography, and cutting. The climax—a crucifixion, with Carradine nailed against the side of a train—was in the script before Scorsese got to it, although he would later match it, shot for shot, in *The Last Temptation of Christ*, where it properly belongs. It has no place here.

Scorsese showed a rough cut of two hours to John Cassavetes, who took him back to his office and laid it out: "Marty, you've just spent a whole year of your life making a piece of shit. It's a good picture, but you're better than the kinds of people who make this kind of movie … Why don't you make a movie about something you really care about?"

"I have this script I keep working on."

"Do that."

"Although it needs a rewrite."

"Rewrite it then!"

Scorsese went looking for "Season of the Witch."

Mean Streets

1973

"You don't make up for your sins in church. You do it in the streets. You do it at home. The rest is bullshit and you know it."

"I just wanted to make, like, an anthropological study; it was about myself and my friends. And I figured even if it was on a shelf, some years later people would take it and say that's what Italian-Americans on the everyday scale—not the Godfather, not big bosses, but the everyday scale, the everyday level—this is what they really talked like and looked like and what they did in the early seventies and late sixties. Early sixties even. This was the lifestyle."

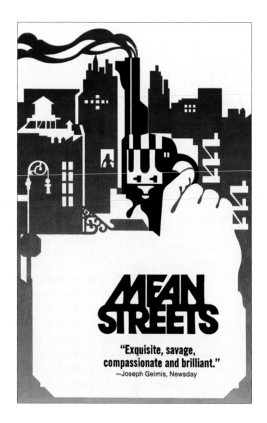

MEAN STREETS

"Exquisite, savage, compassionate and brilliant."
—Joseph Gelmis, Newsday

Above: Charlie (Harvey Keitel) talks business with his Uncle Giovanni (Cesare Danova).

Opposite: Outside a neighborhood pasticceria/gelateria.

Pages 46–7: Scouting for locations in Little Italy.

The title came from Raymond Chandler—"Down these mean streets a man must go …"—and was suggested by Scorsese's friend Jay Cocks, film critic for *Time* magazine. Scorsese thought it a little pretentious at first, and it caused him no end of trouble while on location in Little Italy. People would come up to him, angry, and say, "There's nothing wrong with these streets …" Scorsese would tell them, "No, it's only the preliminary title," but got so nervous he took to wearing white gloves to stop himself from biting his nails. "You had to make deals with everybody," he said. "By the end of it, when my father heard about it he came to me and said, 'You should have talked to me. I could have spoken to so-and-so, and so-and-so. And then he would have talked to so-and-so's father. And we could have made a deal with such-and-such.' I said, 'No, I didn't want to get you involved with it.'"

In one sense, his father couldn't have been more involved, for the story took off from the nightly arguments Marty had heard as a boy between his father and his Uncle Joey. The film is a study of similar familial exasperation, pairing a dangerously soft-hearted hood with his friend Johnny Boy, a neighborhood nut he is constantly having to dig out of trouble, putting off all the confrontations—"the worst thing he could do"—until they boomerang on him. He even named the lead character, Charlie, after his father, and filled the movie with all the sights and sounds that had spilled out of the social clubs and onto the streets in the summers of 1963 and 1964—the Rolling Stones, the Ronettes, the Chantels, Ray Barretto, the Shirelles. "*Mean Streets* was an attempt to put myself and my old friends on the screen," he said, "to show how we lived, what life was like in Little Italy." It was "a declaration, a statement of who I am."

"I remember De Niro at certain dances which were run by parish priests for Italian-Americans … So when it came to *Mean Streets* I thought, 'It's a perfect part for him.' He had an apartment on Fourteenth Street at the time and he had clothes from the old days. I remember him putting a hat on and I said to myself, 'Oh, it's perfect.' I didn't tell him that, I just told him it was good. But when I saw the hat I knew it was Johnny Boy."

Johnny Boy (Robert De Niro) and Charlie may not always see eye to eye, but off screen De Niro and Keitel were fast friends.

The script he had been working on with Mardik Martin all these years, "Season of the Witch," was heavily reworked. Marty's girlfriend at the time, Sandy Weintraub, daughter of producer Fred Weintraub (who had got him out to Los Angeles in the first place), pointed out that the stories he had told her about growing up in Little Italy—letting off firecrackers, a fight in a pool hall over one guy calling another guy a "mook"—were far funnier than anything in the script, which was hung too heavy with Catholic angst. "Why don't you put *those* scenes in the picture?" she suggested. So he took out all the religious stuff and put in the pool hall and the firecrackers.

Much of it was improvised. Working out of the Gramercy Park Hotel, Scorsese spent ten days with his cast, untangling the web of relationships between the main characters—Charlie (Harvey Keitel), Johnny Boy (Robert De Niro), Tony (David Proval), Michael (Richard Romanus), and Teresa (Amy Robinson). They recorded the rehearsals and then used the tapes to further rewrite the script, incorporating what they had improvised. The scene between De Niro and Keitel

in the back of the club was written this way, although when it came time to shoot it, Keitel couldn't remember what he'd done and had to improvise again. The fight with the garbage pails was similarly improvised while shooting. The fight in the pool hall was sketched out but Scorsese had tired of writing the dialogue; George Memmoli (Joey) came up with a gag and they were rolling: thirty-six setups, sixteen hours of shooting straight through. By the end of the day, they had the scene.

Most days they averaged about twenty-four setups: still an astonishing number. Financed on a pittance ($600,000) by Jonathan Taplin, a twenty-five-year-old rock-music tour manager who was looking to get into the movie business, and shot quickly (twenty-seven days in the fall of 1972), *Mean Streets* was filmmaking in the Roger Corman manner, with a crew filled out with graduates from the nearby NYU shepherded by Corman's associate producer, Paul Rapp, who told Scorsese he had only six days and nights to shoot in New York for the exterior scenes at locations such as the old Police Building on

> "People always ask me why I'm interested in characters like the ones in *Mean Streets*. The answer is I grew up with a lot of these people. Before I knew what it was that they did, I thought it was all normal."

Mean Streets made the name not only of Scorsese but also De Niro. The pair would go on to make another seven movies together over the following two decades.

Centre Street and the cemetery at St. Patrick's Old Cathedral. The rest, all the interiors, would have to be done in twenty days in Los Angeles. Scorsese had to piece the whole thing together in the editing room from two or three angles. When David Carradine gets shot in a bar he's in Los Angeles, but the figure we see falling down in the street does so in New York. When De Niro attempts to shoot the lights out of the Empire State Building, he fires a gun from a rooftop in New York and hits a window in Los Angeles. "Bobby, make sure you know exactly where you are so we'll get it," Scorsese told him.

Mean Streets marked the beginning of a collaboration with Robert De Niro that has, so far, taken in eight feature films. They first met at a Christmas dinner at Jay Cocks's apartment, at the behest of Brian De Palma, who had just worked with the actor on *Hi, Mom!* The notoriously monosyllabic De Niro didn't say much through the dinner. Finally, he piped up, "I know you. I know who you used to be with," and started reeling off names—Joey and Curty and some of the other guys Marty used to hang out with as a kid. "How did you know that?"

he asked. It turned out that when De Niro was sixteen, he had been part of his own gang that hung out around Grand Street and Hester. They weren't exactly rivals, but there was "a little bit of frisson" between them, said Scorsese. De Niro had always stood out as the nicest one, the sweet one. That night they quietly struck up the rapport that would last decades, with the two men finishing each other's sentences even when there were no sentences to finish. "It's like we just look at each other, and shake our heads sometimes and move on," Scorsese would say.

De Niro initially turned down the role of Johnny Boy, Teresa's out-of-control cousin. He wanted to play Charlie, the lead, torn between his conscience and the Mob. The film's backers, meanwhile, wanted a star, and were in talks to get Jon Voight, then coming off the Oscar-winning *Midnight Cowboy*. Scorsese held fast to Keitel, for whom he had written the film, persuading De Niro to change his mind and take Johnny Boy. The friendship between the two actors was immediately palpable on screen. "I thought what was going on between Harvey and Bob was great in those three-and-a-half weeks of shooting.

"There was an article in the *New York Times* saying, 'Who the hell cares about these people?' And I just thought: 'Well, *I* do.'"

They understand that, ultimately, the relationship is based on loving each other, but that one was getting more out of it than the other."

Still, Keitel almost lost the part to Voight, who delayed his decision right down to the wire, as the cameras were being unpacked. Keitel understood that if the star committed, it would guarantee wider distribution and he was ready to back out, take a smaller part. Finally, during the San Gennaro Festival, which was to form the backdrop for the film's opening sequence, Scorsese made the call to Voight from a rooftop looking down at the parade, and was told: No, he wasn't taking it. Scorsese turned to Keitel and held out Charlie's coat, bought that day from Barney's.

"Harvey, here's your coat," he said. "Go down. Let's follow him in the street, in the festival …"

They hit the streets and started filming.

Mean Streets feels like that—the film of someone who has just been told that he has seen off the biggest star in Hollywood, a Barney's coat draped around his shoulder and told: Go, go walk the streets of your neighborhood. It is a cock-of-the-walk film, flushed with youth's exuberance and cheek. High Italian society of the sixteenth century had a word for the quality it was most vital for courtiers to possess: *sprezzatura,* the impression of mastery, "a certain nonchalance, so as to conceal all art and make whatever one does or says appear to be without effort and almost without thought" (Baldassare Castiglione, *The Book of the Courtier,* 1528). The acting of Marcello Mastroianni has *sprezzatura,* as does Fellini's *I Vitelloni* and *8½.* And so, too, does *Mean Streets,* a film often mistaken for Scorsese's first, for it has the self-announcing virtuosity of a debut, with Scorsese himself, not Keitel, delivering the opening voiceover: "You don't make up for your sins in church, you do it in the streets, you do it at home, the rest is bullshit and you know it." Barreled along by a young filmmaker's rush to get seemingly everything on screen, the film has the fresh apprehension of a diary. "I like spaghetti and clam sauce, mountains, Francis of Assisi, chicken, lemon and garlic, John Wayne, and I like you," says Charlie to Teresa, while walking on the beach. "I hate the sunshine," he grumbles, anxious to get back to the bars and dives, the cramped

Charlie finds relief from the pressures of gangland in the arms of Johnny Boy's epileptic cousin Teresa (Amy Robinson).

apartments with their constant threnody of traffic noise and police sirens, where Charlie and his gang make the rounds collecting debts, flogging Jap adaptors and cartons of Marlboro, or else stiffing kids for twenty bucks to go to the movies where they sit cackling in the back row. Scorsese whip-pans the camera for every entrance and exit, as if to say: Will you look at this? Will you just look at Manhattan seen from the back of a Thunderbird? Look at this assassin (played by Scorsese himself) letting his hair down before striking. Look at this drunk, refusing to die. Isn't that something? Or smoke rings, blown in slow motion. Or a panther and tiger cubs pacing back and forth

in their cages. Charlie and his gang scatter, only to be drawn back, mesmerized, as if by their own reflection.

American cinema had never seen anything like it. Comparing the film to *I Vitelloni*, the *New Yorker* film critic Pauline Kael wrote:

"Martin Scorsese's *Mean Streets* is a true original of our period, a triumph of personal filmmaking. It has its own hallucinatory look; the characters live in the darkness of bars, with lighting and color just this side of lurid. It has its own unsettling, episodic rhythm and a high-charged emotional range that is dizzyingly sensual … No other American gangster-milieu film has this element of personal obsession;

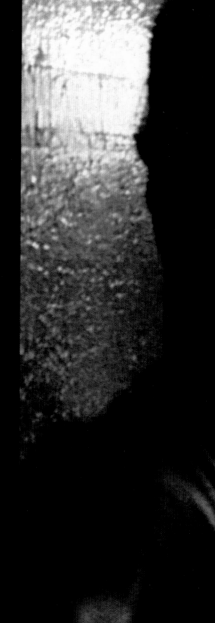

"*Mean Streets* is certainly violent, but that's the lifestyle. What are you going to do about it? These characters live in a violent world, physically and emotionally. If you don't like it, I guess don't look at it."

Left: By pointing a gun at Michael Longo (Richard Romanus), Johnny Boy crosses the line.

Above: "You two-faced, dirty fuckin' bastard! Don't you ever hit me again!" A flare-up between Johnny Boy and Charlie.

"For me, there's no such thing as 'senseless' violence. In the fight in the pool room, I held it long because of the sense of helplessness, the silliness of the whole thing."

Opposite: "I'll give you mook!" A throwaway insult is the cue for violence in the pool hall.

Right: Having carried out the hit on Johnny Boy, Jimmy Shorts (played by Scorsese) and Michael briefly admire their work before speeding away from the scene.

there has never before been a gangster film in which you felt that the director was saying 'this is my story.'"

The Godfather, released just one year earlier, had never managed, nor sought, this level of ebullience, instead heading in the direction of mahogany-hued epic. *Mean Streets* features murders and car crashes and horrible gunshot wounds to the neck, and yet the whole thing feels as light as a bicycle. If *Mean Streets* ousts *The Godfather* as the Mob's favorite gangster film—at least according to wiseguy-turned-informer Henry Hill, Scorsese's source for *Goodfellas*—it may be because crime is not, in fact, its real subject. "Grandiosity, paranoia, and saving face are the movie's subjects, rather than real crime," wrote the ever-perceptive Manny Farber, an early fan of the pool-hall scene in which a fight breaks out between Keitel's gang and the owner, a "feisty fatty in tennis shoes who turns into Toshiro Mifune," in Farber's words. It is all filmed in one continuous take, to the sound of the Marvelettes' "Please Mr. Postman," until the police arrive, at which point peace breaks out and the former adversaries attempt to explain away their knives, "That's a nail file." Then just as they are about to drink each other's health and leave, the fight breaks out again—violence snatched from the threat of conciliation.

Everything in the film stands on a knife-edge, including the tone, which flips from hilarity to menace and back again, frequently several times within the same scene. Moods bleed into their opposite; scenes career into the back of one another. A love scene, shot in tribute to Godard's *Breathless*, explodes with gunshot sound effects; a fight with trashcan lids between De Niro and Keitel ends with the pair wearily climbing into the same bed together at 6 a.m.—"Want me to tuck you in, sweetie?" Of all the actors in the film it is De Niro who makes most use of these switchbacks of mood, riding them like cresting waves before they crash gloriously. From his opening scene, in which he leaves his pants at the coat check, only to have to explain to Charlie where he got the fancy threads, De Niro is a picture of nervy insolence in his porkpie hat, sending forth perfect arias of bullshit ("*Bing! Bing! Bing!* I lose four hundred dollars!") until challenged, at which point he retreats and equivocates, before rallying for another push of bravado.

"See, the whole idea was to make a story of a modern saint, a saint in his own society, but his society happens to be gangsters."

The bloody climax to the film:
Johnny Boy pays the price for pushing
Michael too far, but Charlie manages
to stagger away from the wreck.

It is a performance rich in the comedy of saving face and thin-skinned effrontery, running atop a river of perceived and potential humiliations that would, as time went by, increasingly transfix the actor. It would be a long time before De Niro allowed himself to be this entertaining again.

The film premiered at the New York Film Festival in the fall of 1973, where Scorsese got a standing ovation, although his mother, asked by a journalist what she thought of her son's movie, was keen to establish the fact that, for all the picture's f-bombs, "we never used that word

in the house." The critics were ecstatic. "An unequivocally first-class film," wrote Vincent Canby in the *New York Times*. In his review for the *Chicago Sun-Times*, Roger Ebert wrote that "in countless ways, right down to the detail of modern TV crime shows, *Mean Streets* is one of the source points of modern movies." Embedded in her rave calling it "a true original," Pauline Kael nonetheless sounded a note of caution:

"Though the street language and operatic style may be too much for those with conventional tastes, if this picture isn't a runaway success the reason could be that it's so original that some people will be dumbfounded—too struck to respond."

Alice Doesn't Live Here Anymore

1974

"We never intended it to be a feminist tract. It was a film about self-responsibility and also about how people make the same mistakes again and again."

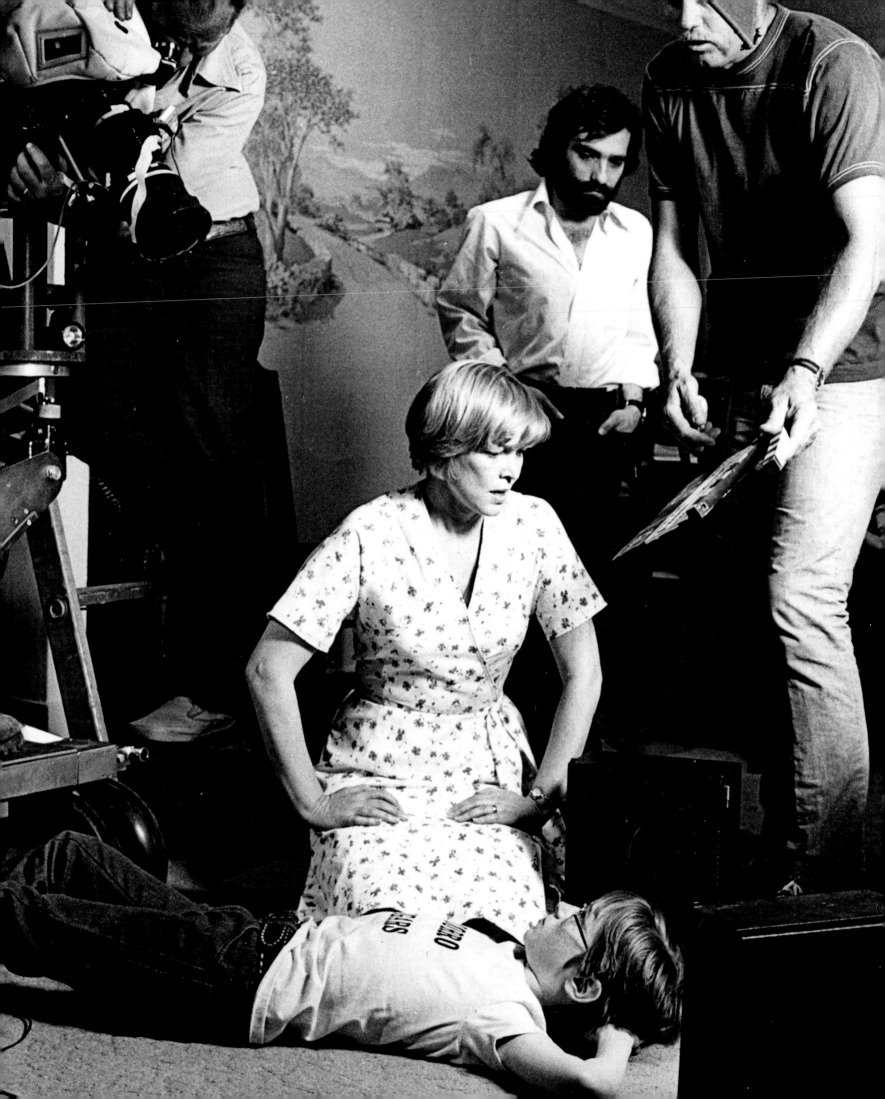

A movie for everyone
who has ever dreamed of
a second chance.

ELLEN BURSTYN and KRIS KRISTOFFERSON in
"ALICE DOESN'T LIVE HERE ANYMORE"

A DAVID SUSSKIND PRODUCTION
and introducing ALFRED LUTTER Written by ROBERT GETCHELL
Produced by DAVID SUSSKIND and AUDREY MAAS Directed by MARTIN SCORSESE
From WARNER BROS. ○ A WARNER COMMUNICATIONS COMPANY TECHNICOLOR®

Page 63: On set with Ellen Burstyn
(Alice) and Alfred Lutter (Tommy).

An unusually calm moment on set with
associate producer and then-girlfriend
Sandy Weintraub.

As Pauline Kael feared, *Mean Streets* stumbled at the box office. Nobody at Warner Bros. knew how to sell the film. They had two posters, one with a gun on it, one with a dead body. Don Rugoff, the influential owner of a chain of art-movie theaters, had told Scorsese, "The ads that don't sell are the ads that have guns and dead bodies." Scorsese couldn't believe his ears. "Don, we just made two ads and those are our ads."

It got crushed by another Warner Bros. film, *The Exorcist*—on its way to an eventual domestic haul of $193 million—although Scorsese would also soon benefit. Ellen Burstyn, the Oscar-nominated star of *The Exorcist*, was looking for somebody young and exciting to direct a script by Robert Getchell called *Alice Doesn't Live Here Anymore*, about a widow and her twelve-year-old son on the road together in the American southwest, looking for a better life. Burstyn went to dinner with Francis Ford Coppola who told her to see *Mean Streets*. She was impressed: *That's the guy*, she thought. *Whoever the director is, he knows how to let actors be real*. She called John Calley, head of

production at Warner Bros., who sent the script to Scorsese, who by that point was getting so many scripts about gangsters he had to ask his girlfriend, Sandy Weintraub, to sort through them. Weintraub read *Alice* and loved it, telling him, "This is one of the few scripts that has any interesting characters in [it]."

"I don't know anything about women," fretted the director at a meeting with Burstyn, Weintraub, and Calley.

"Women are just people," said Weintraub.

Scorsese did like the idea of a woman, married for thirteen or so years, suddenly alone with a kid. Alice's sass reminded him of his own mother. "She was more Old World, but she had that kind of humor, and irony, constantly making wisecracks—constantly hitting your ego. And her own—deflating it." His feelings about his family were going through an evolution. On the one hand, he would finish *Alice* and plunge straight into making *Italianamerican*, a documentary about his parents in which they talked about their experiences as descendants of Italian immigrants. On the other hand, there was a part of him

"Because I was receiving a lot of scripts now, Sandy Weintraub read it first and said it was really interesting. I thought it was a good idea too, dealing with women for a change, only I wanted to improvise some of it and change the third part dealing with the farmer. I was only partly happy with the result, as we really shot a three-and-a-half hour picture and then had to cut it down to less than two hours."

Following her success with *The Exorcist*, Ellen Burstyn had creative control of the project and chose Scorsese as director.

that "wanted to erase everything of where I came from." Since dating Weintraub he had grown his hair and taken to wearing cowboy shirts bought from the retro shops in Los Angeles. The couple moved into a small Spanish house off Mulholland Drive overlooking the Valley, just west of the homes of Marlon Brando and Jack Nicholson, where they fought constantly. "He was a wall puncher. And a phone thrower," Weintraub would later say. "We could not keep a phone in the house."

Scorsese suspected that he had quit his marriage only to make the same mistake all over again, and it was out of this suspicion that *Alice* grew, "a picture about emotions and feelings and relationships and people in chaos," he said. "Which is something very personal to Ellen and me at the time. We felt like charting all that and showing the difference and showing people making terrible mistakes, ruining their lives then realizing it and trying to push back when everything is crumbling … It was basically like analysis for all of us. It's crazy."

Shooting on location in Tucson, Arizona, surrounded by miles and miles of desert, the agoraphobic director "got crazy with the

cactus alone." He hired a crew of mostly women, including Weintraub as associate producer, Toby Rafelson as production designer, and Marcia Lucas as editor. The kid, Alfred Lutter, was pulled out of a casting call of three hundred or so child actors after Weintraub asked him what he wanted to be when he grew up. "A stand-up comedian," he replied. This, Marty had to see. Initially quiet with Scorsese, Lutter opened up with Burstyn in the room. In fact, he wouldn't shut up, pestering her with questions throughout the shoot—"How do you manage to cry like that?"—to the point where she was begging him to leave her alone. "With this kid, she had to hang on," said Scorsese. "She kept looking at me. We kept giving each other looks and writing things down."

With three months of preproduction to play with, even more of *Alice* was improvised than *Mean Streets*: the scene with Burstyn and Diane Ladd in the restroom, and between Burstyn and Kris Kristofferson in the kitchen after they have first had sex. With a budget three times that of *Mean Streets*, this was Scorsese's first film for a

"*Alice Doesn't Live Here Anymore* was the first time in my movie career I was able to build a proper set."

major studio, one whose history he knew by heart. He relished the idea of joining the ranks of journeymen auteurs like Howard Hawks and Nicholas Ray, working within the system to make films that nevertheless bore their own recognizable thumbprint. That Hollywood was, though, on its last legs. *Alice* was the last film to be shot on the old Columbia soundstages on Gower Street, where Scorsese managed to dig up one of the set designers from *Citizen Kane* to construct the set for the film's opening flashback sequence showing Alice as a young girl in Monterey. A wraparound 180-degree set showing the desert at sunset was homage to the sets for classic movies like *Gone With the Wind*, *The Wizard of Oz*, *East of Eden*, and *Duel in the Sun*. "How else are you going to do a flashback?" Scorsese reasoned. The whole thing cost $85,000—more than twice the total budget of *Who's That Knocking at My Door*—and the scene almost hit the cutting-room floor.

The studio wanted the flashback sequence gone. Scorsese told them they could take it out but they'd have to take his name off the picture—the first of many times he would use this threat with a studio.

It worked, but there was another fight about the ending. John Calley wanted a happy ending, with Alice getting her man. Scorsese wanted one where she goes off to pursue her music career. Finally, they came up with a compromise suggested by Kristofferson—the scene in the diner, with Kristofferson telling her "pack your bags, I'll take you to Monterey," to applause from the cafeteria, although Scorsese finally ended the picture with just Burstyn and her son, walking down the street together. His first cut ran to three-and-a-half hours, and included a full hour showing Alice's relationship with her volatile husband, played by Billy Green Bush, which made clear from the outset the cycle in which Alice was stuck. "It was a real odyssey, it was terrific," he insisted. Burstyn disagreed. After showing it to her and hearing a detailed list of her criticisms, he vowed, "I will never allow an actor into my editing room again."

Scorsese's aspirations to auteur status, playing the system from within, had taken a bruising, which may be one reason he has always

undervalued *Alice Doesn't Live Here Anymore*, calling himself "only partly happy" with it. The critical consensus has largely followed suit. *Alice* is seen as the anomaly, the outlier, the one film of Scorsese's that is about "emotions and feelings and relationships" in an oeuvre otherwise dedicated to chiseling away at the rock face of male angst. It makes you curious to know how his career might have gone had he not met De Niro, for, looked at from the vantage point of 1974, *Alice Doesn't Live Here Anymore* continued the investigation of male–female relations that Scorsese started with *Who's That Knocking at My Door* in 1967, continued with *Boxcar Bertha* (1972) and *Mean Streets* (1973)—and which he would finally bring to the boil in *New York, New York* (1977). There's only one film about a solitary male staring into the abyss— *Taxi Driver* (1976)—which leaves the score by the end of the seventies as follows. Movies about emotions and feelings and relationships: five. Movies about solitary male angst: one.

What's more, *Alice Doesn't Live Here Anymore* is a gem, made by a filmmaker fast approaching his creative peak, too absorbed with

"a visceral apprehension about an eager-messy world," in Manny Farber's words, to know yet what a "Scorsese film" was, or what subjects it should confine itself to. The Scorsese who made *Alice* clearly hadn't got the memo that said he didn't understand, or couldn't direct, women: Ellen Burstyn would win the Oscar for her Alice, weary after a hard day's work but still full of spark and rebellion and a self-martyring humor that turns the scenes with her son into oedipal Abbott and Costello routines. "It's not fancy but we like it," says Tommy as they enter yet another fleapit motel. "Okay, I'm off to get rich," announces Alice, having dolled herself up in a bright green cocktail dress. I don't think anyone has ever quite got the fractious, flirtatious patter between a single working mom and her precocious child better. "Who is it?" asks Tommy upon hearing her knock on the door nine hours later. "Diana Ross," comes the droll reply.

That the film got turned into a successful and much-loved sitcom isn't surprising: Alice and Tommy have the parodic, self-dramatizing disposition of people who have been stuck for too long in front of the

Jodie Foster's assured performance as Tommy's friend Audrey booked her a role in Scorsese's next film.

TV set and have now been loosed into the world, rabbiting endlessly about what they find. Their discoveries include: a loverboy with a bolero tie and an unfaltering grin, played by Harvey Keitel, who turns out to be married and violent; a young shoplifting teen who thinks everything is "weird," played by Jodie Foster, who is yanked from a police station by her stepmom with the line "See you later, suckers!" No wonder that after this, one of Foster's first feature appearances, Scorsese came back to her for his Iris in *Taxi Driver*. She delivers a terrific thumbnail portrait of spunky alienation. All the characters in the film have the sap rising in their veins, and all the time they are on screen, they have Scorsese's undivided attention. "A runaway movie," said Pauline Kael. "Scorsese seems to have let the characters go loose; the camera is hyperactive, tracking them."

It's the open-heartedness of the film that strikes you today. Watching it you realize why it was that Scorsese was first in line to write a fan letter to Wes Anderson upon the release of *Rushmore* in 1998: Both films have something of the same blithe, nutty, slightly heartbroken spirit. Because Scorsese was still at that point in his romantic development—maybe the last such point—when he was fully engaged with the opposite sex, even his disappointments feel fresh. The crucial thing here is that missing first hour, because without it Alice's failures with men are good-faith failures. With that first hour in place the repetitiousness of her emotional cycle would have been instantly apparent, clouded by the same pall of inevitability that would later ruin the central relationship in *New York, New York*. Scorsese's opinion of relationships as traps sprung from the slightest

Scorsese gave Warner Bros. a happy ending, but on his terms.

touch was not yet fully formed. That view would require and receive corroboration from another source. Waiting to buttonhole Scorsese on the set of *Alice* was De Niro, clutching a ghosted autobiography of the middleweight fighter Jake LaMotta. It was called *Raging Bull*.

Scorsese couldn't understand De Niro's enthusiasm for the story. Fights in bars he understood, but boxing? "Even as a kid, I always thought that boxing was boring," he said. Sports in general had been a no-no since childhood. "Anything with a ball, no good." Besides, he had his own passion project, which had been burning him up since *Boxcar Bertha*, when Barbara Hershey had introduced him to Nikos Kazantzakis's 1953 novel about the life of Jesus, *The Last Temptation of Christ*. But he agreed to help De Niro with his boxing story, if only to placate him while they made their next picture together.

Taxi Driver

1976

"Travis is right on the edge, you know. Right from the first frame, he's on the edge and we wait the hour and fifty-one minutes for him to go over. But I think that he has right on the surface a lot of the emotions, a lot of the problems, that most everybody has in them."

On every street there's a nobody who dreams of being somebody.
He's a lonely forgotten man desperate
to prove that he's alive.

COLUMBIA PICTURES presents

ROBERT DE NIRO
TAXI DRIVER
A BILL/PHILLIPS Production of a MARTIN SCORSESE Film

JODIE FOSTER   ALBERT BROOKS as Tom   HARVEY KEITEL
LEONARD HARRIS   PETER BOYLE as Wizard
and CYBILL SHEPHERD as Betsy

Written by PAUL SCHRADER Music BERNARD HERRMANN Produced by MICHAEL PHILLIPS and JULIA PHILLIPS
Directed by MARTIN SCORSESE   Production Services by Devon/Persky-Bright

Page 71: Robert De Niro as "God's lonely man" Travis Bickle.

Left: An on-set conference with scriptwriter Paul Schrader and producer Michael Phillips.

"When I read Paul's script, I realized that was exactly the way I felt, that we all have those feelings so this was a way of embracing and admitting them, while saying I wasn't happy about them."

Paul Schrader, a protégé of Pauline Kael, was a film critic from Michigan who in 1972 had hit hard times. He had been kicked out by his wife, lost his job at the American Film Institute and taken to drifting around Los Angeles, living and sleeping in his car—eating junk, watching porn, drinking around the clock. Heavily into guns, he considered suicide. Checking himself into hospital with a stomach ulcer, and hearing himself speak with the nurse, he realized that he hadn't used his vocal cords in weeks. "That was when the metaphor of the taxi cab occurred to me," he said. "That is what I was: this person in an iron box, a coffin, floating around the city, but seemingly alone."

Drawing inspiration from Dostoyevsky's *Notes from Underground* and the diary of Arthur Bremer, the would-be assassin in 1972 of presidential candidate George Wallace, Schrader wrote *Taxi Driver* in two weeks. "The whole conviction of my life now rests upon the belief that loneliness, far from being a rare and curious phenomenon … is the central and inevitable fact of human existence," reads the

epigraph to the script, which he took from the Thomas Wolfe essay "God's Lonely Man." Following the nocturnal wanderings of a New York cabbie—a violent, alienated Vietnam vet—who coasts the streets, cleaning blood and come off his back seat, it was, Schrader said, an attempt to "exorcise the evil I felt within me." Later, he admitted "Travis Bickle is me."

Nobody would touch it. Everyone said, "This is a great script, and somebody should make it—but not us," recalled Schrader. Even Brian De Palma, who loved it, thought, "Who is ever going to see this?" Another of the script's fans was producer Michael Phillips, soon to be riding high with *The Sting*, although after reading it his wife and production partner, Julia, refused to be left in the room alone with Schrader. As early as 1972, they showed the script to Scorsese who felt like he had dreamed it, so intimately did it connect with the anger, loneliness, and alienation he had felt growing up. Schrader wanted to hold out for a bigger name, but after seeing a rough cut of *Mean Streets*, he changed his mind—on condition the director could deliver Robert

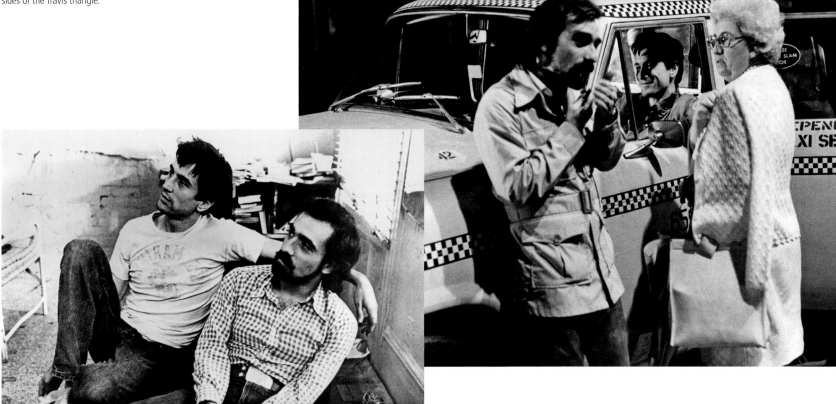

Right: Catherine Scorsese gets her point across.

Below: De Niro and Scorsese—two sides of the Travis triangle.

De Niro. Scorsese had originally wanted Harvey Keitel, but De Niro was rapt by Schrader's script, having been working on a story of his own about a political assassin. He immediately dropped it. "He *was* Travis," said Scorsese.

So that made three of them—"a rather unusual kind of symbiosis," as he put it, all three men playing midwife to this spiritual misfit and self-appointed scourge, Travis Bickle. "The three of us just came together," said Scorsese. "It was exactly what we wanted; it was one of the strangest things." It was the kind of rare, three-way synergy—all three men seeing themselves in the character—that distinguishes the very greatest films. *On the Waterfront* could only happen because Budd Schulberg, Elia Kazan, and Marlon Brando saw something of themselves in Terry Malloy; in *The Graduate* Benjamin Braddock was a unique amalgam of Buck Henry, Mike Nichols, and Dustin Hoffman. And so it would be with *Taxi Driver*, which critics are always holding up as the "The Kind of Film They Couldn't Make Anymore," although the truth is they barely got it made *then*. It took the combined heat

of De Niro, who in 1975 had just won a Best Supporting Actor Oscar for *The Godfather Part II*, Scorsese, who had just helped Burstyn win her Oscar for *Alice*, and Michael and Julia Phillips, still brandishing their Oscars for *The Sting* from the year before—and even then, they only managed to squeeze $1.3 million out of Columbia. Scorsese was convinced they were making a labor of love with no chance of commercial success, and even considered shooting it in black and white to get the tonality of film noir.

The summer of 1975 was hot and humid. There was a garbage strike and everywhere Scorsese aimed the camera there were mounds of garbage and "an atmosphere at night that's like a seeping kind of virus. You can smell it in the air and taste it in your mouth." De Niro prepared for the role by driving a cab—he even got a license. Scorsese drove with him for a couple of nights, up and down Eighth Avenue, and saw how totally disregarded De Niro was by his passengers, "like he was totally anonymous. People would say anything, do anything, in the back of his cab as if he wasn't there."

"The movie deals with sexual repression, so there's a lot of talk but no sex, no lovemaking, no nudity. If the audience saw nudity, it would work like a release valve, and the tension that's been building up would be dissolved."

Left and opposite:
Jodie Foster in the role of Iris,
a teenage prostitute.

Overleaf: "Saw you coming,
you fucking shitheel …"

There was some improv: between Cybill Shepherd (Betsy) and De Niro in the coffee shop, and the famous scene in which De Niro confronts himself in the mirror, shot in an abandoned apartment building at Eighty-Ninth Street that was about to be torn down. In the script it just said: *Travis speaks to himself in the mirror.* De Niro asked Scorsese what he should say. Scorsese told him, "Well, he's a little kid playing with guns and acting tough," so De Niro based his lines on this rap he'd heard an underground New York comedian using around the same time: *Are you looking at me?* Conscious of the fact that they were already five days over schedule on a forty-day shoot, Scorsese crouched at his feet, wearing earphones, worried about the traffic noise.

"Say it again."

Assistant director Pete Scoppa was banging on the door, "Come on, you've got to get back on schedule!"

Scorsese pleaded, "Give us two minutes, give us two minutes, this is really good," and turned back to De Niro.

"Again! Again!"

Finally, De Niro hit upon the line where he admits he's the only one there and must be talking to himself. "That did it," said Scorsese. Within three hours they had wrapped.

They cut and recut the movie until they had a version that worked, only to find the MPAA threatening them with an "X" rating—a virtual death certificate at the box office. At a meeting with Julia Phillips, David Begelman, head of Columbia, and Stanley Jaffe, an executive vice president, Scorsese was told he had to recut his film to get an "R" or the studio would do it for him. Scorsese called an emergency meeting with his friends John Milius, Steven Spielberg, and Brian De Palma at his house on Mulholland. "I had never seen Marty so upset," said Spielberg. "Verging on tears, but leaning toward rage. He shattered a glass Sparkletts bottle all over the kitchen floor. We were holding his arms, trying to calm him down, find out why he was so upset. He finally came out with the fact that Columbia had seen his movie, had hated the ending, and wanted him to take out all the violence, the entire shoot-out."

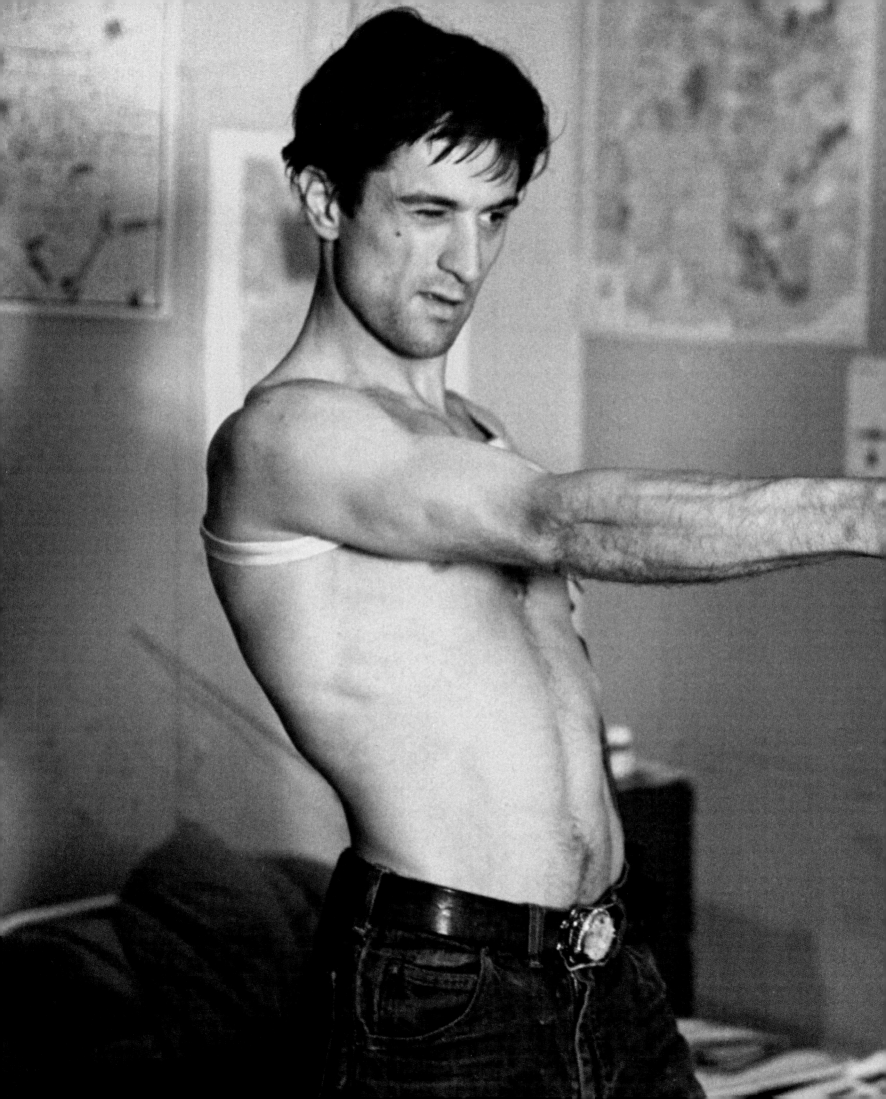

"I thought at the time that we were making sort of a labor of love; a picture that wouldn't necessarily speak to many people—maybe to a darker side of some people— and was surprised when it had such an acceptance."

The art of improv: directing Cybill Shepherd (Betsy; above), Harvey Keitel (Sport; left), and De Niro (opposite).

blood spurting from severed fingers and he desaturated the color—something he'd seen John Huston do on *Moby Dick*—which gave the blood a maroonish tinge that smacked of the *Daily News*.

The night before the film opened, he got everybody together for one last supper, and said, "No matter what happens tomorrow we have made a terrific movie and we're damn proud of it even if it goes down the toilet." Schrader overslept on the morning of the

The Phillipses took the work print to New York to show Pauline Kael, who offered to write an open letter to Begelman in her column if they needed it. When told the news Begelman and Jaffe flipped. Afraid they would seize the print, Scorsese locked it in the trunk of his car and snuck it off the lot, although in the end he agreed to cut a few frames showing

premiere and got to the theater around twelve fifteen to find a line that went all the way around the block. Then he realized: The line was for the two o'clock show, not the noon show. "It was a moment of pure joy," he said. The film was a hit, taking $58,000 the first week in New York and $28 million nationwide before it played out, making it the

seventeenth-highest-grossing film of 1976. Scorsese had the biggest and unlikeliest box-office success of his career.

What weird limbic region of public consciousness did *Taxi Driver* tap into? Of all Scorsese's films, it remains the one that least lends itself to casual viewing. You don't slip it on because you haven't seen it in a while. You don't catch it in reruns. You don't recommend it without a pretty thorough vetting of the interested party: Are they ready for this? Do they know what they're getting themselves into? Do they have plans for after? They should probably cancel, unless it's dinner with another boggle-eyed insomniac who has just survived their first encounter with *Taxi Driver*. Or a priest. You don't mess around with this movie. You get in training for it, the way Travis Bickle does push-ups in his apartment, his flowers for Betsy now ashes in the sink, while, in voiceover, he reads from his diary in that gloriously flat monotone of his—"*June twenty-ninth. I gotta get in*

shape. Too much sitting has ruined my body. Too much abuse has gone on for too long ..." A lesser actor would have blessed Travis with better delivery, but De Niro's line readings are a merciless blend of the reedy and faltering. His is the dead music of autodidacts, ham actors, psychopaths, and bores.

The film has the stillness of a cobra. Abjuring handheld camerawork, Scorsese frequently begins scenes with a head-on framing shot— a diner, a street corner—and then lets motion spill across it, goosing your concentration with little flurries of editing, like the twitches of a paranoiac. "Every scene combines the frantic and the still simultaneously," said critic Manny Farber. Whether alone or in a crowd, at night or in daylight, De Niro is alone in frame, his smallest gesture and movement treated to imperceptible bursts of slow motion, as if he were operating at a different speed from the rest of humanity— subaquatic. Get a stopwatch and measure his reaction times, which get slower as the film goes on, the closer he gets to atrocity, the better to

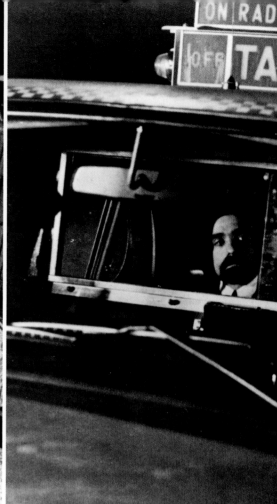

Above: Travis foils a convenience-store robber.

Center: "You must think I'm pretty sick." In a disturbing cameo, Scorsese plays a passenger who explains to Travis exactly how he's going to kill his wife.

Far right: Becoming increasingly deranged, Travis shaves his head into a Mohawk in preparation for his attempt to assassinate Senator Palantine.

savor each fresh indignity, each fresh spur to action. By the end he stares down Keitel as if etching a target on his forehead with a laser. The film ends with a famous spasm of violence, although more chilling is the ashen tableau that follows it, as frozen in time as a Weegee photograph, the stillness broken only by the impotent clicks of De Niro's gun and the whimperings of Jodie Foster cowering behind the sofa, before finally we get the mesmerizing tidal swell of Bernard Herrmann's score—the last he completed before he died in the last days of 1975.

What's amazing about this climax, even after repeat viewing, is not how shocking it is, but how unavoidable. Screenwriters use that formulation all the time to describe the perfect plot twist, but it takes an extremely rare mixture of poetry and pathology to make a three-person bloodbath seem as inevitable as rain. It returns you to the movie to see how they did it, how they sprang the trap, to see if you can spot the point of no return, the point at which Travis could still have pulled back from the edge. And what do we find? That he was perched on that edge the entire time, hiding in plain sight. "What is it?" asks

the cab-company manager who employs him in the very first scene. "You want a second job?" Even *he* knows. Something is just *off* about this guy. Iris (Foster) thinks him a narc. Sport (Keitel) asks if he's a cop. When Travis attempts to come clean to fellow cab driver Wizard (Peter Boyle), he tells him, "I've got some bad ideas in my head," but Wizard advises him to "go and get laid," which is almost the worst thing you could possibly say to Travis, who recoils from the opposite sex into nunnish dreams of cod-gallantry and pornographic fantasy. "There is practically no sex in it," said Kael of the film. "That's what it's about: the absence of sex—bottled up, impacted energy and emotion, with a blood-spattering release."

The taint of loneliness is all over the film like a bad smell. "I think you're a lonely person," Travis tells Betsy. "I saw in your eyes that you're not a happy person—that you need something." Of her workmate (Albert Brooks), he says, "I don't think he respects you." And then this, to Iris: "You should be home." None of these things is true of the people to whom Travis is referring, but they are all true of him. Walking

"A friend of mine who's a priest saw *Taxi Driver* and said he was glad I ended it on Easter Sunday rather than Good Friday."

the streets of New York, he sees only himself. The film adds up to an indelible vision of hell, consisting not of other people, as Sartre said, but other people recast in Travis's image, demons drawn in the blood vessels of one man's eyelids. Scorsese's cinematographer, Michael Chapman, called *Taxi Driver* "a documentary of the mind," a comment that perfectly pegs the film as the high point of the director's decade-long experiment in urban expressionism. Its exteriors don't feel like exteriors—they feel like interiors, the city a shadowland illumined only by Bickle's internal hellfire. "The cesspool panorama of prostitution, rampant drug dealing, architectural dilapidation, and nomadic squalor seen through the windshield of Bickle's taxi is a rebuke to those who romanticize the trashy heyday of Times Square and decry its Disneyfication," wrote James Wolcott in *Vanity Fair* in 2002. "*Taxi Driver*'s Midtown is a pre-Giuliani mess."

Scorsese has two appearances, the first when he is seen ogling Cybill Shepherd on a street corner, and then his famously disturbing monologue, delivered to the back of De Niro's head, about killing his wife with a .44 Magnum—"Now, did you ever see what it can do to a woman's pussy? That you should see." As cameos go, it's an unsettling act of self-excoriation, suggestive of the deep recesses the movie seems plucked from. The director would never match the spooky synchronization he enjoyed with De Niro and Schrader while making it, not even on *Raging Bull*, which never puts the audience behind LaMotta's eyes the way *Taxi Driver* does with Travis. There is more conscious aestheticization in the later film—it knows how beautiful it is, the better to contrast with LaMotta's brutality, as if the only redemption Scorsese could conceive for him was aesthetic not moral. It's hard to be entirely happy with that substitution. *Goodfellas* is the director's most ebullient performance, with its freeze-frames, voiceover, and tracking shots, but Scorsese is fulfilling a childhood dream in that film—a dream of passing muster in the company of violent men. *Taxi Driver* is rich, strange, and unfathomable, a nightmare unfolding in broad daylight, so personal at times you can't believe they got it on film. "Marty gets behind your eyes," said Foster. *Taxi Driver* stays there.

"I was shocked by the way audiences took the violence. I saw *Taxi Driver* once in a theater on opening night and everyone was yelling and screaming at the final shoot-out. When I made it I didn't intend to have the audience react with that feeling, 'Yes, let's do it. Let's go out and kill.'"

Choreographing the inevitable, indelible eruption of violence at the end of the film.

Overleaf: Scorsese used an overhead shot to survey the horrific aftermath.

New York, New York

1977

"I wanted to do it as a real Hollywood film, because the Hollywood film is still something I treasure."

Scorsese was triumphant at Cannes in 1976, where *Taxi Driver* was awarded the *Palme d'Or*—the most coveted prize in Europe for a film director. Looking for a follow-up, he found it in *New York, New York*, a love story between a saxophone player and a singer which he planned as a tribute to the big-scale MGM musicals of the 1940s and 1950s. With Robert De Niro and Liza Minnelli in starring roles, it seemed to have "hit" written all over it. The unexpected success of *Taxi Driver* under his belt, Scorsese wanted to strengthen the line of communication that appeared to have opened up between him and the general public. He wanted his new movie to be a crowd-pleaser, but on his terms, shot with a loose, documentary, *cinéma vérité* feel—Vincente Minnelli by way of John Cassavetes.

"That was the idea! The convention of the Hollywood studio film meets, or crosses with a new style, the Italian cinema, the French cinema, Cassavetes—Kazan, of course, going back to him." He wanted to base it on "myself, our relationships, our marriages. Sure enough, in the picture, the character [Jimmy Doyle], his wife was pregnant,

my wife was pregnant, Bobby's wife was pregnant. It was a crazy time … just madness."

It was during the filming of *Taxi Driver* that a journalist called Julia Cameron had turned up to interview Scorsese, stayed for dinner, then breakfast, and, a few weeks after his thirty-third birthday, had become his second wife. Within a few months, he was staring down the prospect of imminent fatherhood again.

New York, New York began to come together—or apart—as a story about two artists trying to reconcile the irreconcilable demands of family and career. Scorsese was unhappy with the script, by Earl Mac Rauch, so called in Mardik Martin, his old friend and collaborator on *Mean Streets*, to rewrite it but Martin did not finish in time. Liza Minnelli had a commitment to perform in Vegas, so Scorsese went ahead and started shooting without a finished script.

He spent the first two weeks shooting a single musical number, "Happy Endings," with no idea of what ending the movie would eventually finish up with. As a director he had a ball, copying camera

"I wasn't very happy with the improvising. You have to fail in order to know where you're gonna go. The trick of failing is that with smaller films it's easier. But with studio money it's a real problem. We took all those chances on that film."

moves from old Vincente Minnelli movies—particularly *The Band Wagon*—to make the sight of the band playing interesting: "First the camera would track in on the band for a few bars of music before the first cut, with no master shot, which would run for twenty-four bars. Next the camera would track at one angle for twelve bars, and so on back and forth until this became a style." He would subsequently use the same elaborate tracking moves for the boxing scenes in *Raging Bull* and the pool games in *The Color of Money*—it would become one of the most recognized trademarks of Scorsese's style. But after two weeks of shooting with a thousand extras, he had an opening number that ran to one hour all by itself. Mardik Martin still hadn't cracked the ending. "It was a nightmare," he said. "I was writing up until the final frame. You don't make movies like that."

That's when Scorsese made the decision: He would improvise the rest of the movie. "One of the things I will always thank the French for

was giving me that grand prize at Cannes for *Taxi Driver* that allowed me to reveal to myself what a total failure I could be," he would say later.

He lived, slept, and ate at the studio. Holed up in an apartment on the MGM lot in Culver City, he began an affair with cocaine and Liza Minnelli, frequently at the same time. Andy Warhol wrote in his diary that Minnelli and Scorsese showed up at the door of a famous fashion designer demanding, "Give me every drug you've got." One day the director kept 150 costumed extras waiting while he talked to his shrink from the trailer. Meanwhile, all the improvisation was extending the schedule from fourteen weeks to twenty, as Boris Leven, the legendary

"I was extremely disappointed when the movie was finished because I had had a really bad experience making it. But over the years I've been able to see that it has a truth to it. I still don't really like it, yet in a way I love it."

With the script unfinished when shooting started, the structure of the movie became a puzzle that Scorsese was "too drugged out to solve."

production designer of such films as *The Shanghai Gesture*, *Giant*, and *West Side Story*, labored to finish his sets in time. No matter how fast he worked he couldn't keep up with the constant changes. De Niro and Minnelli would start improvising dialogue, and soon they'd improvised themselves out of one set and into another. "Poor old Boris would say 'okay,' go off grumbling, and come back a few hours later to submit his plans," said Scorsese, who then had to go back and improvise some more dialogue to get them back in line to use the original set. "That's one of the reasons why the scenes are so long," said Scorsese, although he later admitted, "I was too drugged out to solve the structure."

Finally, after twenty weeks of shooting they had "something like a movie." The first cut was over four hours long. United Artists feared that it was too dark, but Scorsese refused to change a frame. George Lucas, then putting the finishing touches to *Star Wars*, dropped by the editing room and told him he would gross an additional $10 million if De Niro and Minnelli walked into the sunset as a happy couple. Scorsese knew he would never be able to look himself—or his actors—in the face if

he went down that route. But he could see the logic of what Lucas said: That's how the old MGM musicals used to end. That's when he knew: "I was doomed … I could not make it in this business … I cannot make entertainment pictures, I cannot be a director of Hollywood films."

Beware any film intended by its director as a "love letter to the history of movies." Revisionists now flit in and out of those rusty hulks of 1970s auteurs' excess—Cimino's *Heaven's Gate*, Malick's *Days of Heaven*, Scorsese's *New York, New York*—like fish feeding on coral; and there is much to admire in Scorsese's valentine to the movie musical. "An honest failure," said Pauline Kael. "Scorsese works within the artifices of 1940s movie-musical romances … Evoking the movie past, he's trying to get at the dark side that was left out of the old cliché plots. But the improvisational, Cassavetes-like psychodrama that develops between the stars seems hollow and makes us uneasy, and sequences go on covering the same uncertain ground … The effect is of desperately talented people giving off bad vibes."

Above: Robert De Niro as saxophone player Jimmy Doyle.

Right: Veteran production designer Boris Leven's spectacular sets were one of *New York, New York*'s strong points.

"I wanted to make a different kind of film, about a struggling band in the forties trying to make it, one that was totally personal. I thought there was really no difference between a struggling band in the forties and myself,

"We are just crazy film buffs. It was a direct homage thing, a loving thing to the fifties, early fifties production numbers. Forties, whatever, but they don't want to watch it."

De Niro back in a yellow cab—as a passenger this time. De Niro and Minnelli improvised themselves out of one set and into another.

Not for nothing are De Niro's most memorable scenes opposite mirrors. He is one of the most antisocial talents to work in movies, a true dark star, running on negative charisma, lonely in a crowd, or covering for it with almost psychotic good cheer. He never made for a convincing Romeo. His Jimmy Doyle hits on Liza Minnelli's Francine in the first scene of *New York, New York* with the relentlessness of a rapist; Minnelli acts astonished, and beneath the astonishment we glimpse a people-pleasing urge the size of a planet. The trap is set for these two who will bicker and bully, humiliate, fight, and flee one another in scene after scene, across a series of dazzling sets, unto and beyond the point of exhaustion. Scorsese's big relationship movie is really about the death of love—a worthy theme in almost any other context but one which cuts against the benevolence of the movie musical like barbed wire through wedding cake. The film opened on June 21, 1977, and promptly sank at the box office, taking only $16 million. That year belonged to George Lucas's *Star Wars*, which came out on May 25, and obliterated everything in its path, taking $36 million on its first weekend alone, on course to an eventual $307 million. "*Star Wars* was in, Spielberg was in. We were finished," said Scorsese, stung by the bad notices. Particularly hurtful was "being treated as if I had gotten comeuppance—for what? For making *Mean Streets*? *Alice* and *Taxi Driver*?"

Despite being exhausted after *New York, New York*, he launched straight into production of *The Last Waltz*, a documentary about the breakup of the rock group the Band, another documentary, *American Boy*, and also a Broadway musical with Minnelli called *The Act*, about a workaholic, a "crazy, crazy person who ruins everybody who comes near, marries her, disaster." A flagrant allusion to Julia Cameron, whom Scorsese left soon after their daughter Domenica was born in September of 1976, just like Jimmy Doyle does in *New York, New York*. His marriage over, Scorsese circled the globe, partying, looking for the thing that would lead him back to work. "I have very little time left," he told interviewers, convinced he would not live to see forty.

Raging Bull

1980

"The idea had been to make this film as openly honest as possible, with no concessions at all for box office or audience. I said, 'That's it. Basically this is the end of my career. This is it. This is the final one.'"

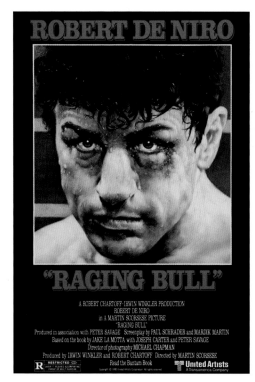

"The poster with the picture of Bob's face all beaten and battered—I mean, if you're a young girl, I don't know if you'd say, 'Let's go see this one.'"

Above: Robert De Niro with the real-life Jake LaMotta.

Opposite and pages 96–7: Scorsese brought the camera in close for the fight scenes, giving the viewer a boxer's perspective.

New York, New York left Scorsese exhausted. "When I look back at that period," he says now, "which was a very troubled period in my life, I know now that what I was really afraid of was that I didn't have anything that I wanted to say any more on film. I didn't know how to become a director, I didn't understand how I could ever show up on the set that early in the morning and deal with the problems for somebody else. I had the joy of filmmaking but not for other people." It was only *The Last Waltz* that kept him from cracking up completely. "That's where I started getting back in line, like a person working in therapy in a hospital," he says. "Things were put back together in my head. But there is no doubt: I did think I'd never find it again. I didn't know if there was any more in me."

During Labor Day weekend in 1978, he decided to attend the Telluride Film Festival, high in the Colorado Rockies, where he collapsed from a mixture of bad coke, prescription drugs, and exhaustion. Returning to New York, he was taken to hospital, bleeding from his mouth, his nose, his eyes. The doctors told him he was in imminent danger of a brain hemorrhage, pumped him full of cortisone, and ordered total bed rest. That's when Robert De Niro came to visit and finally persuaded him to direct *Raging Bull*.

De Niro had been pestering Scorsese for years about the project, but the director wasn't sure he wanted to make another movie together. They were "like brothers" by now, in the best and worst senses, with the closeness and the petty aggravation, too. "De Niro wanted to make the movie, I didn't want to have anything to do with it," says Scorsese. "Bob and I had been through three major movies together. I didn't think I wanted to do any more. I wanted to do *Gangs of New York*, I wanted to do *Last Temptation of Christ*. I didn't know anything about boxing."

"Bob came to me in hospital and said, 'Come on, what is it you want to do? Do you want to die, is that it? Don't you want to live to see your daughter grow up and get married? Are you gonna be one of those directors who makes a couple of good movies and then it's over for them?' He said, 'You could really make this picture.' I found myself saying 'okay.' Ultimately, finally, when I was down and out, I realized,

"Knowing Jake personally at that time, he was a very interesting man, he was very subdued. It's an odd thing. Sometimes I'll look at an animal and the animal is at peace. Sometimes fighters are like that, real fighters who get in the ring every day. Part of the brutality, part of being human, I don't know what it is, but Jake had gone through a terrible journey and come out the other side alive and reached some kind of understanding of himself."

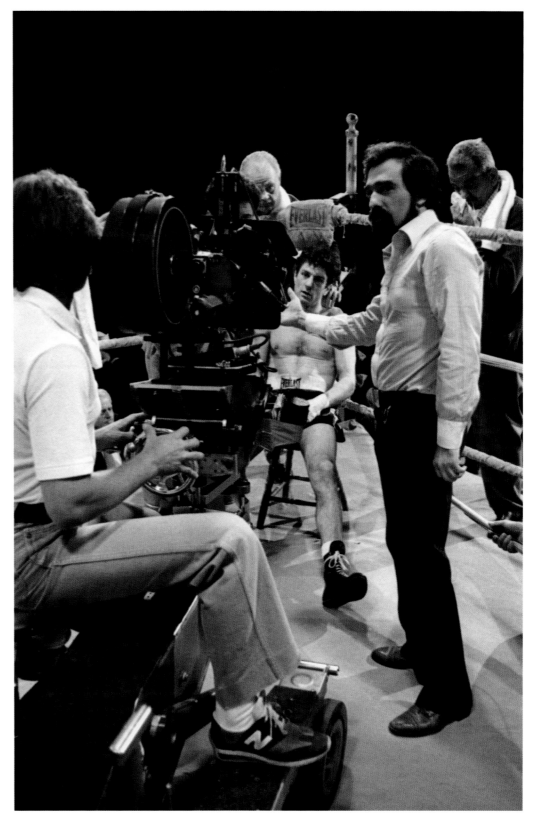

yes I should do this movie. I became obsessed with it. Going down in flames meant that if it was going to go down, let it go down. I didn't care anymore. I just knew this was the last thing to say. If I could say anything, this was the last chance to do it."

Raging Bull wasn't really about boxing. It was about self-destruction. *That* he knew about. "For me, here was a person who had gone through terrible times, had treated himself badly, treated everybody else around him badly, and then evolved to the point where he was at some sort of peace with himself and the people around him," he said. "I thought that *Raging Bull* was kamikaze filmmaking—we threw everything I knew into making it, and I really thought that was the last movie I was going to make."

The first thing De Niro did was whisk the convalescent director off to the island of St. Martin in the Caribbean, where they rented a villa for a few weeks—"sort of like a spa, like *8½*," said Scorsese. De Niro would rise early to run along the beach, then wake up Scorsese, make him coffee, and the two men would spend the day hashing out the film, scene by scene, writing up the new material on yellow legal pads in the afternoons. In the evenings, De Niro and Scorsese would head out in a golf cart to have dinner at one of the small restaurants nearby.

"Raging Bull is the story of a man who is facing a wall … Here's a man who is methodically destroying himself, who is pulling others down with him, who falls into the deepest hole—and who pulls himself up again. Pulls him up again toward what? It doesn't matter. To live with a strip-teaser? Yeah, so what? Are you better than a strip-teaser?"

De Niro and Joe Pesci as brothers Jake and Joey LaMotta—the actors would also work together in *Goodfellas* and *Casino*.

It was "total concentration," said Scorsese of the experience. "Everything was done at that little table with that silly cabana umbrella and we're looking out at the ocean."

The first writer to take a pass at the script had been Mardik Martin, Scorsese's old NYU friend and co-author of the *Mean Streets* screenplay, who delivered a conventionally chronological biopic: boyhood, adolescence, triumph in the ring, then defeat, fleshed out with anecdotes drawn from Scorsese's youth in Little Italy. This draft displeased De Niro, so it was discarded and De Niro approached Paul

Schrader, then shooting *Hardcore*, to do a draft. Relations were "a little touchy" with the writer, after the way *Taxi Driver* had been celebrated at Cannes as a De Niro–Scorsese collaboration, but Schrader saw the shortcomings of Martin's script immediately. "One reason it was so flat was it had no Joey LaMotta. It was just a cavalcade of events," he said. In real life, "they'd made this unspoken deal that Joey would manage and get the girls, while Jake would fight, and they would split the money, which was a surefire recipe for disaster. So now I had a sibling story, and I knew how to write that."

Scorsese thought Schrader's draft, which junked the beginning and started the picture right in the middle, was "brilliant." Jake is obviously winning a fight; he knocks the guy down … but he loses. Why? "Because he's not going to give in for the wiseguys. Not because of honor, but because he doesn't want them to share his money." But there was still work to be done: Schrader wanted more depth, Scorsese more aggression. At a script conference in Manhattan's Sherry-Netherland hotel, "Bobby started dictating stuff to me," said Schrader, "and I blew up and threw the script at him. I said, 'If you want a secretary, you'd

better hire a secretary. If you want a writer, I'll be up in my room.'" Finally, he separated from the project, but before he did, he told Scorsese, "You pulled *Mean Streets* from your guts. Do it again, but this time limit yourself to two or three characters. You won't be able to handle four."

On the island they merged two characters—LaMotta's brother Joey and a close friend, Pete Savage—into one, and came up with LaMotta's lowest point, when he hits rock bottom, in the police cell. Schrader had him masturbating, but De Niro nixed the idea. In New York, the actor

"Before shooting, I went to two boxing matches, five-round matches between unknown boxers. The first evening, even though I was far away from the ring, I saw the sponge red with blood, and the film started to take form. The next time, I was much closer, and I saw the blood dripping from the ropes. I said to myself that this sure doesn't have anything to do with any sport!"

To prepare for *Raging Bull*, Scorsese referred back to classic noir movies of the forties and fifties.

had come up with an alternative: hammering against the wall of his cell with his head and fists. Scorsese was certain that "the language is in the body, the language is right there." Replaying the scene again on St. Martin, he was sold. "When I looked at it there I saw the scene," he said. "I saw the shot—what you see in the film. A number of times I wished I had a camera. I would've shot it immediately."

Before production started, he screened several films for De Niro—an impromptu film-history lesson that would turn into something of a tradition for the director and his actors. The program included Henry Hathaway's *Kiss of Death* (1947), Abraham Polonsky's *Force of Evil* (1948)—De Niro's favorite, about two brothers deep in the numbers racket in New York—and Robert Rossen's *Body and Soul* (1947). Interestingly, only one of these—the Rossen—was about boxing. Scorsese was particularly impressed by the way cinematographer James Wong Howe, the man responsible for the monochrome glitter of *Sweet Smell of Success*, mounted his cameraman on roller skates to circle the ring with the boxers. All of the old newsreels shot from outside the

ropes. He wanted something similar, except using a Steadicam brace to follow De Niro around the ring. One afternoon, Scorsese was watching footage with Michael Powell, when Powell said: "There's something wrong about the red gloves." "You're right," said Scorsese. "I've got to shoot this in black and white."

Principal photography commenced in April of 1979, in New York, where most of the film was shot, except for the fight scenes which were filmed at the old Olympic Auditorium in Los Angeles. De Niro trained with LaMotta for nearly a year, boxing some thousand rounds in a gym on Fourteenth Street, and adding twenty pounds of muscle to his 145-pound frame. (He added sixty pounds to do the film's later sequences.) He got so good that LaMotta scheduled three professional bouts for him, under an assumed name, and De Niro won two of them. Watching the dailies of the actor getting pounded, first from the right, then from the left, take after take, hour after hour, Thelma Schoonmaker, who won an Oscar for her editing, was astounded. "I've never seen anyone more connected to the earth," she said.

"I wanted to do the fight scenes as if the viewers were the fighter, and their impressions were the fighter's—of what he would think or feel, or what he would hear. Like being pounded all the time."

De Niro's preparation for the movie involved a year's training at LaMotta's gym. He even fought three professional bouts under a pseudonym.

Scorsese shot nineteen takes of the film's climax, in which LaMotta delivers Brando's "I could have been a contender" speech from *On the Waterfront* to a mirror. De Niro favored one of the more emotional versions. Scorsese picked out a flatter one. So they watched both, back to back, but failed to change each other's mind. Scorsese chose his. "I still think the one I have in is best," said the director. "All right," said De Niro, "let it go." Said Scorsese, "You can only do that with someone you trust, because the bottom line is the guy could say, 'You've got to use the take I want. Because the picture was made because of my name.'"

Who was right? We'll never know, although that single choice may have been what separated even admirers of Scorsese who found LaMotta loathsome and those who found him properly tragic. To this day, few things divide aficionados more starkly than the question of whether Jake does, or does not, find redemption at the end of the film. If there is redemption, it is eked out under extreme pressure, extreme duress: *Raging Bull* comes from the most embattled, uncompromising corner of Scorsese's psyche. It is the movie that gets called his "masterpiece" more than any others, which is not to say that it is his best. It is shot in black and white, every frame a beauty, features the intermezzo from Pietro Mascagni's *Cavalleria rusticana* on its soundtrack, and concerns a man who rains destruction down upon himself—the time-honored subject of American masterpieces from *Citizen Kane* right through to *There Will Be Blood*, as if the flip side to American freedom were the freedom to destroy yourself. The film feels almost like revenge on the audience that had abandoned Scorsese over *New York, New York*, an act of psychic doubling-down ("You didn't like *that*? Try *this* …") that trashes anyone expecting sympathetic heroes, or character arcs or third-act redemptions. *Raging Bull* may not tower over eighties filmmaking to the extent that its admirers maintain, but it certainly beats it bloody. It is *punishment*, in both the Catholic and pugilistic senses.

Round one. Technique. Over the course of the film, Scorsese stages the fights with increasing levels of abstraction, as if tracking Jake's retreat from the world, until finally the bouts seem to be taking place

Jake and Vickie (Cathy Moriarty) share a tender moment.

"Up to a certain point in your life, you'll kill everybody around you. You're killing yourself. And that's ultimately what I saw in the picture."

inside his own pulverized skull—boxing his own shadow. The first fight, against Jimmy Reeves in Cleveland, is breathtaking enough: a fierce welter of close-ups and crane shots that weave in and out of the fighters like sneaky blows to the kidney. The second fight, a title decider against Sugar Ray Robinson in Detroit, is a Steadicam-and-slow-motion coronation, the rounds flying by, with more Mascagni, and LaMotta doused in water like a saint—sweet victory! By the time of the third bout, a rematch with Robinson, the crowd has all but disappeared beyond the edges of a vast ring. The light dims. The opponent is a devilish silhouette winding up his fist in a vertiginous corridor of track-and-zoom camerawork. We hear nothing but Jake's breath, and flashbulbs, through whistling wind. He might as well be alone, with his demon—the minotaur become his own maze.

Round two. The love story. Yes, there is one, if only to show love's occlusion and eventual eclipse. "If you re-encounter *Raging Bull* today, after a long absence, you will find it far more tender than you remember—even, at times, rather sweet-spirited," says Richard Schickel. And it's true, the love scene—with Vickie (Cathy Moriarty) tracing her lips up and down the ridges and bruises of her new lover's body—is among the most tender sequences Scorsese has filmed. The more you watch *Raging Bull*, the more compelling Moriarty becomes, with her broad swimmer's shoulders, hefty frame, and low, dulcet voice. Watch her in the scene where she packs to leave, flattening herself while De Niro roars, freezing the moment he touches her, waiting patiently until released, and continuing her packing—the body language of a woman expert in the art of not getting hit. The consensus

is that Scorsese doesn't understand women, but he has a granular understanding of a certain type of woman—the kind, like Vickie, attracted to brutes, or turned on by violence, like Karen (Lorraine Bracco) in *Goodfellas*, or victimized by it, like Lori (Illeana Douglas) in *Cape Fear*. Such women exist; Scorsese's portraiture is sympathetic, penetrating, and candid.

Round three. The knockout blow. Administered not by Scorsese but De Niro. From the beginning, "it was Bob's film," said producer Irwin Winkler. The Academy famously snubbed Scorsese at the Oscars—Best Picture and Best Director awards went that year to *Ordinary People*—but De Niro picked up his second Best Actor trophy. "By the end it became evident that much of *Raging Bull* exists because of the possibilities it offers De Niro to display his own explosive art," wrote Richard Corliss in *Time*. "What De Niro does in this film isn't acting, exactly," dissented Pauline Kael in the *New Yorker*, "though it may at some level be awesome." The key word here—the pivot uniting the film's friends and foes—is "awesome," in the proper sense

of the word: inspiring or deserving of awe. Stars had transformed themselves for roles before. Once the studio system began to come apart in the 1950s and 1960s, actors took more control of their image, subverting it like Tony Curtis dulling his baby blue eyes and gaining twenty pounds to play the title role in *The Boston Strangler* (1968), or Rod Steiger, soaring past 230 pounds on two dinners a day for *In the Heat of the Night* (1967). De Niro's performance in *Raging Bull* was something else again, of another order of magnitude—an act of self-deconstruction, of lacerating self-graffiti that opened the door for the fleshy transformations and transmogrifications of Charlize Theron in *Monster*, Christian Bale in *The Machinist*, and Natalie Portman in *Black Swan*. De Niro had issued an open retort to the high-tech spectacle that was George Lucas's *Star Wars*. How could the actor compete? By quite literally making a spectacle of himself—turning himself into his own special effect. De Niro was *morphing*. He had also given independent filmmaking the rationale by which it would hold its own in the era of the blockbuster.

The King of Comedy

1982

"The amount of rejection in this
film is horrifying. There are scenes
I almost can't look at."

KODAK SAFETY FILM 5063
8A
9
9A
10
10A
11
11A
12
12A
13
13A
14
14A
15
15A
16
16A
17
17A
18
18A
19
19A
20
20A
4 9 3
21A
22
22A
23

Above: Robert De Niro played Rupert Pupkin, a would-be comedian stalking talk-show host Jerry Langford (Jerry Lewis).

Page 109: As well as following Langford literally, Pupkin also apes his hero's stage patter, mannerisms, and fashion sense.

At the end of 1979 Scorsese returned to New York, his lengthy sojourn in Los Angeles seemingly at an end. He moved into a small one-bedroom apartment in Lower Manhattan and filled it with functional furniture—metal bookcases, cheap metal-and-rattan chairs—to give the illusion of someone at home. He would wake up, check the TV listings to see what classic films were on, then go to see his therapist—five days a week, with phone calls on weekends, wondering aloud if his career was over. "I must say I can understand why people eventually stop making pictures," he said, "because to make films in such an impassioned way you really have to believe in it, you've really got to want to tell that story and after a while you may find that life itself is more important than the filmmaking process."

The King of Comedy came to him from Robert De Niro, who first gave him the script by Paul Zimmerman when Scorsese was filming *Alice* in 1974. It seemed to him to be a film about one gag: the kidnapping of a talk-show host. "I didn't understand it," he said.

"I was too close to it." But he had since become something of a celebrity himself, fêted by film festivals around the world for *Mean Streets* and *Taxi Driver*, only to see *New York, New York* dumped on. He understood something of fame's weird vortex—the way it buckled your world, seemed to bend the light. Reading the script again in 1979, he got Rupert Pupkin's absurd, pathological will to succeed.

"It's the same way I made my first pictures," he noted, "with no money and with constant rejection—going back and going back and going back until finally, somehow, you get a lucky break. I remember I'd go anyplace, do anything, try to get into screenings, get into any kind of social situation to try and talk up projects."

While shooting, he had Pupkin (De Niro) call Jerry Langford (Jerry Lewis) from the very same payphone he had used to pester producers in the early seventies. But he also understood Langford—his guardedness and paranoia. Scorsese had seen close up the way De Niro was besieged by fans after the success of *Mean Streets* and

"Rupert? What are you doing down there?" If Mrs. Pupkin (voiced by Catherine Scorsese) only knew …

"I felt it was De Niro's best performance ever. *The King of Comedy* was right on the edge for us; we couldn't go any further at that time."

The Godfather Part II. One in particular had somehow obtained the actor's telephone number and used to call him up at all hours of the day, sometimes during meetings. "Bobby, my man, how are you? What are you up to? Do you want to come to dinner tonight?" At first evasive, De Niro grew so curious that eventually, during the shooting of *Raging Bull*, he met up with the man, who was waiting for him with his wife, a shy suburban woman who was clearly embarrassed by the situation. The man wanted to put De Niro in a car and drive him to their house, two hours outside New York.

"Why are you stalking me?" the actor asked the man. "What do you want?"

"To have dinner with you. Have a drink, chat. My mom asked me to say hi. My friends, too. They'd like to know if …"

And off he went: question after question. Even afterward, he continued to call. During the shooting of *The King of Comedy*, De Niro tried a little role reversal with autograph hunters—part research, part

fan jujitsu. He would set about them, stalking *them*, nagging *them* with questions. It was, after all, the theme of the film: the fine line between celebrity and fan, between obsessive and obsession, the two conflicting sides of Scorsese's own personality.

Even Scorsese had occasion to regret *The King of Comedy.* "We had explored everything that we could do with each other on *Raging Bull,*" he said of his fourth collaboration with De Niro. "I should have waited for something that came from me." The critical reaction ranged from the dismissive to the perplexed. "*The King of Comedy* is one of the most arid, painful, wounded movies I've ever seen," said Roger Ebert in the *Chicago Sun-Times.* And he was one of the movie's fans. "De Niro in disguise denies himself a soul," wrote Pauline Kael, who was not. "It is not merely that he hollows himself out and becomes Jake LaMotta, or Des the Priest in *True Confessions* or Rupert Pupkin—he makes them hollow too, and merges with the character's emptiness."

Kael didn't mean her description as a compliment, but such is the funhouse mirror of *The King of Comedy*—wherein everything is upside down, or distorted into its opposite—that it comes very close to nailing the genius of De Niro in this film. It's not that he's a chameleon—quite the opposite. His greatest performances rest on the observation that we are, most of us, very bad actors. And Rupert Pupkin is the worst of the lot, a ham of a human being, a distillation of all the nowhere men the actor had given us to this point, the original absence from which the others are scooped out. He could be Travis Bickle's no-hoper cousin, or Jake LaMotta reborn as a people-pleaser, all his pain and violence repressed behind that knotted tie and his expressionless observations. "Is that cork?" he asks Langford's secretary. "You know, she died tragically alone like many of the world's most beautiful women," he says of Marilyn Monroe, on his first date with Rita. "I don't want to see that happen to you," failing to realize that the person more likely to suffer that fate is him.

The whole movie is like that—it's a Hobbesian vision of a New York filled with passive aggressors who backbite and snipe at one another. As the "sexual terrorist" Masha, Sandra Bernhard screws up her face like a pug, as if permanently offended by someone else's stink, while Jerry Lewis radiates hostility like dry ice, as unamused by the goings-on as only a great comedian can be. He gives a superb performance, "worthy of a book by Wittgenstein, the nonentity everybody knows" in critic David Thomson's formulation. "There is a sequence where he walks down the street—in public, waiting to be mobbed, but not quite—that is perhaps the gentlest, finest comedy Lewis ever did."

The King of Comedy opened and took a nosedive, earning back only $2.5 million of its $19 million budget. At dinner with his friend Jay Cocks at the end of 1983, Scorsese heard someone on TV refer to the movie as "the flop of the year" and figured it was the end of an era for his kind of filmmaking. But *of course* it flopped. How else to greet a film about flop sweat? What better debut for Rupert Pupkin than a groan

"I wanted to look at what it's like to want something so badly you'd kill for it. By kill I don't mean kill physically, but you can kill the spirit, you can kill relationships, you can kill everything else around you in your life."

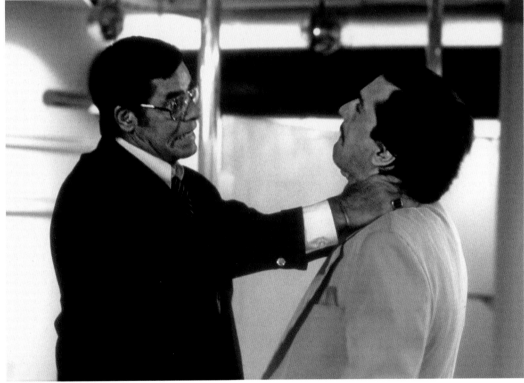

Opposite: Masha (Sandra Bernhard) gets wind of Pupkin's plan.

Right: An imaginary scene in which Langford invites Pupkin to a swanky lunch and asks him to cover as host of his talk show (top) could not be further from the true nature of their relationship (bottom).

in a half-empty theater? What better opportunity to pick himself up, dust himself off, paste that grin on his face, and press on? And *The King of Comedy* has pressed on, growing more prescient with each passing year. By the time it had come out, John Hinckley, drawing inspiration from *Taxi Driver*, had attempted to assassinate Ronald Reagan. The next two decades would see the advent of meta-showbiz satires like *The Larry Sanders Show* and *Curb Your Enthusiasm*, as well as the spread of reality TV, bequeathing us a culture rich in warrantless aspiration and the halting comedy of excruciation. Rupert would get the last laugh—and sound like he'd counted the "ha"s in the script.

After Hours

1985

"I realized you can't let the system crush your spirit. I'm a director, I'm going to be a pro and start over again. I'll make a low-budget picture, *After Hours*."

Pages 114–15: A night in SoHo on location for *After Hours*, New York, 1985.

Above: A conversation about Henry Miller triggers the strangest night that Paul Hackett (Griffin Dunne) has ever known.

Opposite: "After *Last Temptation* was cancelled in '83, I had to get myself back in shape. Work out. And this was working out."

Scorsese was supposed to follow *The King of Comedy* with *The Last Temptation of Christ*. It had taken him six years to finish Nikos Kazantzakis's novel about the internal struggles of Jesus Christ, after Barbara Hershey gave it to him on the set of *Boxcar Bertha*. He kept picking it up, putting it down, rereading it, absorbed but slowed by Kazantzakis's hypnotic language, before finally finishing it in 1978 while visiting the Taviani brothers in Tuscany while they were making *Il Prato* (*The Meadow*), where he also met his third wife, Isabella Rossellini. The way the Gospel had been taught to him in school, Jesus was a figure so holy he virtually glowed in the dark. The Jesus of Kazantzakis's novel was a very different figure, wracked by human frailty and doubt, whose sermons are pulled from his breast only after intense self-interrogation—much like Scorsese himself.

The film was originally to be made for Paramount, then led by president Michael Eisner and head of production Jeffrey Katzenberg, who provisionally approved a budget of $12 million and a shooting schedule of ninety days. Every other week, it seemed, Eisner would phone Scorsese and tell him, "There's a green light on this picture. It's a 'go' picture and Jeffrey is really behind it," only for Katzenberg to call later and say "Michael Eisner is fighting for you to make this picture." Fighting with whom? Scorsese couldn't figure out why the two top executives at the studio were trying so hard to convince him they wanted to make the picture.

He began scouting for locations in Morocco and Israel, a day and a half's journey from Los Angeles. Eisner and Katzenberg, both wary of letting a big-name director loose in a faraway location—the *Heaven's Gate* fiasco was burned into every executive's brain—wanted Scorsese to shoot closer to home: San Francisco, say. Nor were they sold on the idea of Aidan Quinn playing Jesus. It didn't help that the religious right had started bombarding Gulf+Western, who owned Paramount, with letters protesting that the proposed movie would defile Christ, depicting him as homosexual—untrue—or that Irwin Winkler's budget projections had started to climb, from $12 million, to $13 million, then to $16 million. Scorsese had flights booked to Tel Aviv,

in readiness, every day. Finally, in October of 1983, Winkler went to Paramount asking for another $2 million. It was the week another Winkler-produced film, *The Right Stuff,* had come out and tanked. Barry Diller, chairman of Paramount, met Scorsese in a hotel in New York and asked him why he wanted to make the picture.

"Because I want to get to know Jesus better," replied Scorsese.

It was the wrong answer. Diller smiled. "Marty," he said, "the reality is that UA theaters wouldn't show the picture. I'm sorry, I'm going to have to pull the plug on it because if we spend $18 to $19 million on a movie, it has to be showing some place."

In the old days, Scorsese would almost certainly have done something crazy—overturned some furniture, thrown a phone against a wall. This time, he was too shocked to react. "I was beyond responding," he said, "as if a spring had broken, or as if something was dying inside of me." He met his old friend Brian De Palma, himself depressed over the reaction to *Scarface,* for lunch at Hugo's restaurant in West Hollywood.

"What are we doing here?" asked De Palma. "What could we do? Become teachers maybe?"

They looked at one another.

"I don't know," said Scorsese. "We can't go on like this. They don't want to make pictures that we want to make."

For a few weeks, his agent, Harry Ufland, kept his hopes alive, trying to find another backer for the film at half the cost and half the shooting schedule, but he got nowhere. Scorsese realized he had to make another film—any film—just in order to stay alive. Desperate to appease him, Katzenberg and Eisner offered him *Beverly Hills Cop* and *Witness,* but he just couldn't see himself directing a fish-out-of-water comedy about a cop in LA ("What's a fish out of water?" he asked), or fitting in with the Amish in rural Pennsylvania. Returning to New York, Scorsese was finally handed a script by his lawyer, Jay Julien. Called "A Night in SoHo," it had been written by Joseph Minion, a recent graduate of Columbia, and concerned a young office worker led on a wild-goose chase around SoHo at night by his attraction for

"I thought it would be a parody of film noir, and also a parody of a thriller. The angles themselves are parodies—the angles, the cuts, and the Fritz Lang–type shots, the Hitchcock parodies."

Left: Rosanna Arquette's Marcy is a kookily captivating femme fatale.

Opposite: The Munch-like sculpture helps to express Paul's mounting fear and frustration.

a kooky blonde. It was more of a novel than a script, "amateurish, but in a good way," said Scorsese. "You felt it had a lot of heart."

Still numb from his *Last Temptation* bruising, he delighted in the script's sick humor, the way it piled misfortune upon misfortune on its luckless hero, Paul, a scenario with which he could identify. However, the moment the girl, Marcy, died the story fell apart; the original ending had Paul going out with June, the middle-aged lonely heart, to buy an ice cream. At Scorsese's prompting, Minion came up with another ending in which June grows to a massive height, and Paul disappears up her skirt, returning to the womb—a surreal Freudian twist. That version of the script took its title from Marcy's riff about *The Wizard of Oz*: "Surrender, Dorothy." "Marty, you can't do that, you're out of your mind," David Geffen told him. Steven Spielberg suggested that after Paul is mummified in a papier-mâché mold to protect him from the angry mob, he should fall out of the back of a truck, causing the mold to shatter. Michael Powell thought he should fall out of the truck and wind up at work again. Terry Gilliam told

him to lose the whole thing. Almost everyone seemed to agree Paul should fall out of the truck.

Scorsese storyboarded the entire movie—five hundred shots, sixteen setups a day, as opposed to the five he had managed on *The King of Comedy*—and filmed it in forty days flat, financed with a bank loan taken out by the movie's star, Griffin Dunne, and actress-producer Amy Robinson, who had played Teresa in *Mean Streets*. Scorsese edited it in four months. Scorsese wanted to parody Hitchcock with lots of close-ups—nothing special, just fingers on light switches, say—to put the audience on edge, and camera movement to give Paul's predicament a vertiginous swing. He told Dunne, "There are a lot of crazy shots here. You have to answer the phone with your left hand and talk this way. Please, if you can't do it, if you feel uncomfortable, just tell me." Dunne was fine with it; Scorsese was back in his groove. "It was kind of a miracle," he said. *The King of Comedy* had been a depressing experience, from start to finish. On *After Hours*, "every time I put my eye to the viewfinder, I was happy."

Linda Fiorentino as Kiki Bridges, Marcy's sculptor roommate.

"It was all shot at night, eight weeks of night shooting. That's great. I used to edit at night, too. I prefer the night because you don't get the phone calls."

With new wife, Barbara De Fina, and parents, Charles and Catherine, at a private screening of *After Hours*.

Comedies are not famous for their camera angles. Preston Sturges starts *Unfaithfully Yours* with a long crane shot that circles the orchestra before closing in on Rex Harrison, conducting *con brio* from the front, but Wilder and Hawks filmed their busiest scenes in master shot, at eye level, as if to better contain the wildness within the frame. Now, of course, we have the Coens, who think nothing of tracking the camera along a bar and hopping over a sleeping drunk as they do in *Blood Simple*—their brand of dark comedy seems to demand a cock-eyed angle on the world—but as the brothers were still zipping up their first body bags, Scorsese was panning, tilting, craning, and tracking his way through Lower Manhattan in *After Hours*.

It's one of his slighter works—a black comedy that spins in ever tighter circles, like someone rolling a penny around Dante's Inferno—but no less brisk and buoyant for that, with the director at his most comically Catholic. Griffin Dunne is a perfect mixture of furtive lust, apology, and silent agony and Rosanna Arquette is glorious. "I confess it was Rosanna Arquette's scenes that I most enjoyed filming," said

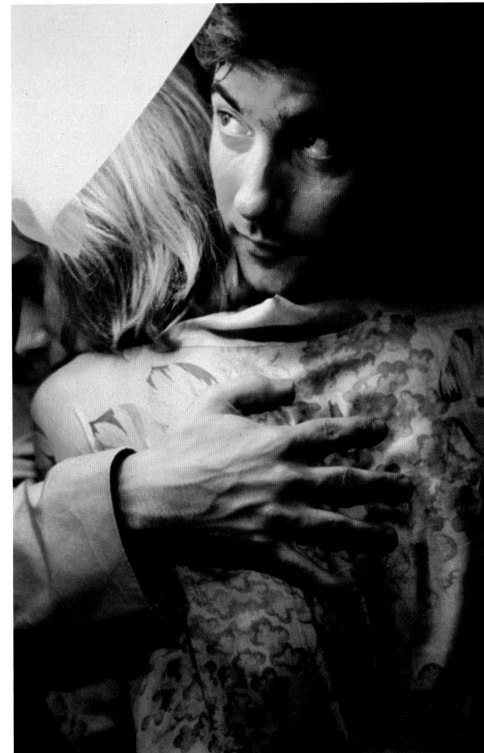

Paul holds Marcy, with lust still on his mind.

Scorsese, who probably came the closest he ever would to outlining his sexual ideal in the form of Marcy—a screwball coquette, skittish, damaged, endlessly puzzled by male desire, her giggling fits departing as mysteriously as they arrive, like a sudden rain shower. It's a beautifully ticklish performance, Arquette's reactions bubbling up from such a spontaneous place, she seem to catch *herself* by surprise. Scorsese had three sirens lined up to torment Paul—you can't help but notice that equals the number of marriages Scorsese had racked up by this point—but once Arquette leaves the picture, some of the life goes out of it, despite memorably dotty turns from Teri Garr and Catherine O'Hara, in ascending order of psychosis.

The film served its purpose: A quick pick-me-up, shot outside the system for $4 million, it got Scorsese's blood flowing and even earned him the Best Director Award at Cannes in 1986. The ending finally adopted by Scorsese, with Paul breaking out of his papier-mâché chrysalis by falling out of the truck slap in front of his uptown office gates, repeated a similar image of Jerry Lewis breaking free of his cocoon at the conclusion of *The King of Comedy*. That made two films in a row that ended with an image of mummification, liberation, and rebirth. Something was cooking.

The Color of Money

1986

"With *The Color of Money*, working
with two big stars, we tried to make
a Hollywood movie. Or rather, I tried
to make one of my pictures, but with
a Hollywood star, Paul Newman.
That was mainly making a film
about an American icon."

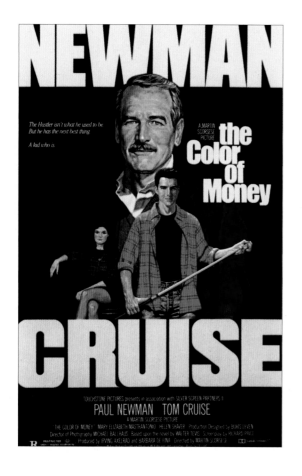

"The film concerns a being who changes his lifestyle, who alters his values. His arena is a billiard room, but what it is does not matter. The film concerns delusion then charity, perversion then purity."

Above: On set with Paul Newman, one of Scorsese's screen idols.

Page 123: Tom Cruise (Vincent Lauria) and Newman (Eddie Felson) go head to head.

Scorsese was in London on a press tour when Paul Newman called. The star had two words for him.

"Eddie Felson."

"I love that character," said Scorsese.

"Eddie Felson reminds me of the characters you've dealt with in your pictures," continued Newman. "And I thought more ought to be heard from him."

"Who's involved?"

"Just you and me."

"What have you got?"

"I've got a script."

Newman's script was very much a typical sequel, featuring clips from the first film, *The Hustler*, but Scorsese sought out novelist Richard Price for another draft. If *After Hours* marked the beginning of Scorsese's career rehab—a piece of expressionism on the cheap, shot outside the system in just forty days—*The Color of Money* showed the director fast approaching match fitness. A studio film, with a bigger budget, two stars, the whole thing came together, in one of the great instances of eighties deal-making, under the aegis of Newman's agent, Mike Ovitz, who also happened to represent Tom Cruise. "I was up against stronger powers," said Scorsese. "I wanted to prove to myself that I could survive within the system by conducting a film costing $14 million with a much bigger crew, an army of extras, a more elaborate visual choreography, and two stars who could have held me at their mercy if they had decided to be temperamental, or improvise, or just arrive late on set."

An interesting flinch of mistrust. Newman had written Scorsese a fan letter saying how much he liked *Raging Bull*, although he mistook the director's name for "Michael Scorsese." Scorsese had idolized the actor since he was fourteen and saw *Somebody Up There Likes Me*, Robert Wise's biopic of middleweight boxing champion Rocky Graziano. Newman seemed to hail from an entirely different world— he drank beer and was crazy about sports and liked the outdoors, whereas Scorsese spent most of his time lurking in darkened movie

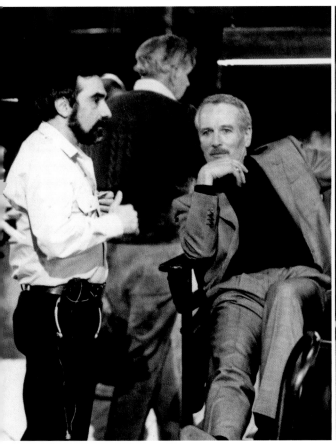

The actors played all their own pool shots.

theaters and jumped if you showed him a cactus. But something about Newman intrigued him: "Here's a … guy who keeps improving with age. He races automobiles even if he doesn't win. He can't beat the top Formula One drivers. I wanted to know why he took the risk of racing if he knew he'd never be number one?"

He sensed that the answer to that question would be the key to unlocking Eddie Felson: Why would this guy start playing pool again at fifty-two, twenty-five years after the action of the first film? At their first meeting, he asked Newman: "Why do you race if you don't win every time?" The star looked at him, unable to answer. "That's the picture," said Scorsese. He knew Eddie would never be able to walk away from the pool table, as seemed to happen at the end of *The Hustler*. "He has it in his blood," he said. Richard Price agreed: Felson would never have quit. He would have simply become a hustler of a different type, maybe not playing pool himself but hustling younger talent. The idea of an older man corrupting a younger one, and in the process regaining his own taste for the game, fascinated Scorsese.

He and Price presented the idea to Newman in February of 1985 at the actor's rented house in Malibu. Chatting on the sundeck overlooking the Pacific Ocean, and seeing Scorsese in his New York clothes, encased in the boiling sun, Newman burst out laughing. "I had the impression he thought I was Nosferatu," said Scorsese, but the actor also loved the pitch, and thus was born a working method, with Price writing on his own, bringing what he had written to Scorsese, both men then going to Newman for his input, with occasional breaks for the actor to go and race cars. Scorsese kept telling Price, "we're making a three-piece suit for the man. He's the main character and the reason we're involved in this thing. He's got to look a certain way and the words have to come through his vocal cords."

Determined to bring the film in on schedule and under budget, the director planned the production "like a military campaign." His tight production team included Newman's lawyer and producer, Barbara De Fina, who was by then Scorsese's fourth wife. Portions of Scorsese's and Newman's fees were put up as insurance against going

"This was my first time working with a movie star. A movie star is a person I saw when I was ten or eleven on a big screen. With De Niro and the other guys it was a different thing. We were friends. We kind of grew together creatively … But with Paul, I would go in and I would see a thousand different movies in his face"

Opposite: *The Color of Money* was Scorsese's first experience of directing a genuine star vehicle and resulted in Newman's first Oscar for Best Actor.

Right: Eddie pays out to Moselle (Bruce A. Young). Money was the main issue on and off screen. Scorsese saw the film as "a calculated business move" to prove that he was a player worth backing.

over budget. At Newman's request, Scorsese rehearsed the actors extensively, blocking the scenes as they went, and storyboarding all the pool games in two or three days, so that by the time cameras rolled, they could really hit the ground running.

Shot during the cold, dirty Chicago winter of 1985 to 1986, with Newman and Cruise playing all their own games, *The Color of Money* was an exercise in fast, lean, pinchpenny filmmaking. Scorsese watched costs right down to the last phone bill. Everyone got trailers, but while Newman and Cruise got phones Scorsese did not. He collected quarters and made calls from the payphone on set, until other people came along and threw him off. It grew a little embarrassing, until one of the teamsters asked him if he wanted his own phone. He still asked people to call him back.

Instead of fifty days, they finished in forty-nine. Instead of $14.5 million, they spent $13 million. "That's the stuff of sainthood in Hollywood," Scorsese told interviewers proudly. There was no mistaking his purr of satisfaction. "I enjoyed making it immensely."

The Color of Money is a good movie: a fast, tight blues riff about an old dog learning new tricks. If Scorsese purists tend to praise it only faintly, or underrate it—as Scorsese does himself—it may be because it is so many things other than simply "A Martin Scorsese Picture." It's a sequel, and a star vehicle, and not just any stars but Paul Newman, and Tom Cruise in his *Risky Business* phase—uncool. Not only that but it made $52 million in America, four times its budget, making it Scorsese's most profitable film to date. In short, for those who would force the director into a zero-sum showdown with popular success from which only one can walk away triumphant, the film represents a huge victory for the forces of mammon. Hell, it's even got money in its *title*.

Phooey. Of all the films Scorsese made in the mid-to-late eighties, it is the best, just as *Taxi Driver* was his best seventies film, and for much the same reason: the rare three-way synergy enjoyed by director, lead actor, and writer. All three—Scorsese, Newman, and Price—saw themselves in Fast Eddie Felson, and all felt the need for his comeback as keenly as if for themselves. Their hunger is there on the screen—

"*The Color of Money* was a good commercial exercise for me.
I learned a great deal about structure and style."

in the slate-gray light hanging over Chicago's motels, back rooms, and eateries. It's there in the watchful hawk-like gaze of Eddie Felson, the once great pool-hall prodigy turned liquor salesman, who senses a fast buck when he meets Vincent (Cruise), a local hotshot cleaning up at the pool table for the amusement of his girlfriend, Carmen (Mary Elizabeth Mastrantonio). It's there, too, in Scorsese's whip-pans as Eddie cranes his neck to see what's going on—his technique working hand in hand with Price's taut, savvy script to set up the central triangle of the film, as swiftly as a player racking up the balls before a game.

Cruise gives one of his finer performances as a rooster too busy crowing to see how he's being played by his girl. Eddie sees it immediately, of course, making the scenes between Newman and

Mastrantonio the finest in the film—the actors have the easy, immediate rapport of two leopards arguing over who gets to eat lunch first. Wait for the moment when Eddie reprimands Carmen for flirting with him, all the stillness of Newman's performance suddenly gone in a burst of speed and naked aggression. He moves like a cat. Scorsese had directed acting vehicles before—both *Raging Bull* and *The King of Comedy* had been directed at De Niro's behest—but *The Color of Money* was his first true star vehicle, and maybe he couldn't have done it for an actor trailing any less celluloid history: For once, his roles as director and archivist were as one. The result is a wonderfully grooved character portrait, running on Newman's trademark blend of intensity and mellowness—it won him his first Oscar for Best Actor—but with an added bite of desperation that was

Opposite: "You make him feel good, I teach him how to run." With the help of Carmen (Mary Elizabeth Mastrantonio), Eddie schools Vincent in the art of the hustle.

Right: His credibility restored, Scorsese was now embraced not only by Mastrantonio but by Hollywood.

Scorsese's, too. When Eddie looks up at the camera through his shades in the film's final shot, says "I'm back," and then makes a killer break, he spoke for his director as much as himself.

Scorsese saw the crossroads he was at clearly. "The question was: Are you going to survive as a Hollywood filmmaker? Because even though I live in New York I'm a 'Hollywood director.' Then again, even when I try to make a Hollywood film, there's something in me that says, 'go the other way.'" Of all his films, *The Color of Money* splits the difference with the least amount of fuss, sending a driver down the middle of the table with a resounding crack. There's a tendency to overlook the films Scorsese made during this period—*The King of Comedy, After Hours, The Color of Money*—his "rehab" pictures,

made while in recovery from the seventies, in preparation for his comeback proper at the beginning of the nineties. It's a mistake, I think, and not just because of the discipline Scorsese internalized in the course of making them: All three films sit low to the ground, giving off a hard, compacted, graphite glitter. There's not a wasted shot among them. If *The King of Comedy* grows more prescient by the minute, and *After Hours* anticipates the Coens, *The Color of Money* foretells the alliance of Quentin Tarantino and John Travolta in *Pulp Fiction*, of Darren Aronofsky and Mickey Rourke in *The Wrestler*, and all the other instances in which a director and a star have hooked up to hustle for a suitcase of studio money. Scorsese wasn't just surviving—he was mapping out the contours of the independent film industry to come.

The Last Temptation of Christ

1988

"I made it as a prayer, an act of worship. I wanted to be a priest. My whole life has been movies and religion. That's it. Nothing else."

Page 131: "It is accomplished." Willem Dafoe as Jesus in the harrowing depiction of the Crucifixion.

Above: Jesus flanked by Mary Magdalene (Barbara Hershey) and Judas Iscariot (Harvey Keitel).

Opposite: Scorsese finally got to make *Last Temptation* five years after the project was canceled by Paramount.

After Paramount pulled the plug on *The Last Temptation of Christ* in 1983, Harry Ufland had shopped around a stripped-down version of the film, keeping hopes alive, just, but the film had become the laughing stock of cocktail parties in Hollywood. "Big people in the business were turning around and saying 'Yeah, I know the pictures you make,'" said Scorsese. "One guy introduced me to someone who was the head of some company. He says 'This guy's gonna make *Last Temptation*.' The guy looked at me and laughed in my face. Walked away. 'Yeah right. Call me next week.' I mean, I'd come through all those years for *that*? It was like a kick in the heart."

The savior of the project, in the end, was Mike Ovitz, the man who had made the deal for *The Color of Money*, and who had by the late eighties become—as co-founder of CAA—the most powerful man in Hollywood. His collaboration with Scorsese would change forever the course of his career, not just getting projects like *The Last Temptation of Christ*, *Goodfellas*, and *The Age of Innocence* off the ground but allowing the director to set up his film foundation at his

office in uptown Manhattan, complete with editing suite and screening room. "That was all Mike," Scorsese would tell visitors. "I owe pretty much everything to Mike Ovitz."

One night in the fall of 1986, Ovitz invited Scorsese over to his house in Brentwood Park, Los Angeles, a big white neo-Georgian mansion hung with Picassos and Dubuffets.

"You know you can get paid for this," Ovitz told him.

Scorsese laughed. At this point, he didn't care about the money. On *Raging Bull* he and De Niro had split salaries as a sign of trust. On *The Color of Money* he had put his salary up as insurance.

"What do you want done most?" asked Ovitz.

"*The Last Temptation of Christ*," replied Scorsese.

Ovitz smiled. "I'll get it made for you."

Scorsese didn't believe it for a second, but within three months Ovitz had pulled together a deal with Tom Pollock at Universal, in conjunction with Garth Drabinsky, the head of Cineplex Odeon Theatres. He called Scorsese in January of 1987.

"I never imagined the reaction against doing something like this would be so vociferous. It may be hard to understand now, but at the time I first decided to do it, I really thought a film of this nature would be quite acceptable."

"What's the price?" he asked.

Scorsese told him the movie's new price tag: $6 or 7 million—almost nothing.

"They want to do it," Ovitz told him.

Still, Scorsese had to pitch to Pollock. He was nervous before the meeting, uncomfortable with his new role as supplicant. "How are you feeling?" asked Ovitz. "Get in there tomorrow and do your lunch meeting, and give them your idea."

"I don't know," he said, "I don't know if I can."

"What do you mean 'you don't know'?" replied Ovitz. "You're going to go in and tell them you're going to make the best picture ever made. That's how you do it."

The next day Scorsese walked out of Pollock's office with a deal.

He had recruited a cast back in 1983 and most of it was still in place—Harvey Keitel as Judas, Barbara Hershey as Mary Magdalene, Vic Argo as St. Peter—but this time he had Willem Dafoe, not Aidan Quinn, as Jesus, and David Bowie, not Sting, as Pontius Pilate. Paul Schrader had condensed Nikos Kazantzakis's six-hundred-page novel into a script, removing most of the historical context and focusing on the relationship between Jesus and Judas, turning the movie into a fascinating study of twinned, opposing souls: the preacher and the revolutionary, the man of spirit and the man of action, the betrayer and the betrayed—a theme that Scorsese would pursue further in *Goodfellas*, *Gangs of New York*, and *The Departed*. Over a period of several months, he and Jay Cocks rewrote Schrader's dialogue to make it plainer, more idiomatic. "Jesus lived in the world," he said. "He wasn't in the temple. He wasn't in church. He was in the world. He was on the street."

Two months before the shoot in Morocco, Scorsese simplified his 1983 storyboards. Back then he'd envisioned a sweeping epic with lots of wide angles, crane shots, thousands of extras. With a budget of just $7 million, and a schedule of only sixty-two days, the production

"The whole point of the movie is that nobody is to blame, not even the Romans. It's all part of the plan. Otherwise, it's insane. I mean, the Jewish people give us God, and we persecute them for two thousand years for it."

Left: It was Hershey who introduced Scorsese to Nikos Kazantzakis's source novel during the making of *Boxcar Bertha* back in 1972.

Below: Jesus in the wilderness, where he is tempted by the Devil in various guises.

was run like a commando operation, everything planned down to the last detail, to get around the short days in the desert. The crew had to be in place before the sun rose. At four thirty in the afternoon the light began to fade, and by six it was night and they were in the dark on silent, deserted trails that hadn't changed in two hundred years. "When you're in Morocco, and the sun's going down, and the generator's breaking, and the actor's wig is coming off, and you know you don't have $26 million and the ten thousand extras like Bertolucci—that's discipline."

The shooting schedule changed daily. Scorsese lost a few pounds and even got a tan, something that had never happened to him before, not even when he was in Arizona shooting *Alice Doesn't Live Here Anymore*. "On *Alice* I had the bars at least," he only half-joked. In Morocco, there were no bars, no phones, nothing. They couldn't even see any rushes. They had to shoot the film "blind," sending the footage back to Thelma Schoonmaker to edit, then grilling her about what they had. "What does it look like?" Scorsese would ask her. "Does this or that happen in the scene?"

Filming in the Moroccan desert presented
singular challenges.

The John the Baptist sequence was completed in a single day.
To make the most of good weather, the Crucifixion was shot in the
middle, over three days with sixty different camera setups, without
interruption, no stopping for lunch. It would have been impossible
without Scorsese's storyboards. Dafoe could only stay up there for
two or three minutes before he started to find it difficult to breathe.
"The only things missing were the nails," said Scorsese. He shot three
versions of the ending, unable to decide what Christ's last words
should be. "It's over"? Too Roy Orbison. "It is consummated"? Too
sexual. "It is finished"? "It is completed"? In the end they decided to
use Kazantzakis's version: "It is accomplished." Or, as Scorsese, giddy
with relief at finally bringing the film to the screen, translated for the
benefit of one interviewer: *Ididit! Ididit! Ididit!*

"Motion pictures were not born in religious practice," writes Paul
Schrader in his superb book *Transcendental Style in Film: Ozu, Bresson,
Dreyer*, "but instead are the totally profane offspring of capitalism

and technology." Photographing only people's outsides, not their
insides, cinema draws closest to the realm of the spirit only by an act
of self-renunciation, argues Schrader, who finds that renunciation in
the "aesthetic of paucity" pursued by directors such as Yasujirō Ozu
and Robert Bresson—the cinematic equivalent of sackcloth and ashes.
The rest is kitsch. In Cecil B. DeMille's *The Ten Commandments*,
God power-pitches some small, whirling fireballs across the screen
accompanied by a whizzing sound and some angelic choirs. The fireballs
build in size, and then in a puff of smoke—*poof!*—Moses's tablets are
engraved with the Commandments. God seems to share his spirit of
showmanship, and design sense, with Wladziu Valentino Liberace.

The best thing in Scorsese's film are the miracles. In Scorsese's
version of events, Jesus (Dafoe) is eating an apple while Judas (Keitel)
sleeps, and tosses the core into the desert. Next we see a fully formed
tree. The shot is held in silence for a few seconds, then it is gone.
The same with the cobra, the lion, and the pillar of flame in which
forms the Devil manifests himself to tempt Jesus—gone, with one

"There were things to be decided on the spot. How does an apostle walk up and ask for something? I don't know. I had to work all that out."

Jesus and the apostles arrive
in Jerusalem.

snip of the editor's scissors, the most basic magic of the movies, Scorsese's budget enforcing its own aesthetic of paucity. The crowd listening to Jesus deliver the Sermon on the Mount is no more than a small throng, close enough to hear each individual doubt, not least Jesus's own. He seems to be talking himself into belief, into action.

Much of the film is like that: an argument scratched in dust and blood. It is also, for long stretches, baffling. The conflict between Jesus and Judas is up and running before the movie starts, and is never clearly delineated. Jesus's argument with God, meanwhile, is the first thing we witness. "First I fasted for three months," says Dafoe in voiceover, as we see Jesus curled in a fetal crouch on the ground. "I even whipped myself before I went to sleep. At first it

worked. Then the pain came back. And the voices …" The central conflict of the film is thus internal, invisible, off-camera. Only in the final sequence—the last temptation of the title—does the film attain anything like true dramatic shape. Nailed to the Cross, Jesus conjures an alternative path for himself, one in which he settled down with Mary Magdalene and started a family, only to be witness to her death, the sacking of Jerusalem, and the baleful reproach of Judas. What an ending: as powerful and wrenching as anything in the director's work, prefiguring the mazy torment—and final-reel deliverance—of *Shutter Island*. There is a vein of heartbreak, and regret, in Scorsese that has to do with men realizing too late the miracles hiding in plain sight.

The final section of the film, in which Jesus receives a vision of an alternative outcome to his life.

The movie's release brought denunciations from far-right Christian groups, accusations of blasphemy, demonstrations. The film did poorly at the box office, taking only $8 million. "There was nothing I could say or do," said Scorsese. "In the end I think *Last Temptation* was out of my grasp because I naïvely thought I was supposed to have taken some sort of spiritual journey with it. But it may have been the wrong material to deal with in that way—dealing with Jesus as a man, the carnality, the physicality." He had for so long been directing films about saviors—Charlie in *Mean Streets*, Travis Bickle in *Taxi Driver*—using his Catholicism as subtext, as shadow, that by the time he got around to flushing it out into the open, beneath a searing Moroccan sun, the subtext had died on the vine. *The Last Temptation of Christ* is as good

an argument as any, in fact, against the more hardcore variants of auteur theory. Sometimes directors need forcibly restraining from getting to film their passion projects. Steven Spielberg didn't need to make *Hook*: He had already shown us he was Peter Pan in *E.T.* David Cronenberg didn't need to make *Naked Lunch*: The match-up with William S. Burroughs was too exact. Director and author canceled each other out.

Scorsese didn't need to make a film about Christ—he had already made it, many times. He had almost lived it, getting the film to screen. Apparently one of those self-punishing souls who needs to make life difficult for themselves, if only for the release it affords them afterward, Scorsese could now get *The Last Temptation of Christ* out of his system, cut loose, and enjoy himself.

"I wanted him to be a character you cared about when he died."

Portraying Jesus as a flesh-and-blood human being brought him closer to the audience, but angered conservative Christians.

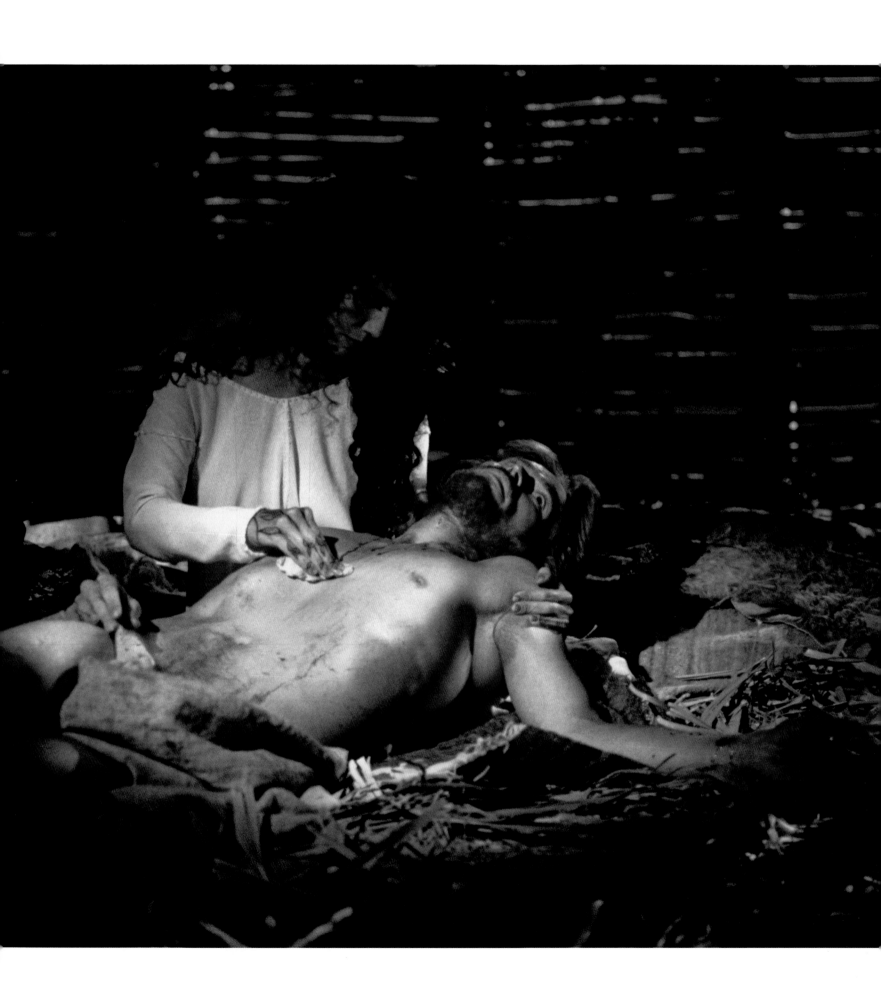

Goodfellas

1990

"What fascinated me most were the details of everyday life. What they eat, how they dress, the nightclubs they go to, what their houses look like, and how, around that, life organizes itself, day by day, minute by minute."

"*Goodfellas* is an indictment. I had to do it in such a way as to make people angry about the state of things, about organized crime and how and why it works. Why does it work? What is it in our society that makes it work so well and operate on such a grand scale? Major gangsters aren't usually convicted. I have no idea why."

Opposite: Ignoring Marlon Brando's advice, Scorsese could not resist adapting Nicholas Pileggi's book about mobster Henry Hill.

Page 141: "To be a gangster was to own the world." Robert De Niro (Jimmy Conway), Joe Pesci (Tommy DeVito), and Ray Liotta (Henry Hill).

At the height of the controversy over *The Last Temptation of Christ*, Scorsese took the film to the Venice Film Festival. Walking out of his hotel on the lido, surrounded by a half-dozen or so bodyguards, he saw Ray Liotta across the lobby. "Ray, how are you?" he called, having just seen the actor's audition tape arrive at his office back in New York. "I got the tape. I haven't been able to view it yet." As Liotta came toward him, one of the bodyguards grabbed the actor's arm. Scorsese noticed something interesting about his reaction: He held his ground, but made them understand he was no threat. "I liked his behavior at that moment, and I saw, Oh, he understands that kind of situation." He thought: *Goodfella*.

The director had been in Chicago shooting *The Color of Money* when he first came across a review in the *New York Review of Books* of *Wiseguy*, Nicholas Pileggi's account of the rise and fall of Henry Hill and his hoodlum associates. He got a copy of the book in galley and loved the "wonderful arrogance of it … Just straight ahead. Want. Take. Simple." Hill seemed to speak in his own voice, his own rhythm,

almost that of a stand-up comedian—*Business bad? Fuck you, pay me. You had a fire? Fuck you, pay me. The place got hit by lightning? Fuck you, pay me.* The lower down the ladder you went, the louder the mouth. That's what he'd noticed as a kid in Little Italy. The toughest guys always had the best manners. Either way, you stepped aside when they showed up. "You could just feel the flow of power from these people, and as a child you looked up to this without understanding it." That was the impetus behind *Goodfellas*—"It's what I thought about these people when I was eight."

Still, he had reservations about returning to this subject matter. Marlon Brando told him, "Don't do another gangster picture. You've done *Mean Streets*, you did the gangsters in *Raging Bull*. You don't have to do that." At first, Scorsese agreed. He told Michael Powell, "I don't think I can do this *Goodfellas* thing," but Powell took the script home with him and had Thelma Schoonmaker read it aloud to him, so bad was his eyesight at that point. Scorsese was in his editing suite at the Brill Building when Powell called. "This is wonderful,"

he raved. "It's funny and no one's ever seen this way of life before. You *must* do it."

Shepherded again by Mike Ovitz, the project found a home at Warner Bros., who initially wanted Tom Cruise and Madonna for the leads, but after Venice Scorsese knew he wanted Liotta to play Henry Hill—he'd also been a big fan of his performance in Jonathan Demme's *Something Wild*. He hesitated over who to cast as Jimmy Conway until Robert De Niro suggested himself, and with De Niro onboard they were able to squeeze a few more million from the studio. After meeting Lorraine Bracco at his apartment on Fifty-Seventh Street, Scorsese cast her as Henry's wife, Karen, and with Joe Pesci in place as Tommy DeVito, Pileggi put the word on the street that they were looking for extras with real-life Mob connections. They held an open audition at Rao's restaurant in Harlem—dozens of guys showed up and by dessert they were all trying to outdo each other's stories: *I knew a guy who beat someone up, I knew a guy who stole this, who stole that* … More than a half-dozen of them were eventually put on the Warner Bros. payroll, although they balked

at giving up their social security numbers. "One two six, uh, six seven eight, uh, four three two, one seven eight …" they would go. "They just kept reciting numbers until they were over," said Pileggi. "Nobody ever figured out where that money went or who cashed the checks." During filming, only De Niro had real money in his pocket; everyone else had counterfeit cash. They even caught somebody pushing it as the real thing. "Let's say we had a lot of set visits from certain people," said Illeana Douglas, who played one of the other gangster's wives. "There were a lot of people in the film where it was, nudge-nudge, wink-wink, 'Make sure she gets on camera, otherwise Local 19 is going to be a little upset with us.' There was a great sense of blurring the lines."

Coming off the stylized expressionism of *Life Lessons*, his contribution to the 1989 *New York Stories* anthology film, Scorsese wanted movement, lots of it, and kept going back to Dziga Vertov's 1929 silent classic *Man with a Movie Camera* for inspiration. The famous tracking shot through the Copacabana nightclub came about, originally, because the management wouldn't allow them to come

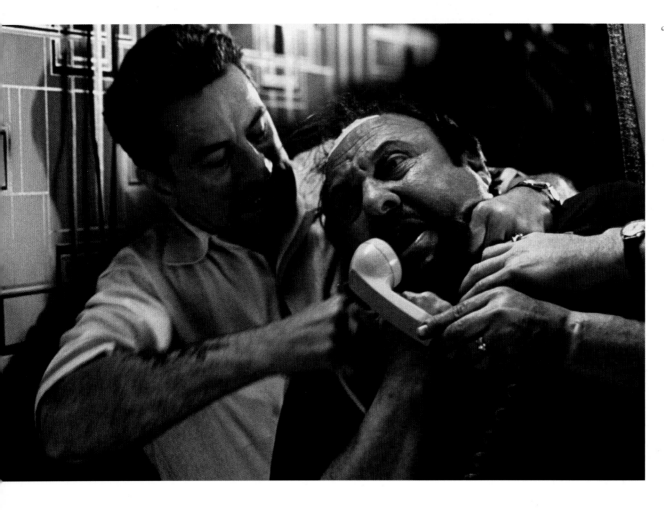

Jimmy puts the squeeze on Morrie Kessler (Chuck Low).

in through the main entrance, only through the back. They did it in eight takes, and then only so many because veteran comedian Henny Youngman—who was playing the club comic—kept blowing his lines. Scorsese kept telling the crew, "Make sure you move in such a way that we see the money—or at least the hand gestures, a tip to the right, a tip to the left, a tip here, a tip there …" It was like a magic act: Everything had to arrive as if from nowhere. "When the table comes in, it's got to *fly* in!" he said. "I came here as a kid and I saw this!"

Much of the dialogue was improvised—the scene where Tommy shoots Spider (the only scripted line of which was "Why don't you go fuck yourself, Tommy"), the impromptu art criticism over the dog painting ("One dog goes one way, and the other dog goes the other way. And this guy's saying, What do you want from me?") and the famous "Do you think I'm funny?" exchange between Tommy and Henry, which came from a story of Pesci's. He'd been working at some restaurant in Brooklyn, or the Bronx, and offhandedly said to one of the customers, "You're funny," and the guy turned on him, "You think

I'm funny?" The only way Pesci got out of it was by doubling down and making fun of the whole thing. "We've got to use that," said Scorsese, who conducted a rehearsal with the rest of the cast and recorded it, as he had done on *Mean Streets*, then constructed the scene from the transcript. The editing was crucial. "The key moment was how long we waited before Ray says, 'Get the fuck outta here, Tommy,' in an attempt to break it," said Schoonmaker. "We kept screening it over and over again to get just the right beat for that one incredible moment where Ray knows if he doesn't make this work, he's going to get shot."

More than any Scorsese film since *Raging Bull*, *Goodfellas* would find its form in the editing room. It took Scorsese and Schoonmaker back to their early days cutting documentaries together, using slow motion, fast motion, freeze-frames for emphasis—a fireball, for instance, followed by the words "they did it out of respect" to convey the impact it would have on the eight-year-old Henry. Scorsese showed Pileggi the beginning of Truffaut's *Jules et Jim* to show him the effect he was going for. "I wanted *Goodfellas* to move as fast as a trailer or

Right: Tommy does not let Spider live to regret insulting him.

Below: Scorsese and Thelma Schoonmaker brought *Goodfellas* to life in the editing room.

"There are moments, especially when you work with some very gifted actors like I've been blessed to work with, when certain scenes just come together in the cutting. The music hits, and the camera moves right, and the actors are in there, it's—well, it happens in the cutting. That moment—that's what makes it worth it."

"One night, Bobby Vinton sent us champagne. There was nothing like it. I didn't think there was anything strange in any of this." Seduced by the high life, Karen (Lorraine Bracco) soon learns not to ask questions.

the opening of *Jules et Jim* and to go on like that for two hours," he said. "The trick in the picture was to sort of ignore the danger, make it a rollicking road movie in a way—like a kind of Bob Hope and Bing Crosby picture, with everybody on the road and having a great time."

Scorsese knew which songs he wanted in the film three years before he shot it. He wanted the soundtrack to play like one of the old jukeboxes he had heard pumping music out into the street back in Little Italy, and then to age in real time, alongside the characters—the Sex Pistols version of "My Way" playing over the end credits, for example, rather than the triumphant Sinatra version. Elsewhere, the soundtrack shows Scorsese masterfully juggling the apposite and the ironic. The line "I'm a flea-bit peanut monkey and all my friends are junkies" from the Stones' "Monkey Man" plays over the sequence involving a baby, drug-smuggling, and a stroller, while the killing of Billy Batts takes place to the sound of "Atlantis," a song by Donovan. "Though gods they were," sings the famously vegetarian, pacifist singer-songwriter, as Tommy returns to the bar to beat Batts's head to pulp.

"They *are* like gods, and gods fall," said Scorsese. "It's the American Dream gone completely mad and twisted."

Obliged by the studio to preview, they had a disastrous screening for an audience in Orange County, Southern California. About seventy people walked out. "They thought it was an outrage that I had made these people look so attractive," said Scorsese. "A lot of the preview audience were agitated by the last-day sequence, but I argued that they *should* be agitated." Bob Daly, the Warner Bros. chairman, had to go countless times to argue Scorsese's case to the ratings board. In response, Scorsese tightened the last two reels and shifted a couple of sequences around. They were supposed to open in two thousand theaters. Warner Bros. opened it in a thousand—real B theaters, too, with fewer seats and grungy decor, convinced they had a bomb.

Instead, they had a meteor. Is there a faster two-and-a-half-hour movie in existence than *Goodfellas*? As critic David Thomson has pointed out, the film "rushes down its slope like a great musical and a wild comedy."

"Whenever we needed money, we'd rob the airport. To us, it was better than Citibank." Scorsese had not always found his work so profitable, but Goodfellas made $46 million at the box office.

It marks Scorsese's most ebullient performance as director, with editing, camerawork, and sound all working at full tilt to create a great, rolling, runaway ribbon of celluloid—cinema as guitar riff—that surges, chugs, and kicks like a Keith Richards guitar lick. "The moviemaking has such bravura you respond as if you were at a live performance," said Pauline Kael. "All you want to talk about is the glorious zigging camera, the freeze-frames and jump cuts. That may be why young film enthusiasts are so turned on by Scorsese's work: They don't just respond to his films, they want to be him."

Up to a point. That Steadicam shot through the Copacabana is a show-off piece of filmmaking, but it works because Henry himself is showing off in order to seduce Karen—so Scorsese seduces the audience, too. His exuberance is born of the vitality of his hoodlum antiheroes, who even as they dish out death are themselves full of life—vibrant, awful, vulgar life, with their wide suits and hot cars, their lacquered women and their terrible taste in home furnishings. But what really assured the film's popularity—and *Goodfellas* is by a

wide measure Scorsese's most popular film, regularly heading up top-ten lists and on almost permanent loop on TV—was the way it used all this anthropological detail to fill out a fantasy the director had nursed since he was a kid, watching all the neighborhood action, asthmatically, from the sidelines. What if, instead, he got to join in the fun? And it *would* be fun, wouldn't it, to be a gangster? To steal people's cars, and abscond with their daughters, and stamp on their heads when they disagreed with you?

Goodfellas is a boyish fantasia of inclusion—an exact, loving recreation of what it might feel like to be welcomed by the Mob, to feel their hands on your back and their laughter in your ears—and a reminder of just how buoyed by bonhomie Scorsese can be when he's not wearing his loneliness like a stain. That seesaw, between wild gregariousness and haunted isolation, has been within him from the beginning. It was there in the eyes of Harvey Keitel, torn between the allure of the streets and the guilty tug of his conscience, but how different again is the unbridled hedonism of Scorsese's goodfellas,

"There were filmmakers and critics who felt I was morally irresponsible to make a film like *Goodfellas*. Well, I'll make more of them if I can."

Planning the shot: Henry realizes
he's next on Jimmy's hit list.

who rob and kill and maim their way to the top without so much as a backward look, unless you count the furtive glances Henry makes into his rearview mirror as he feels the FBI closing in. *Goodfellas* is not about guilt, or Catholicism, or even America in the way that *The Godfather* was about America. It is, as critic Owen Gleiberman observed, "a movie devoted to the hedonistic lure of criminality."

Scorsese's sense of criminality is luscious, tactile, entropic, organic. *Goodfellas* has the bloom and decay of a plant or flower ripening in its own rot—a gangster *nature morte*. His script begins in the middle, the gang's lawbreaking in full flow, then tracks backward for an hour, before arriving where it started and beginning the long slide down to that single frantic day in which Hill attempts to make spaghetti sauce, snort coke, meet with Jimmy, and avoid the Feds, all at the same time. The film doesn't end so much as self-immolate—a shooting star breaking up in its own heat. Scorsese could almost have been tracing the shape of his own career, as if finding a second act in the dramatic

arc shaped by his first. How the mighty fall: He knew *this* theme from the inside out and would return to it in movie after movie.

Goodfellas was a hit at the box office, taking $46 million, as well as with critics, even if it fell at the Academy Awards to *Dances with Wolves*—the loss only confirming Scorsese's position as the neglected saint of American movies, the *poète maudit* of blood and pasta, the uncrowned, exiled king. Everyone was convinced he would win. Illeana Douglas, who was dating the director at the time, even got him a little table where he would put his Oscar. When he lost, all he could think about was his mother. "They put me in the front row with my mother, and then I didn't win," he said, "They don't like me. They really, really don't like me." So be it. A triumphant return to form, *Goodfellas* also marked a rampant ramping up of that form: Scorsese's mature style, a polyphonic legato of movement and rhythm, was there for all to see. The question for the director, going forward, was how to find material that matched it.

"People think gangsters kill people. Yes, of course they do. But the main purpose of the gangster, especially in *Goodfellas*, is to make money. That's why, in *Goodfellas*, Tommy is killed. After a while, he was making more noise than money."

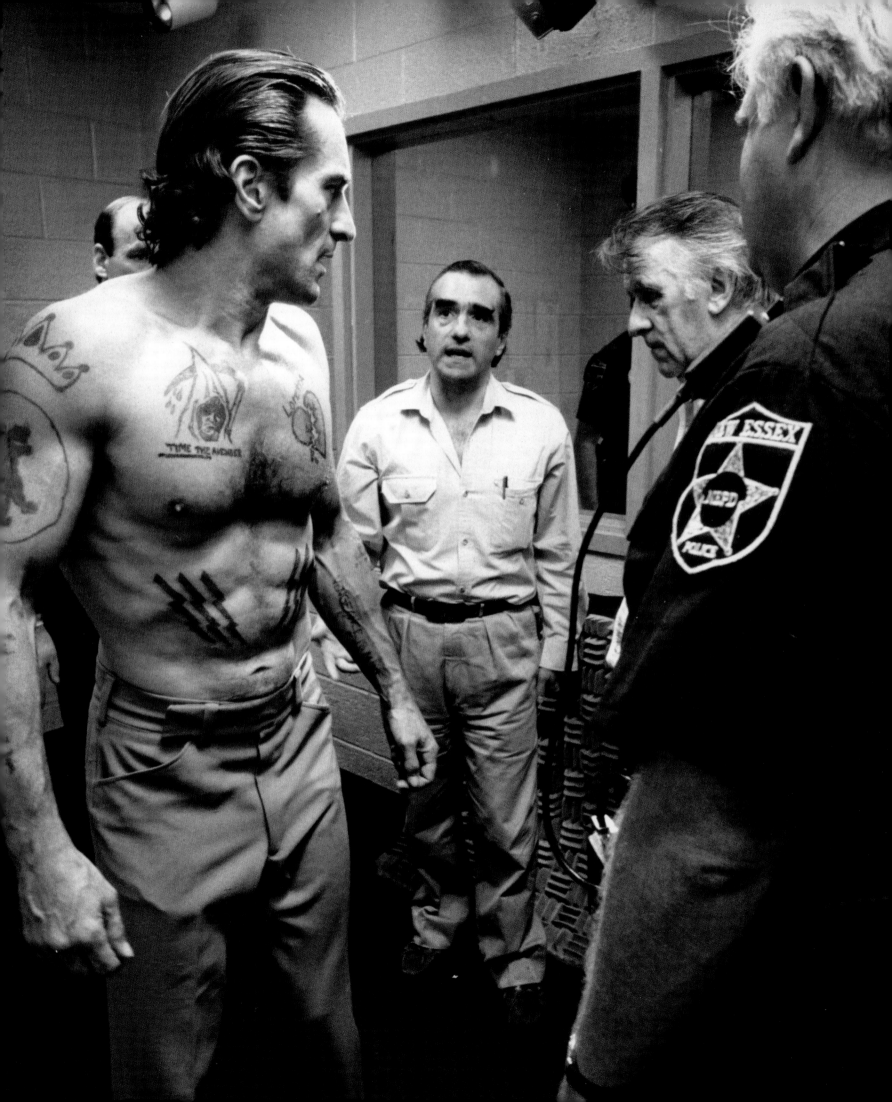

Cape Fear

1991

"*Cape Fear* really felt like going to work in a way, I wasn't really exploring anything new there. Except a Hollywood theatricality, with the thriller and boat aspect. It was really a hard picture for me to make."

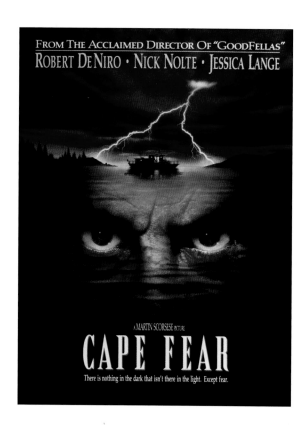

FROM THE ACCLAIMED DIRECTOR OF "GOODFELLAS"

ROBERT DE NIRO • NICK NOLTE • JESSICA LANGE

A MARTIN SCORSESE PICTURE

CAPE FEAR

There is nothing in the dark that isn't there in the light. Except fear.

Page 152: Scorsese back at work with Robert De Niro, as violent ex-con Max Cady.

Above and opposite: As soon as he gets out of jail, Cady tracks down his attorney, Sam Bowden (Nick Nolte), whom he blames for the severity of his sentence, and prepares his revenge.

Scorsese tried his damnedest not to get involved with *Cape Fear*. Universal had backed *The Last Temptation of Christ* on the basis that he would also do a more commercial project for them, and it was while he was editing *Goodfellas* that Steven Spielberg approached him with a script for a remake of the 1962 studio thriller *Cape Fear*, which had starred Gregory Peck as a lawyer named Sam Bowden and Robert Mitchum as his murderous client Max Cady. Scorsese read it three times, "And three times I hated it. I mean really *hated* it."

Originally written with Spielberg in mind, Wesley Strick's script featured lots of scenes of the Bowden family sitting around the piano singing happily. "They were like Martians to me," said Scorsese. "I was rooting for Max to get them." For his next project, he had *Schindler's List*, the adaptation of Thomas Keneally's Holocaust novel, lined up, but after the furor over *Last Temptation* he didn't feel like taking on another sensitive subject. Spielberg, meanwhile, didn't want to do *Cape Fear*—"I just couldn't find it inside me," he said—so they decided to swap projects. "Steve said, 'If you do this, what are you going to do with

the family?'" recalled Scorsese. "'Is the family going to live at the end?' I said, 'Yes, they'll live. Otherwise there's no point to it.' And he said, 'Well, then you can do anything you want up to that point.'"

He commissioned twenty-four drafts from Strick before they arrived at their final shooting script, shifting the focus to the emotional pathology of the Bowdens: the father's infidelity, the wife's anger, their teenage daughter's sexuality and contempt for her parents, with Max Cady emerging as "sort of the malignant spirit of guilt, in a way, of the family—the avenging angel. Punishment for everything you ever felt sexually. It's the basic moral battleground of Christian ethics." A scene that was originally to have been a chase between Cady (Robert De Niro) and Danielle (Juliette Lewis), the Bowdens' daughter, through the basements of her school—what would have been a tour-de-force Spielberg pursuit, ending with Danielle hanging from a ledge—became an unsettling seduction. Scorsese wanted the scene to be about "the violation of the kid, it should be quiet, it should not be a chase." Right before shooting started De Niro had the idea of

"If every picture I made was about Italians in New York, people would say 'That's all he can do.' So I'm trying to stretch."

putting his thumb in Lewis's mouth. Scorsese loved it. "Just do it," he told De Niro, "don't tell her."

Shot with a budget of $34 million, *Cape Fear* was the first film made under a six-year deal between Universal and a director who had never had more than a two-picture deal, ever. Scorsese's association with Mike Ovitz was beginning to pay off, but the responsibilities weighed on him heavily during the shoot, which he later described as an "unpleasant experience because I was uncomfortable with the genre." Working in Panavision for the first time—an unusual choice for a thriller, the format being more commonly associated with widescreen epics like *The Robe* and *The Ten Commandments*—Scorsese and his veteran English cinematographer Freddie Francis pulled out all the stops, using split screens, special filters, matte painting, optical effects, and a device called a Panatate, which allowed the camera to flip over to follow Max Cady as he hung from the ceiling in one scene.

"What I hopefully will do will be to try to blend the genre with me, in a sense, with my expression of it, with the elements that I'm

interested in and see if it doesn't derail it too much," said Scorsese, painfully aware of what had happened the last time he attempted such genre revisionism, on *New York, New York*. He would spend much of his time in press interviews going back and forth between the genre's needs and his own—unable to quite come to rest. "I never intended to make a straight genre film," he would say. "You work within that framework and it's like a chess game. You see if you can really be expressive within it. I don't know if you can, because I always have that problem: Loving the old films, I don't know if I can make them."

There is a strain of seamy, insinuating nastiness to *Cape Fear* that in most thrillers is confined usually to the villain. It certainly starts there: De Niro gives one of his most mesmerizingly repellent performances as ex-con Max Cady, a demon in a floral shirt, brandishing his obscenely stubby cigar while he quotes the Bible to Sam Bowden (Nick Nolte) as if reading pornography. "There isn't a hell of a lot else

Having poisoned the family dog, Cady next brutally assaults and rapes Bowden's lover Lori Davis (Illeana Douglas).

Cady also turns his attention to Bowden's teenage daughter, Danielle (Juliette Lewis), but she is more resourceful than he had expected.

"Maybe [De Niro] thought it would be a good film for me because of its themes of guilt and retribution. Who's right and who's wrong, all the things you dread coming back to haunt you and your family. It's fascinating."

to do in prison except desecrate your flesh," he says in his Southern Drawl, his vocabulary as artificially pumped by his time inside as his tattooed body. But the rot spills and spreads far beyond Cady. Lounging in his car, he flirts with Bowden's wife (Jessica Lange), who brims with anger over her husband's many affairs. He viciously assaults Bowden's most recent mistress (Illeana Douglas), but she, too, is an accident waiting to happen: hypersexualized, promiscuous, a victim looking for a victimizer. And in the audacious seduction scene between Cady and Bowden's daughter, when De Niro inserts his thumb into the mouth of the unsuspecting Lewis, she sucks it like a lollipop—a wonderfully unsettling piece of improv.

The idea of turning Cady into an avenging angel punishing Bowden for his moral hypocrisy is dramatically sound—just the kind of thing Hitchcock might have snuck past the studios, back when he was making his most Catholic pictures, *I Confess* and *The Wrong Man*, in the 1950s. With its nods to Hitch, its Elmer Bernstein score and Saul Bass titles, its cameos for Peck, Mitchum, and Martin Balsam (who all starred in the original movie), Scorsese's *Cape Fear* is a film buff's delight, but his self-estimation was essentially right: He loves the old films, but cannot make them himself. He lacks the shamelessness of the great manipulators—that weird out-of-body ability of a Hitchcock or a Spielberg to direct their movie from the front row of the theater. He directs through one set

Cady grapples with Bowden's wife, Leigh (Jessica Lange).

"The films I make are very personal films. I don't make thrillers or genre pieces. I think it requires a great deal of humility to make a thriller and I can't do that. I promised Universal I'd make them a picture. I'm not excusing the film; I tried a lot of things with it—some successful, some not—and quite honestly I don't know if it works or not."

of eyes: his own. It's what makes him a great film artist but it also makes him a sloppy and sometimes hysterical disciple of genre. A hothead who cannot wait to bring everyone else to the boil, Scorsese lacks the cooler temperament of the great thriller makers.

A small example: A shot of a teddy bear, wired to a window to signal Cady's entry, is held not in silence, to build tension, but assailed on all sides by the screeches of Bernstein's violins. The violins let us know how *Scorsese* is feeling, as he approaches his big shock moment, but they deny the audience any element of suspense. *Cape Fear* is that weirdest of creatures: a thriller plugged into the nerve endings, not of its audience, but its director, who can't get out of his own way, bringing the same level of intensity to the shutting of a car door as to an act of strangulation. No matter: The film took $79 million at the box office, scooping Scorsese out of the debt he had incurred making *The Last Temptation of Christ*, and paving the way for more ambitious, personal projects.

The movie culminates in a desperate struggle between Cady and Bowden in the Cape Fear River.

The Age of Innocence

1993

"What I wanted to do as much as possible was to recreate for a viewing audience the experience I had reading the book."

Pages 160–61: "All Wharton and yet all Scorsese," as critic Roger Ebert described *The Age of Innocence*.

Right and opposite: "Is New York such a labyrinth?" For those who misstep in this society, the consequences are severe.

I n 1980, Jay Cocks gave Scorsese a copy of Edith Wharton's novel *The Age of Innocence*, telling him, "When you do your costume piece, when you do your romance, this is you." The book tells the romantic tragedy of Newland Archer, an up-and-coming young lawyer who is engaged to marry sweet, pretty, well-behaved, well-connected May Welland. Then one night at the opera, he sees his cousin Ellen, Countess Olenska, a childhood playmate who has returned to New York after a disastrous marriage to a Polish count that has left her reputation tarnished. Archer initially resists but then acts as her lawyer in the divorce proceedings and falls in love with her, but ultimately realizes that he cannot escape the destiny that New York high society has laid out for him. "It was the spirit of it," said Scorsese, "the spirit of the exquisite romantic pain. The idea that the mere touching of a woman's hand would suffice. The idea that seeing her across the room would keep him alive for another year. That's something I guess that is part of me. [Jay] knew me, by that time, fairly well."

"In the subculture I was around when I grew up in Little Italy, when somebody was killed, there was a finality to it. It was usually done by a friend. And in a funny way, it was almost like ritualistic slaughter, a sacrifice. But New York society in the 1870s didn't have that. It was so cold-blooded. I don't know which is preferable. I grew up thinking in one way, but in my own private life the past ten years, I've started to appreciate the ability to say a little in certain emotional situations and mean a lot."

At the time, he was finishing *Raging Bull*—not great prep for a story of unrealized romantic longing—but eventually got around to reading the book in 1985, in England, as Merchant Ivory's *A Room with a View*, featuring Daniel Day-Lewis, was sweeping cinemas. Scorsese liked the unconsummated nature of Wharton's romance, and the way Archer ends up checkmated by all the women—a strain of male paranoia which followed neatly on from *After Hours*, which he had just finished. For two years, Scorsese and Cocks worked on the structure, Cocks coming over once or twice a week to hash it out, although they ended

up making very few changes to the book, and even kept the idea of a non-diegetic narrator for the story, almost as if the voice of society itself were speaking up. The executives at Columbia were confused. "Who is the narrator?" they wanted to know. "Who cares," said Scorsese and chose Joanne Woodward—a key casting decision, for it would be Woodward's languid voice, reading Wharton's lapidary prose, that held the picture together. "I love that idea of a female voice, taking us through, very nicely, and setting us up for the fall."

As production designer he hired Dante Ferretti, whom he had first met on the set of Fellini's *City of Women*. Eighteen months of research produced twenty-five reference books of period detail for them to consult. In what was now firmly established as his working method, Scorsese screened a short season of films for inspiration, including Albert Lewin's *The Picture of Dorian Gray* (1945), Jack Clayton's gothic classic *The Innocents* (1961), Luchino Visconti's *The Leopard* (1963), and William Wyler's *The Heiress* (1949), which his father had first taken him to see when he was nine or ten. The brutality with which Ralph

Richardson points out to his daughter, played by Olivia de Havilland, that Montgomery Clift must be marrying her for her money, not her beauty, had stayed with him all these years. "No blood is spilled. But aren't the relationships marked by violence? How to suggest what goes on below the surface? That was the question I asked myself right away. And the answer: by using camera movement and editing to express the emotions that the characters themselves cannot express."

During filming, Daniel Day-Lewis asked not to hear the directions Scorsese gave to Michelle Pfeiffer—so the miscommunication between them was real. Their emotions were partially expressed through bursts of pure color—red, yellow—"sort of like a brush coming through and painting bits and pieces of color, swishing by," said Scorsese. "Texture, it's all about texture."

The film took twelve months to edit—longer than *Goodfellas*. The scene in which Archer declares his love, for example, took five or six days to shoot but much longer to edit: How long does it take him to answer her question? Twenty seconds? Did they need to add or cut

"I was interested in the use of color like brushstrokes throughout the film, the sensuality of painting, how the characters expressed themselves by sending each other flowers."

Left: In the relationship between Newland Archer (Daniel Day-Lewis) and his fiancée, May Welland (Winona Ryder), it is naïve-seeming May who holds the reins.

Opposite: Exuding warmth, color, and spontaneity, Ellen Olenska (Michelle Pfeiffer) stands out from the stiffness of her surroundings.

a few feet of film? In the scene where Archer finally confronts May (Winona Ryder) to break it off with her, only to be outmaneuvered by the revelation of her pregnancy, Scorsese showed her rising from her chair in three cuts, three separate close-ups, one at twenty-four frames, one at thirty-six, and one at forty-eight, in order to convey the intensity of the moment: "He'll never forget that moment for the rest of his life," he said. "Everything rests on the tension between the emotion and the mask, and it was at the editing stage that we achieved that."

Would all this be enough to convey the emotions being held in check? Toward the end of principal photography, as they filmed the final scene in which Archer, now an old man, walks away from the Countess Olenska's apartment in Paris rather than going up to see her, even Scorsese's director of photography, Michael Ballhaus, was

puzzled. "Oh, why can't he go upstairs?" he asked. "He can't," replied Scorsese. "He can't go up. That's what she loved about him. What are you going to do, be inconsistent at the last minute?" Jay Cocks later told the director that audiences never forgave the fact that Daniel Day-Lewis and Michelle Pfeiffer "don't get to make love in the film. But that's the story."

Most of the problems people had with *The Age of Innocence* were problems with Wharton's original novel. Tales of doomed passion can make for great films—David Lean's *Brief Encounter*, Wong Kar-wai's *In the Mood for Love*, Clint Eastwood's *The Bridges of Madison County*— but such are the matchmaking properties of the movie screen that the forces of doom must be readily explicable. Scorsese goes at the task

"Newland. You couldn't be happy if it meant being cruel. If we act any other way, I'll be making you act against what I love in you most. And I can't go back to that way of thinking. Don't you see? I can't love you unless I give you up."

with a vengeance, bringing a full armory of techniques to bear on the riptides of gossip, propriety, and innuendo keeping Newland Archer and Ellen Olenska apart. His camera swoops and glides with the grace of Max Ophüls's, picking out the rustle of silk and the bloom of boutonnières like a nosy houseguest, or a time-traveling anthropologist. We are as far from the tidy decorousness of Merchant Ivory as can be—this is a world in which the sight of a woman walking across a room to sit next to a man sends shockwaves ricocheting across the city. This is Fifth Avenue's equivalent of the Mob, the violence all taking place behind closed doors, where fires flicker and cigars are stubbed out, like reputations, or romantic hopes.

Michelle Pfeiffer moves with a freedom seemingly denied everyone else in the film—a living figure among waxworks. Arriving to meet Archer flushed and out of breath, Ellen's effect on him is palpable—the laughter she pulls from him almost a church giggle. Scorsese renders their courtship rapturously, through shots of hands, clasped, caressed, or—in one remarkable scene in a carriage—peeled tenderly

"That's what I found so moving about the book. He may not have Ellen, and Ellen may not have him, but he has the memory of Ellen. The memory of that incredible passion, that beautiful love. Ultimately, there is a part of me that thinks memory might be better than actuality."

The film conveys the strength of Newland's passion subtly but unerringly. A recurring motif is the touching and caressing of hands.

from gloves. They might as well be nude. The reasons for Ellen's refusal are clear enough: She knows only too well the outcast life they would share together. Hugging her like a child at his mother's waist, Day-Lewis gives off the exquisite throb of an impacted molar. "He is carnality defeated, nobility tamed and tired," said Anthony Lane in the *New Yorker*.

At the Countess Olenska's farewell dinner, where Archer is forced to sit next to her, making small talk, "there is huge devastation in his eyes, which are wet not with tears but with pure pain, as if somebody were chewing his leg off beneath the table."

For some Archer's passivity was the deal breaker: the film felt as shut in as its hero. "The material remains cloaked by the very propriety, stiff manners, and emotional starchiness the picture delineates in such copious detail," said *Variety*'s Todd McCarthy. An ambiguity persists: Was Scorsese's sinuous direction an expression of the passion simmering beneath the surface of this "hieroglyphic world" or of the forces of formality hemming his lovers in? Beating heart or hieroglyph?

Fresh from *Bram Stoker's Dracula*, Winona Ryder gets one magnificent late scene, her eyes glittering blackly as if this time *she* were the vampire, sucking the life from her husband—one of the great scenes of emotional betrayal in Scorsese's work, as violent in its way as the hit jobs that spatter the final acts of *Goodfellas* and *The Departed*.

Certainly, *The Age of Innocence* is not a film for the young. It is all flickering embers and simmering regret—plenty of age, not so much innocence. "I had a late adolescence in a way," said Scorsese, "right up to the point where I started making *The Age of Innocence*. It has made me think, at the age of fifty, what if I'd been a different type of person, one who could have handled things easily? Would my life have been very different?" This vein of loss and longing, first touched on in *The Last Temptation of Christ*, would be dealt with in projects as various as *Shutter Island*, *Hugo*, and the George Harrison documentary *Living in the Material World*. But the film was not a commercial success, recouping only $32 million of its $34 million budget. More immediately, Scorsese needed a hit.

Casino

1995

"This is the oldest story in the world. It's people doing themselves in by their own pride and losing paradise. If they handled it right they would still be there."

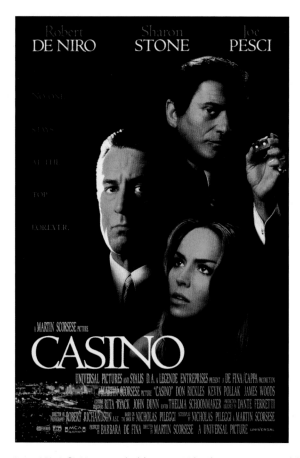

Pages 168–9: "In Vegas everybody's gotta watch somebody else." Sam "Ace" Rothstein (Robert De Niro) lets nothing get past him.

Right: Sharon Stone in one of the forty costumes she wore as Rothstein's wife, Ginger McKenna.

Below: *Casino* begins with a bang.

Casino came to Scorsese through Tom Pollock at Universal, to whom he still owed two films. The idea was from Nicholas Pileggi, author of the source material for *Goodfellas*, who had a deal for a nonfiction book about mobster Frank "Lefty" Rosenthal, his wife Geri McGee, and right-hand man Anthony "The Ant" Spilotro, and their careers riding the rollercoaster of Mob influence in Las Vegas in the 1970s. The only problem: Pileggi hadn't written it yet. He just had a seven-hundred-page, single-spaced factual chronology into which he had crammed four years of research. "The plan was, book first," said Pileggi, but after Scorsese passed on directing Richard Price's *Clockers* (it eventually went to Spike Lee), a window in his schedule opened up and "when Marty has a window, you better jump through it before five million other people do."

In February of 1994, the two men holed up in the Drake Hotel in Midtown Manhattan, close to Scorsese's office. The idea was to stay there until the script was written, incorporating interviews that Pileggi had already done with witnesses under FBI protection, including some with Rosenthal himself, conducted over the phone without a tape recorder with Pileggi scribbling furiously. Every time the film needed more detail, he would go off and do another interview. Their hotel room was a mess of papers, transcripts, and newspaper clippings, the two men "consuming, consuming, consuming," said Scorsese. The film was going to be an epic, three hours at least, but fast, as fast as *Goodfellas*.

At the end of six months they had a screenplay. It originally opened with the events described in the first newspaper clipping Pileggi had showed him: the police arriving to quell a domestic dispute on the lawn of a Vegas McMansion. From that fight unraveled an entire ten-year history, but Scorsese and Pileggi both realized it required too much context, and didn't create enough dramatic tension, so they started with the detonation of a car, throwing Sam "Ace" Rothstein—the character based on Rosenthal—up into the air, in slow motion, over the flames, "like a soul about to take a dive into hell." It would form the basis for Saul Bass's title sequence— a shimmering palimpsest of falling silhouettes, flames, and neon, to the sound of Bach's *St. Matthew Passion*. As he had with *Goodfellas*, Scorsese binged on Soviet filmmakers during production: Sergei Eisenstein's *The General Line*, Vsevolod Pudovkin's *The End of St. Petersburg* and *Storm Over Asia*, Lev Kuleshov's *By the Law*, Alexander Dovzhenko's *Arsenal*—"pure cinema," said the director. "It reminds you of all the possibilities."

They shot in a real casino. Producer Barbara De Fina (Scorsese's fourth wife until 1991) worked out that given the extra time it would take to build a casino set, it probably would not cost any more to use a real one, so that is what they did, shooting during working hours, capturing all the electricity and life and casting real-life veterans of the Strip—more than seven thousand extras, from go-go girls to hotel clerks, the largest cast of Scorsese's career, all of them requiring costumes from Rita Ryack and John Dunn. Joe Pesci needed twenty to twenty-five changes of costume, Sharon Stone forty, Robert De Niro a staggering fifty-two—sports jackets in blinding primary hues, silky haberdashery, white socks, turquoise alligator loafers—and even then they had to tone down some of the more vivid outfits the original Lefty had worn.

Editing *The Age of Innocence* had been hard, but with *Casino* Scorsese and Thelma Schoonmaker felt like they were juggling fireballs: a three-hour picture, with multiple narrators, and large sections of faux-documentary material. It took them eleven months, with the

"When I was making *Casino* I was angry at the extraordinary place that Vegas was. All that greed seemed like a reflection of Hollywood at the time, a reflection of American culture."

shooting script pinned to the wall, sequence by sequence—264 at the last count, another career high for Scorsese. "That's not possible," he joked. "There must be someone over there who is still shooting this film." Whole sequences were moved around. The money-skimming section was originally an hour into the film, but each time they came to it, it seemed like a change in direction, so they kept moving it further up to the front, eventually splitting it off into two parts, with the facts outlined at the beginning so you knew from the outset how it all worked. "It's a story of empire, and the story of, again, the seeds of destruction in our own selves," said Scorsese. "Gaining paradise and losing it, through pride and through greed—it's the old-fashioned Old Testament story."

As an example of cinematic skill, *Casino* is consummate, a maestro flourish as pure as anything practiced by the Soviets, although it's an easier film to admire than to like—technically bravura but a little joyless. Sometimes it can seem as if the only person really having fun is Scorsese. Thematically, the film aims big—*Goodfellas* writ large, with louder shirts, in flashing neon. This time, we get three narrators, one of whom, like William Holden in *Sunset Boulevard*, doesn't survive the film. We get Edenic expulsions and Shakespearean falls, the whole thing coming on like a kind of gangster's *Paradise Lost*, complete with that Luciferean tumble from grace in the opening titles.

A colder, more reptilian film than *Goodfellas*, it lacks the rapscallion charm of Ray Liotta to serve as an entrée into the gangster lifestyle. Scorsese seemed done with such niceties. Lit with the tungsten glare of Robert Richardson's top lights—which turn bars into interrogation rooms and men into islands in the gloom—De Niro and Pesci seem wrapped in distrust from the get-go. Playing a former bookie, De Niro has the dour, businesslike affect of an accountant, tamping down his emotions in every scene—as if only the dullest of men could succeed in so gaudily tempting an Eden. As Rothstein's enforcer Nicholas "Nicky" Santoro, Pesci is a mad dog whose f-bombs and acts of violence—including squeezing a man's head in a vice until his eyeballs

"Ultimately, it's a tragedy. It's the frailty of being human. I want to push audiences' emotional empathy with certain types of characters who are normally considered villains."

Opposite: With her marriage and her liquor on the rocks, Ginger starts an affair with Rothstein's right-hand man, Nicky Santoro (Joe Pesci) …

Right: … and gets up to no good with her pimp ex-boyfriend Lester Diamond (James Woods).

pop—are among the most genuinely repellent Scorsese has filmed. There is little surprise when these two vipers turn on one another.

What fresh turf the movie turns is largely down to Sharon Stone as Rothstein's wife, Ginger McKenna, the coke-snorting hustler whose druggy connection with James Woods's dissolute moocher, Lester Diamond, feels like the closest the film has to an emotional center, their hushed voices on the phone forming a single pool of mutual dependency. Stone "gnaws at the film like a mongoose with a grip on a cobra's neck," said critic David Thomson. "She is incessant, forlorn, trashy, and human." The film is absurdly watchable—it sucks you in. Schoonmaker's editing is propulsive, while the soundtrack—ranging from "Stardust" and soul to the Stones and Devo—leaves the usual

scorch marks. It's almost impossible to wander in halfway through and not watch the film to the end, even if it relinquishes you feeling bleary-eyed and sullied by the violence of its final scene, in which Nicky and his brother are brutally clubbed to death in front of one another.

"There was nothing more to do than to show what that way of life leads to," said Scorsese with a finality that seemed to go beyond the death of Santoro. He seemed done with the Mob. *Casino* did good business at the box office—$116 million worldwide—but still didn't make enough money to satisfy Universal. "It was clear that it no longer pays for studios that are owned by major corporations to make a $50–60 million profit on a movie. They want to make more. So that was the end of that kind of picture for me."

Above: "Are you out of your fucking mind? You tie up our kid and lock the fucking door?" Rothstein queries his wife's approach to parenting.

Opposite: Things end badly for Ginger, who dies of a drugs overdose (top), and Nicky, who is beaten to a pulp and buried in a field (bottom).

"Even though you may not like the people and what they did, they're still human beings and it's a tragedy as far as I'm concerned."

"I'm watching Joe Pesci and his brother, their characters, get beaten to death with baseball bats. I just shot it straight, no camera moves or nothing. Just reportage. Because that's where it leads and that's the end of it, that's the end of life. That's the end of that way of thinking and that's the end of violence for me. I don't think I could do it anymore."

Kundun

1997

"It was almost a retreat making this film … It simplified things, made me think what was important in my life, helped me accept the changes."

"What interested me was the story of a man, or a boy, who lives in a society which is totally based on the spirit, and finally, crashing into the twentieth century, they find themselves face to face with a society which is one of the most anti-spiritual ever formed."

Pages 178–9: Having sickened himself with the venality and violence of *Casino*, Scorsese chose a more spiritual theme for his next project.

In October 1993, the week that *The Age of Innocence* opened, Scorsese visited Harrison Ford and his then wife, screenwriter Melissa Mathison, at their house in Wyoming. Also among the guests was the fourteenth Dalai Lama. Scorsese had been following the Dalai Lama's story ever since His Holiness was given the Nobel Peace Prize in 1989, but he was now considering filming a script about his life, written by Mathison. They talked for two days, Mathison facilitating, in the course of which the Dalai Lama told Scorsese about a dream he had had in which he stood in a sea of dead monks, and a fish pool filled with blood. Scorsese was surprised at how comfortable he felt in his presence. As he was leaving, they shook hands, and as he looked at the Dalai Lama, he felt the rest of the room fade away. "I could hear my heart beat," he said. "After that meeting, I knew I would have to make that film."

Scorsese liked the simplicity of Mathison's script. It wasn't a treatise on Buddhism or a historical epic, but was, like her two previous scripts, *The Black Stallion* and *E.T.: The Extra-Terrestrial*, very much a child's-eye odyssey. "I realized that I should probably try to do everything from the child's point of view," said Scorsese. "Not just low-angled shots or camera movement that's low-angle, but [with a recognition] that as the child is growing, everything around him is seen by him, so the audience shouldn't be privy to a lot of information that the boy is not privy to."

Mathison went through fourteen drafts of the script before Scorsese approved it. They tried to include more historical context, more political intrigue, but Scorsese realized that a lot of it was unnecessary and asked Mathison to scale it back down again. They knew they were on the right track when the last draft resembled the first again. For inspiration, Scorsese watched Vittorio De Sica films like *Bicycle Thieves* and *The Gold of Naples*, some Roberto Rossellini, a lot of Satyajit Ray, particularly *Pather Panchali* and *The Music Room*, and also some of the new Chinese directors—Zhang Yimou, Chen Kaige, Tian Zhuangzhuang's *The Horse Thief*.

"One of the first things Marty and I agreed on was that there would be all Tibetan people," said Mathison, although the prospect of a largely

The adaptable Moroccan landscape this time doubled as Tibet rather than the Holy Land.

subtitled film, shot with just Asian actors, and no stars, caused Universal to balk. Just about every other studio passed until Disney stepped in, and with a budget of $28 million Scorsese set out for the same patch of Morocco he had filmed *The Last Temptation of Christ*, only with four more weeks in the schedule this time. The pace of the picture was very much dictated by the Tibetans. Scorsese was forced to slow down, go with the flow, focus on their faces, see what they told him. "They directed the picture, in a sense," he said. "Very often, the Tibetans had to show me what their behavior would be in a particular scene, and certainly what the rituals would be like," said Scorsese. "I already had angles planned, but I would improvise and work with them. I was being put into their world, you see, not the other way around."

For the first week and a half they rehearsed in a hotel with the youngest of the actors cast as the Dalai Lama, who was just two years old. By the end of day five, the other Tibetans had learned about hitting their marks, and saying their lines, making sure the light hit them the right way. Then came D-day. They put the boy in the middle of a wide shot, and started playing with him, but when Scorsese gave the

signal for dialogue, the child simply looked at him, wondering what was happening. Several days went by like this. Eventually, they built a canopy to hide the camera and painted clowns on it. For the shot in which the camera pulls back from his closed eye, they had to wait until he fell asleep, then crept back, the camera crew working in almost religious silence.

The first cut of the picture confirmed all the doubts Scorsese had harbored since he took the project on. It lacked power. Edited in straightforwardly linear fashion, the Dalai Lama's escape from Tibet and arrival in India simply weren't gripping. "We have to shuffle scenes," Scorsese told Thelma Schoonmaker. They left the first section with the two-year-old Dalai Lama pretty much alone, but in the section with the five-year-old, who meets the Lord Chamberlain, they began to reorder the narrative. The same with the twelve-year-old's scenes. The Chinese invasion was moved up, thus increasing the impact of what followed. By the time they reached the eighteen-year-old Dalai Lama,

they were cutting the picture purely on an emotional level, almost like a documentary, without worrying what monastery they were in, or what part of the world, turning certain scenes into dreams, and vice versa, without marking where the dream started or stopped.

"For the last thirty or forty minutes of the film, we were in free fall," said Schoonmaker. "Marty explained it in musical terms: We had to play with the scenes like musical notes and create crescendos of emotion by making certain juxtapositions." Whole passages were built around Philip Glass's music, using dissolves—as many as 250—to give the movie the feeling of remembrance. They edited throughout 1997, from January to August and on into October. Scorsese ended the film with an audacious cut. Normally you would end a movie with a fade to black. "Not on this film," he said. "I want a sudden cut." The idea was to rip the audience from a mountaintop vista just as the Dalai Lama had been when forced to leave Tibet. "Who else would end a film that way?" said Schoonmaker.

Opposite and above: Filming such young actors required patience and inventiveness.

The future Dalai Lama passes the test set by the searching lamas.

Apart from Richard Corliss's rave review in *Time*, the critical reception for *Kundun* upon its release on Christmas Day 1997 ranged from the merely polite to the mocking. "Lovely as it is, *Kundun* is of very little dramatic interest—it's an extremely beautiful, boring movie," wrote David Edelstein in *New York* magazine. Even the usually faithful Roger Ebert conceded that the movie was "made of episodes, not a plot."

Poorly promoted by Disney, *Kundun* took $6 million at the US box office and disappeared.

It may be Scorsese's most underrated film—a sinuous, meditative poem which ranges from vast mountaintops to intricate mandalas, the film bears only the scantiest resemblance to a traditional biopic, although the events in the life of Kundun, as the Dalai Lama is known

"These people were so committed to telling their story. They weren't acting, they were living. There was no artifice."

"I dedicated the film to my mother because the unconditional love that she represented to me in my own life somehow connected with the idea of the Dalai Lama having a compassionate love for all human beings."

Pages 184–5: Four actors of different ages played the Dalai Lama, including the five-year-old Tulku Jamyang Kunga Tenzin.

Left: Tenzin Thuthob Tsarong took the role of the adult Dalai Lama.

Below: Scorsese receives the International Campaign for Tibet's Light of Truth award from the real Dalai Lama, April 30, 1998.

to Tibetans, are certainly there on the screen. At the age of two (played by Tenzin Yeshi Paichang) he is discovered and, after performing a series of tests for the searching lamas, is brought to the Potala Palace in Lhasa. His Holiness is a curious, fidgety, at times pesky child, pulling faces at the monks gathered around him. The mood is tranquil but rapt, a little like leafing through the pages of an illustrated storybook, Mathison's script hovering at the edges of fairytale without ever stepping fully in. Most of the scenes are no more than a minute long, the hypnotic flow of images keeping time with the pulses and arpeggios of Glass's score.

Working with lots of natural light, cinematographer Roger Deakins illuminates the interiors like a Vermeer, filling in with some beautiful deep blacks. We see the Dalai Lama's education at the ages of five (Tulku Jamyang Kunga Tenzin) and then twelve (Gyurme Tethong) and the daily routines of the monastery, only for them to be rudely shattered when the Chinese invade. We don't ever see the bombers, merely the splintering

The Chinese invasion of Tibet in 1950 jolted the country—and the film—out of its gentle rhythms.

masonry—and the sight seems wholly foreign, almost Martian, so carefully have the preceding two hours cast their hush. "They have taken away our silence," says Kundun. The easiest of Scorsese's films to deride—a paean to peace from cinema's most caffeinated jitterbug—it also casts the gentlest of limbic spells. Maybe only a filmmaker as hard-wired to his reptilian brain could have made it.

Ten years later, in October 2007, the Dalai Lama was in Washington to receive the Congressional Gold Medal. Scorsese was invited to the ceremony. There he met a Tibetan monk—very small, with a chubby face and glasses, wearing golden robes—who saw him and took his hand.

"I thank you so much for making that film. Thank you so much," the monk said. "I saw your other movie, *New York Gangs*. Violent, violent."

Scorsese frowned apologetically.

"But it's alright," continued the monk. "It's in your nature."

Scorsese, with tears in his eyes, was blown away by "the acceptance of it," he later told Richard Schickel. "If it's in your nature, okay, it's in your nature. I mean, that's the movie. That's the feeling."

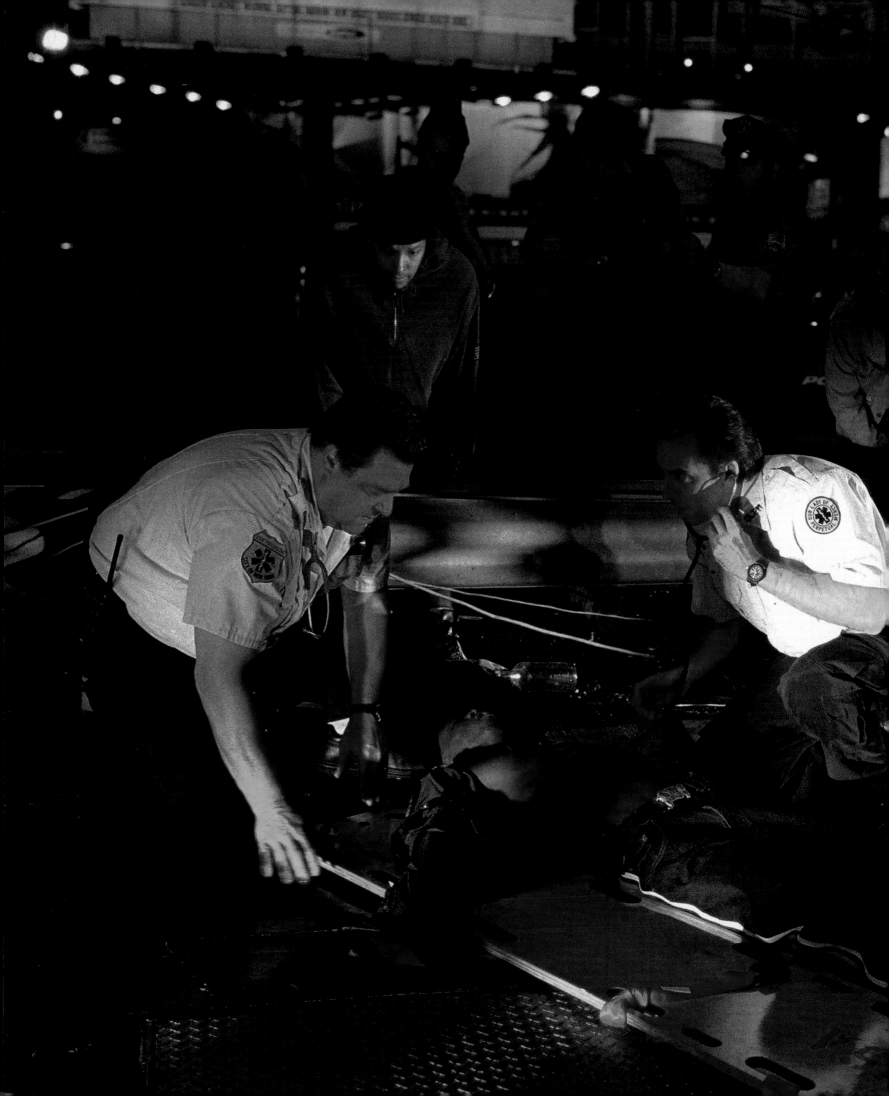

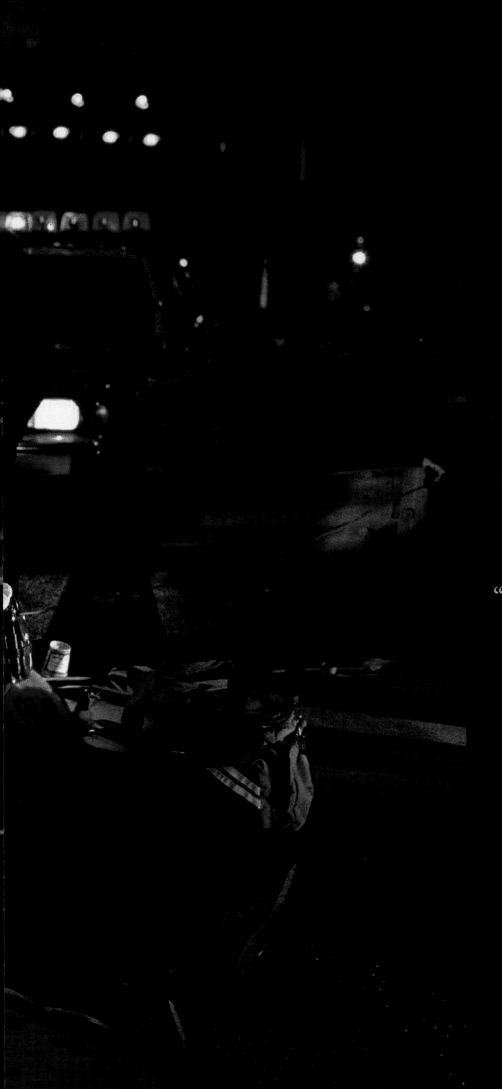

Bringing Out the Dead

1999

"I don't think I could have done this picture nine years ago. It had to come out of the experience of going into emergency rooms in the middle of the night … My father's death, my mother's death."

"If anyone had told me I was going to make this film, I would have said they were crazy: It just wasn't planned. But I responded to the beauty of the book and had such an identification with the story, and I loved what Schrader did with the characters."

Above: Scorsese knew Nicolas Cage would be perfect as overworked paramedic Frank Pierce.

Opposite: And Paul Schrader was his go-to screenwriter.

Pages 188–9: Frank and his partner, Larry (John Goodman), attend another call.

When producer Scott Rudin sent him the galleys for Joe Connelly's 1998 novel *Bringing Out the Dead*, a scorchingly vivid account of a New York night-shift paramedic named Frank Pierce who is stretched to breaking point, Scorsese immediately thought of Nicolas Cage's face and eyes. Cage, he decided, would be the perfect witness to the parade of shooting victims, crackheads, and drunks who wind up in the over-packed emergency room of a hospital that Connelly called "Our Lady of Misery." Scorsese had met Cage a few years previously through the actor's uncle, Francis Ford Coppola, and liked him. Brian De Palma had also told Scorsese that Cage was great to work with. "He's inventive and he goes from an expressive style, almost like silent film, like Lon Chaney, whom he adores, to something extremely internal," said Scorsese.

There was also only one person Scorsese thought of to write the script: Paul Schrader, his old collaborator on *Taxi Driver*, *Raging Bull*, and *The Last Temptation of Christ*. They met for dinner, and Schrader liked the book although he warned Scorsese about some of the more

overt religious overtones to the film. "The heroine's called Mary. Watch out for the Catholic symbols. You've already done that in *Mean Streets* and *Raging Bull*." Schrader wrote a final scene that wasn't in the book, in which Frank (Nicolas Cage) begs for forgiveness the spirit of Rose, a young Hispanic woman whose life he was unable to save. "Nobody told you to suffer," he is reminded by his friend Mary (Patricia Arquette). "It was your idea." When Scorsese read that, he was in heaven. "Oh, of course … That's the connection between us. We never really discuss it, but over the years, we've had this similarity to each other. I said to him, 'It's so beautiful. And you're right, because you can't forgive yourself. You want everybody else to forgive you.' We're tied to each other with this sort of thing."

Scorsese holed up in the countryside for a week to design the film, shot by shot, scribbling in the margins of the script. "In *Taxi Driver* Travis cast a paranoid eye on the world, and I framed it from his point of view," he said. "In Frank's case, it's the images of the outside world, hallucinatory images, that assail him, invading his field of vision and

lacerating his psyche. After some time, reality is reduced to these visual aggressions: bodies strewn on the sidewalk, faces twisted in pain or withdrawal."

He went again to Robert Richardson, his director of photography on *Casino*, and also a frequent collaborator with Oliver Stone. Richardson filled the movie with his characteristic *chiaroscuro* contrasts between darkness and bright, haloed light. The film was shot in Hell's Kitchen on Manhattan's West Side, whose grittiness

production designer Dante Ferretti amplified to create a nightmarish vision of the city. For the first time in many years, Scorsese found himself tramping up and down Ninth Avenue and Fifty-fourth Street at night. "You become part of the city's nocturnal fauna," he observed. "They were out; they were there, those people. And if some of them aren't on the streets, believe me, they gotta be someplace. I saw some of the places where they are. You don't wanna know. It's like underneath the city in a hole. Under the railroads. It's the end of life.

> "Frank is not an avenging angel and instead of killing people, our protagonist is trying to save people. We were all about thirty years old when we made *Taxi Driver* and now we're in our mid-to-late fifties. It's a different world and we're different, too."

This page: Robert Richardson's distinctive cinematography conjured up a nightmarish vision of Manhattan's West Side.

Opposite: Marcus (Ving Rhames) leads the prayers while Frank battles to revive an overdose victim.

It's the dregs. It's down. You can't get any lower." People kept telling him, "New York looks a little different now." Mayor Giuliani had cleaned up Hell's Kitchen since Scorsese was last there. He would reply, "But you're looking at the surface. This is not about New York. This is about suffering, it's about humanity. It's about what our part is in life."

Even from its title, *Bringing Out the Dead* feels like an attempt to exorcise old haunts—to summon the old devils. A companion piece of sorts to *Taxi Driver*, it displays that mixture of stylistic brio and thematic over-determination that marks much of Scorsese's later work—the old expressionist style looking for an occasion to throw itself a party. Nearly twenty-five years after Travis Bickle's Dantean descent into New York's scum-filled streets, the neon lights streak past not with the eerie, dreamlike flow of *Taxi Driver* but with a much faster, amphetamine-jag intensity—as Frank drives his ambulance through streets slick with rain. Taking patients to an embattled, blood-stained emergency room seemingly modeled on a hellish limbo, he doesn't

know whether to laugh or cry and the film follows suit, flipping between sorrow and gallows humor to arrive at a volatile, mordant tone that is all its own. "I'd always had nightmares, but now the ghosts didn't wait for me to sleep," says Frank, echoing Travis's sleeplessness. He is a figure that goes back even further in Scorsese's work, to Charlie in *Mean Streets*: the self-appointed saint who believes he has been set down on Earth to save others, when it is his own soul that needs saving.

Frank gets three partners, of increasing levels of pathology. The first, played by John Goodman, worries only about when he's going to eat or have his next nap; then we get an excitable con artist (Ving Rhames) with an outrageous tent-revivalist style; finally a paramilitary bullyboy (Tom Sizemore), who is basically a violent crime waiting to happen. It's almost as if Frank is drawing demons out of the woodwork. Night after night, he has visions of Rose, whose face stares accusingly at him from the shoulders of passers-by. It's not that he can't forgive himself for not having saved her life, he can't forgive himself for having grown indifferent. This feels a little worked up, a literary conceit—a pose of

"I don't expect it to be a blockbuster, but thank God we were able to make it. I guess it's not going to be for everybody, but I wanted to literally have the audience go through this moral and spiritual rollercoaster ride …"

Opposite: "I'd always had nightmares, but now the ghosts didn't wait for me to sleep." Frank is haunted by the faces of the people he was unable to save.

Right: But he finally finds peace in the arms of Mary (Patricia Arquette).

guilt rather than the thing itself. At this point in his career, Scorsese doesn't seem willing to distinguish between the two. Does Mary slip back into drug addiction because of some internal realignment or simply because Frank, at this point in the story, needs another soul to save? Or because Scorsese fancies a descent into a druggy inferno? The sequence ends spectacularly enough, with the dealer impaled on railings like Christ. While medics try to cut him free, the sparks intermingling with the fireworks in the distance, he recites an ode to New York—a truly gonzo sight, certain of a place in Scorsese's career clip reel—but nothing in Arquette's quietly compassionate performance has hinted at the possibility of relapse.

"Scorsese doing Spike Lee doing Scorsese," is the way J. Hoberman put it in the *Village Voice*. "The mood is less angst-ridden than hypercaffeinated, as Scorsese keeps cranking the velocity-bloodbath in the reggae inferno, exploding skyline *pietà*, climactic white light of redemption." What calms an otherwise over-frenzied film are the actors. Cage delivers one of his most soulful performances, pallid and

drawn, like an El Greco saint, while Arquette exudes a beautiful hush that soothes Frank like a balm; they seem to communicate in whispers. Sharing an ambulance ride, they sit side by side saying nothing. It's a lovely scene whose unexpected tranquillity bears the after-trace of *Kundun*, as if each new picture Scorsese made at this point in his career were a skin that is never sloughed, but a layer on top of the last. The ending is a beaut, as an exhausted Frank ascends the stairs and climbs into bed with Mary, laying his head on her breast and falling into a deep sleep. No Scorsese film before or since has ever finished on quite the same note of weary, well-deserved peace.

Gangs of New York

2002

"I've been dying to make this picture for years because it's more about the history of the city, and the history of the city being the history of America really, I think."

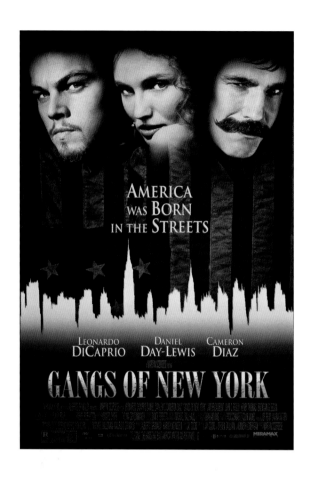

AMERICA WAS BORN IN THE STREETS

LEONARDO DiCAPRIO DANIEL DAY-LEWIS CAMERON DIAZ

GANGS OF NEW YORK

"Originally what we had on paper was more novelistic, more literature than cinema, in a sense, at least that's the way I saw it. There was just so much background. Every page was just so rich. And it took a long time."

Pages 196–7: Priest Vallon (Liam Neeson) in the heart of the battle.

Opposite: Scorsese on set with Leonardo DiCaprio (as Vallon's son, Amsterdam), who has starred in all but one of the director's subsequent features to date.

At the turn of the millennium, Scorsese's stock in Hollywood was at the lowest it had been since the late seventies. He had not had a hit since *Cape Fear* in 1991. *The Age of Innocence* had not recouped its costs for Columbia; *Casino* had not done as well as Universal had hoped; nor had *Bringing Out the Dead* worked out well for Paramount. As his box-office receipts dwindled, projects began to slow down, but Mike Ovitz, ever in Scorsese's corner, sent two top executives from his newly formed Artist Management Group to meet with him in New York.

"If you could do anything, what would it be?" they asked him.

"*Gangs of New York*," replied Scorsese.

The project dated back thirty years to 1970, when, staying with some friends at New Year, the director found a copy of Herbert Asbury's 1928 history *The Gangs of New York*, about the incredibly violent years in the city between 1830 and the Civil War, when gangs ruled the streets of Lower Manhattan, including the Bowery, very close to where Scorsese had grown up. He read the book in one

sitting and passed it on to Jay Cocks. "Marty said, 'Think of it like a Western in outer space,'" said Cocks, who came up with a draft that ran to 179 pages—"sweeping, almost Dickensian" in its scope, heavily influenced by Federico Fellini's *Satyricon* ("science fiction in reverse") and Stanley Kubrick's *A Clockwork Orange*, whose star, Malcolm McDowell, was even at one point proposed as their lead. Then, five days after *Raging Bull* premiered in 1980, Michael Cimino's *Heaven's Gate* opened and belly-flopped, taking down United Artists with it, and the prospects for a reverse-engineered, period–sci-fi gangland epic from the director of *New York, New York* disappeared overnight.

The project resurfaced at Warner Bros. in the 1990s, in the wake of *Goodfellas*, only to have the plug pulled again, and then reappeared at Disney, until the depressed box-office performance of *Kundun* gave them cold feet. After that, every major studio turned it down. Only when Ovitz visited Scorsese on the Hell's Kitchen set of *Bringing Out the Dead* in 1998 and offered up Leonardo DiCaprio as a potential star, did *Gangs* finally begin to look bankable. It was Robert De Niro who

first alerted Scorsese to the young star's talent, having acted opposite him in *This Boy's Life*. "I remember seeing the film, of course," said Scorsese, "and De Niro was the one who told me about Leo. He said, 'I worked with this kid in this film. You should really work with him someday.' And he doesn't usually do that."

De Niro turned down the role of the film's villain, Bill "the Butcher" Cutting, so Scorsese approached Daniel Day-Lewis, then working as an apprentice cobbler in Italy, in semi-retirement. Day-Lewis was not, however, a fan of Harvey Weinstein, the movie's eventual backer at Miramax. The bulky indie-movie impresario had been waiting to work with Scorsese for years and jumped at the chance, but the clash of styles between the two men was clear from the outset. Weinstein brought in Steve Zaillian, the Oscar-winning screenwriter of *Schindler's List*, to rewrite the script, then when the threat of a writers' strike loomed, he advanced the first day of the shoot to September 18, 2000. This gave Scorsese only four weeks for rehearsals. "I should really have had two additional weeks of preproduction," said the director afterward.

"I was so convinced that the film wouldn't be made that I was caught off guard. I had to scramble and round up my collaborators at the last minute."

He would later describe the shoot as "nightmarish." Principal photography commenced on schedule at the Cinecittà Studios in Rome, where *La Dolce Vita*, *Cleopatra*, and *Ben-Hur* had been filmed. The set, nearly a mile long, recreated the Five Points neighborhood of Lower Manhattan before the Civil War: a rabbit's warren of breweries, bars, factories, churches, opium dens, underground saloons, and secret tunnels, stretching in every direction as far as the eye could see. Scorsese whirred around the twisting streets among hundreds of Italian extras in a golf cart, parking long enough to explain to the costume people precisely how much dirt to grind into each garment. Working at a snail's pace, shooting less than a page a day, he soon pushed the budget beyond its agreed $83 million.

Weinstein took at least six trips to oversee production, spending up to sixteen weeks on set. For one scene, Scorsese insisted on a

"I was obsessed with the story of the city. There were so many wonderful elements to it, so many anecdotes, different characters, so much I wanted to show. It just never settled satisfactorily in my mind. I felt I had to sacrifice too much of all that, and I never felt comfortable about it."

Right: The mile-long set at Rome's Cinecittà Studios was a spectacular re-creation of the Five Points area of Manhattan.

Overleaf: Scorsese saw *Gangs of New York* as "an attempt to contribute to the tradition of the American epic film."

historically accurate "rat pit," in which a single terrier fought against dozens of sewer rats while onlookers placed bets. For another, he demanded a jar of human ears on the bar of Bill's brothel headquarters, Satan's Circus. "Harvey didn't want the rats. He didn't want the ears," Scorsese said dismissively. "I mean, you give an ear, you get a drink. That's the way it was. You don't have to *dwell* on it." Finally, the two men had a blow-up row over the way the director had styled Day-Lewis with prosthetics and oiled hair. Weinstein wanted a marketing campaign that featured a good-looking Day-Lewis. Why cast two of Hollywood's premier heartthrobs then cover them in grime? What's with that bizarre stovepipe hat? What about his garish plaid trousers? Miramax sent out ceaseless memos detailing Weinstein's concerns. "It was constant," moaned Scorsese. "There was one that said there was 'too much oil in the hair,'" said Day-Lewis. "So I said, 'Great, let's put some more oil in.' When I bumped into Harvey on the stairs at Cinecittà, I said, 'Harvey, I got the message about you wanting more oil in my hair. Is it okay now?'"

On more than one occasion Scorsese threatened to walk from the set and let someone else finish the film. He eventually had mirrors affixed to the video monitors to alert him to Weinstein's approach. He and DiCaprio also agreed to pay a combined $7 million to help defray the cost overruns, but by this point Miramax had already spent at least $10 million more than they intended, as the film's budget ballooned to more than $103 million. Shooting dragged on for so long that Cameron Diaz's next movie, *The Sweetest Thing* (for Columbia), demanded her release from the set. That prompted another big fight with Weinstein. "I had to release Cameron," said the producer. "Marty said, 'you can't do that.'"

"Marty, you can't have an actress who worked practically for free, stayed four-and-a-half months straight, six months overall, and then about to come into a $15 million pay day and not release her."

Scorsese offered to talk to Columbia himself.

"Do whatever the fuck you want," replied Weinstein, who recalled, "He called Columbia and they said 'fuck you.' He got mad at me, overturned what he thought was my desk but he threw down [production consultant] David Parfitt's desk by mistake."

Jay Cocks was there to witness the last week of shooting. Props were being taken away, extras were leaving. "The pressure on Marty was extraordinarily intense," he said. "He was shooting the final confrontation between Daniel and Leo, and they actually made him stop before he got all the shots. They said, 'That's it, that's it!' It's like you're running the vacuum cleaner and they pull the plug out."

"Imagine *Gone with the Wind* as narrated by Travis Bickle," said *New York* magazine, and the *difficulty* in imagining that testifies to both the audacity and ultimate failure of Scorsese's film, which is heartbreaking in the way that only missed masterpieces can be: raging, wounded, incomplete, galvanized by sallies of wild invention. The movie begins in 1846 with a brutal street fight in the snow between two rival gangs.

"*Gangs of New York* is the beginning of the gangster film overlapping with the end of the Western."

Amsterdam squares up to McGloin (Gary Lewis), a racist thug.

The American-born Nativists, led by Bill the Butcher, vie with the Dead Rabbits, a horde of Hibernians led by Priest Vallon (Liam Neeson). The fighting is ferocious, bloody, and at close quarters—a human scrum, viewed from a series of jabbing, low-angled close-ups, that leaves the snow reddened. It's a perfect reminder of what Scorsese does best: conflict, shown so close up that the shots feel like blows to the viewer's own kidneys. He's always been the most agoraphobic of directors, a spidery urban expressionist, scurrying between shadow spots, as bored of wide-open spaces as Harvey Keitel and his gang are of the countryside in *Who's That Knocking at My Door*. *Mean Streets* was shot almost entirely without establishing shots; by the time of *Taxi Driver*, the city of New York had become almost a state of mind.

The sweeping showmanship of a film like *Gone with the Wind*—with its grand historical vistas, its feel for the way spectacle amplifies emotion—works from an entirely different visual grammar, and for the first hour of *Gangs of New York* you can feel Scorsese trying to hammer out some compromise between Selznickian display and his own trademark intensity. Cinematographer Michael Ballhaus and production designer Dante Ferretti go for a dark palette with low, smoky skies, beneath which sits a jumbled, claustrophobic maze of listing wooden shacks and cobblestone streets winding in and out of muddy paths. It's a stunning set, halfway between Chinese opera and David Lean's London in *Oliver Twist*, but it doesn't take long for the audience to figure out where its edges lie—a slightly disconcerting feeling if the expansiveness of historical epic is the aim. Maybe psychological interiority is too much Scorsese's default register: He wasn't happy until he'd brought that set down to size. It could also be that he simply couldn't resist showing it off: There are some crane shots here whose splendid redundancy would have warmed the heart of Cecil B. DeMille.

Perhaps unsurprisingly, the film finds its firmest footing underground. Scorsese seems to love it down in the catacombs, where his tracking shots can go exploring, and where Vallon's

Right: One of the flashpoints in Scorsese's troubled relationship with producer Harvey Weinstein was sparked by Cameron Diaz's commitment to shoot another film.

Below: Diaz played Jenny Everdeane, a petty criminal who falls in love with Amsterdam.

son, Amsterdam (Leonardo DiCaprio), spends sixteen years in a reformatory sharpening his retribution on Bill the Butcher for murdering his father. The first two thirds of the movie shape up as a classical revenge drama, with Amsterdam insinuating himself into Bill's gang where, in spite of himself, he finds himself drawn to the charismatic older man. "It's a funny thing being under the wing of a dragon," he says. "It's warmer than you think." It's a great line, and the trouble for the movie is that the audience thinks so, too. As with *Hamlet*, the indecisiveness of the protagonist would seem to be the point, but Amsterdam's pusillanimity unbalances the film's central conflict. In full flight from *Titanic* when he shot Scorsese's movie, DiCaprio gives a performance that seems largely centered in his frown. He is easily outclassed by Day-Lewis who chews the scenery as if intent on devouring the entire movie. Squashing his eyes and curling his lower lip under his thick handlebar mustache, he strides through the sets in his plaid yellow trousers, as if borne along by the

Left: "You tell young Vallon I'm gonna paint Paradise Square with his blood. Two coats." Daniel Day-Lewis's extravagant portrayal of Bill "the Butcher" Cutting dominated the movie.

Opposite: Amsterdam's showdown with Bill is entwined with the 1863 Draft Riots.

same spirit of outlandish poetic extravagance that conceived of this Looking-Glass Gotham in the first place. In Day-Lewis's performance alone can you see the film Scorsese had in his mind's eye—a fractured national epic, star-spangled and bleeding, a howl from the streets—rather than the wounded animal we eventually got.

The final reel is a straightforward mess. After what seems an eternity, Amsterdam and Bill finally face off against one another, only to be interrupted by the 1863 Draft Riots—cannonballs fly, federal troops arrive, and the two men struggle to keep their deathly appointment with one another. Weinstein was essentially right: The story seems hijacked by its own historical backdrop. "Scorsese is caught in a conceptual bind: He is trying to make a movie that is hyperbolic, almost hallucinatory, in its historical perceptions, and yet also realistic in human terms," said *New York*'s Peter Rainer, although many were able to look past these flaws, or take them as a sign of the film's near-greatness. Here was a messy, sprawling, imperfect epic about a messy, sprawling, imperfect time in America's history—tidy perfectionists be damned! "*Gangs* may

be the epic's last gasp," said Richard Corliss in *Time*. "If so, it is a gasp that sings, howls, like a grand tenor at an Irish wake." In the *New York Times*, A. O. Scott found the film "brutal, flawed, and indelible."

At the 2003 Academy Awards, *Gangs of New York* was nominated for ten Oscars, including Best Picture, Best Director, Best Actor (for Day-Lewis), and Best Original Screenplay, but won none. The picture took $200 million worldwide but stalled in a sea of red ink and landed Scorsese in debt, from which he would not acquit himself until *The Departed*. Never mind. He had found a way out of the impasse of the late nineties, survived a brawl with one of Hollywood's biggest bruisers and now entered his fifth decade in the movies. "For me, filmmaking is literally getting in the ring and fighting," he told me when I visited him during the editing of *Gangs*. "I'm in the middle and there's smoke and there's guns and fire over me, and people lobbing grenades. And I'm just going to come out of a foxhole to present a little offering and I get shot at or I get praised, I don't know. What is this now, thirty years? Can't be. I look back and it's like a battlefield out there."

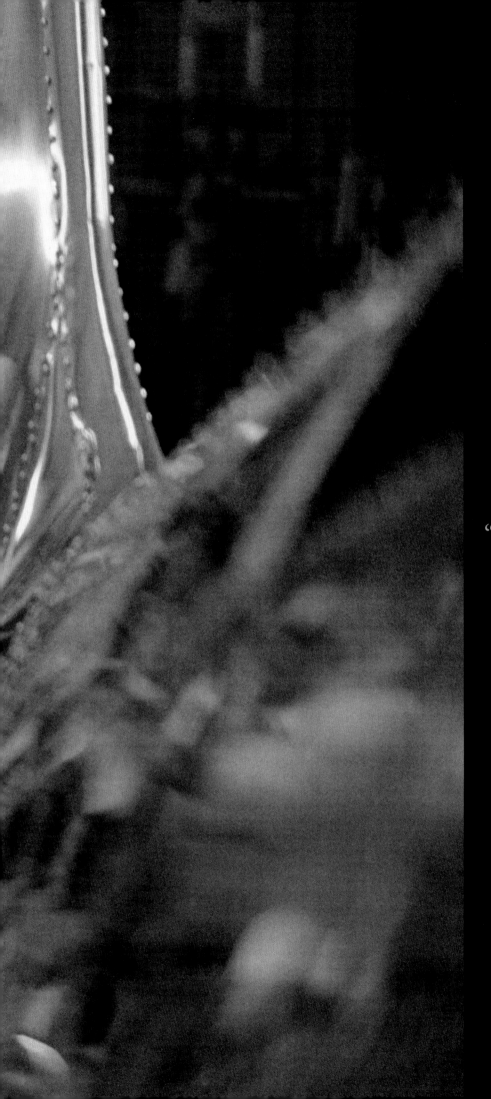

The Aviator

2004

"*The Aviator* is probably the last big movie that had themes that I could feel good about and relate to and want to go to the set to shoot with so many actors and with a crazy schedule—we shot this in ninety-one days and came in on schedule, by the way."

The making of *Gangs of New York* had brought Scorsese and Leonardo DiCaprio closer together. What at first had been an alliance of necessity had turned into something more affectionate, collegial. "Leo and I share a certain sensibility," said Scorsese, "a temperamental affinity." He resolved that if ever a project came to him that he thought the young actor would be good for, he'd do it, in much the same spirit that he decided to make *Alice Doesn't Live Here Anymore* for Ellen Burstyn in 1974. He was just trying to get *Silence*—a film about Jesuit missionaries in Japan—off the ground

when a script came to him from his agent, Rick Yorn. It was called *The Aviator*. He thought: Now *there's* a word that hasn't been used in years.

The first scene snagged his interest: a boy being bathed standing up by his mother, who warns him that the world is a dirty, plague-ridden place and then teaches him to spell "quarantine." It brought back his own fears of disease as a kid, when he had heard the words polio, diphtheria, and cholera on everyone's lips, along with mention of the dreaded iron lung. Between 1880 and 1900, Elizabeth Street, where he grew up, had had the highest rate of infant mortality in New York.

"I was attracted to the story because it told me things I didn't know about Howard Hughes … He had all the money in the world so he could do exactly as he pleased. He was a visionary and obsessed with speed and he was a man with a tragic flaw who ultimately does himself in."

Left and pages 208–9: *The Aviator* consolidated the close working relationship that Scorsese and Leonardo DiCaprio had built during *Gangs of New York*.

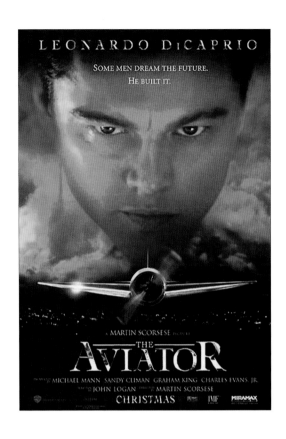

It was twenty pages before he realized the script was about Howard Hughes. Scorsese knew nothing about Hughes. He didn't even like flying, often shifting his schedule around to avoid storms, and if he couldn't track the weather patterns, he wouldn't get on the plane (that's why he missed picking up his prize for Best Director, for *After Hours*, at the Cannes Film Festival in 1986). He was aware Hughes had made *Hell's Angels* and that he had died in a hole somewhere looking kind of strange at the end. That was it. If he thought of him at all, it was as someone else's obsession. Warren Beatty had been talking about a Howard Hughes picture for decades now; he'd even talked to Scorsese about it at one point.

The Aviator was the product of a three-year development deal between DiCaprio, screenwriter John Logan, and director Michael Mann, but after making *The Insider* and *Ali*, Mann did not want to do

a third historical project and so offered it to Scorsese. By the time he finished reading the script he was won over. He liked the way Logan had concentrated on just two decades, from 1927 to 1947, before Hughes's dementia set in for good. You got to see the pioneer aviator pushing west, the rebel who wanted to take Hollywood by storm but with a fatal flaw that would eventually bring him down. "So it was Hollywood spectacle combined with internal conflict, and the destruction of this man—at least the seeds of it."

There was endless discussion about whether to show Hughes at the end of his life—DiCaprio kept on bringing up the subject—but Scorsese felt Logan had made the right choice. He liked the emphasis on this vibrant young man but told Logan, "You've got to deal with all the things he did with the women." The question was: which one? Katharine Hepburn was one whole story, Ava Gardner another. Then there was the woman invented to represent all the others— Faith Domergue. The prime interest was Hepburn, but Scorsese added one scene where Gardner threw an ashtray at him, and also introduced

Left: Scorsese shot the first section of the movie in shades of red and cyan to evoke the Cinecolor film stock of the period, so that in Hughes's game of golf with Katharine Hepburn (Cate Blanchett) the grass appeared blue on screen.

Opposite: The obsessive-compulsive Hughes lurks by the bathroom door waiting for someone to come in so that he can slip out without touching the doorknob.

the men in white gloves who close in on him at the end. "In my mind, his obsessive-compulsive disorder is like the labyrinth that he gets stuck in—sort of like the minotaur," he said. "He seemed happiest when he was up there flying alone. That sense of being locked off, hermetically sealed from the world below, away from the germs, all the difficulties and the shyness and the extraordinary need and hunger for fame, all of that is like a god flying in the air."

At the same time, the film was to be an intentionally glitzy tribute to Hollywood's golden era—a pick-me-up after the ordeal of *Gangs of New York*. "Movies like *The Age of Innocence* are what my wife calls eat-your-spinach movies," Jay Cocks told the *New York Times*. "*The Aviator* is not an eat-your-spinach movie. This is dessert." Scorsese wanted the color tone of the film to change as it went along: For the first fifty minutes, scenes would all be shot to imitate the look of two-color film stock, Cinecolor, with objects appearing only in shades of red and cyan blue. For the scene with Hepburn on the golf course they dropped the yellow entirely. The scenes taking place after 1935 were treated to

"Having just made the biggest picture I'd made in my life, which was *Gangs of New York*—well, the biggest next to *New York, New York*, which was pretty big, too—I had no idea this would not be a smaller, independent movie. However, there was something about the character of Hughes that began that process all over again. It had certain themes that I seemed to be drawn toward: his self-destructive element, whether it's intentional or genetic; the depiction of Hollywood in the twenties, thirties and forties; the aviation; and the relationship with the women."

emulate the saturated appearance of three-strip Technicolor, with the changeover coming during the scene with Louis B. Mayer in the bathroom, where Hughes can't touch the doorknob.

"It's a history of color in a way," said Scorsese. Using the big screens at the Sony Studios lot, he showed a print of Max Reinhardt's 1935 version of *A Midsummer Night's Dream* to demonstrate the beauty of black and white; then examples of two-strip Technicolor and three-strip Technicolor, including *Robin Hood*, *Becky Sharp*, a clip of *East of Eden* in its original CinemaScope print, *Ryan's Daughter* in 70 mm, *The Divorce of Lady X*, *Blithe Spirit*, and *Leave Her to Heaven*, in which Gene Tierney's wardrobe provided costume designer Sandy Powell with inspiration for some of Ava Gardner's clothes in the film. Scorsese also showed the colors to his director of photography, Robert Richardson, telling him, "You see the way the light is reflecting off the gun? That's the blue we want."

Working with a budget of $115 million, his largest to date, he directed the actors at speed, drawing inspiration from *Mystery of the*

Wax Museum and *His Girl Friday*, which he had everyone watch in 35 mm. The story of the obsessive Hughes brought his own obsessive tendencies scurrying to the fore. Dante Ferretti never stopped telling him "But this is all about you!" They spent nine days and nights shooting the scenes with Hughes locked up in his screening room, his nails and hair grown long, running the same movie over and over. DiCaprio's body makeup alone took seven hours, which cut into shooting time, taking it from twelve hours a day down to five. "It was hell, absolute hell," said Scorsese, although when he saw the rushes he was delighted, and excitedly showed them to DiCaprio in his trailer. "You have to see this stuff," he told him. "There's no need to film Howard Hughes as an old man. There he is. We *did* the old Howard."

One of the best scenes in *The Aviator* takes place high above the Hollywood hills at night. Howard Hughes (Leonardo DiCaprio) takes Katharine Hepburn (Cate Blanchett) for a spin in his gleaming biplane; while she takes the controls, he sits back, admiring her profile while

Left: Holed up in his screening room, Hughes talks business with aeronautical engineer Glenn Odekirk (Matt Ross).

Opposite, top: Blanchett's memorable performance as Hepburn was rewarded with an Academy Award for Best Supporting Actress.

Opposite, bottom: The XF-11 crashes on a test flight and Hughes sustains horrendous injuries.

in the air, head thrown back to loose her braying laugh, she delivers a spinning top of a performance, whirling in and out of rooms as if driven by sheer centrifugal force.

Scorsese's interest in Hughes seems a little more faked. In his early films Scorsese felt almost umbilically connected to his protagonists—their obsessions were flush

sipping on milk—an intriguing blend of infantilism, voyeurism, and high altitude. Next to *New York, New York*, it is probably Scorsese's glossiest movie, a film of luxuriant surfaces, from Hepburn's alabaster back to the gleaming aluminum skin of Hughes's H-1 Racer, and for the first hour or so the film performs acrobatically—a love letter to the movies of the 1930s and 40s, from its dazzling coloration and plush period ambience to its screwball-speed patter. Enjoying a *Bringing Up Baby*–ish round of golf with Hughes, Blanchett seems to draw as much from Hepburn's own performances as from the woman herself—nose

with his—but it's hard to imagine what he saw of himself in Hughes, the millionaire dilettante flogging his hobby horses across the finishing line. In his review for *Slate*, David Edelstein guessed that Scorsese was "galvanized by the superb pacing (and nonjudgmental tone) of Steven Spielberg's *Catch Me If You Can*—which offered the rebuke of a wonderful DiCaprio performance while the actor was floundering on neighboring multiplex screens in Scorsese's *Gangs of New York*." This is acute and illuminates the slight cross-purposes at which star and director seemed to be working. They had both fallen in love with

"What mainly attracts me is the man obsessed—obsessed with flying and being the fastest man in the world: a real, wonderful, obsessive madness. And we live today with so many of the results of his obsessions. I'm also fascinated by the mythical aspect of his downfall—whom the gods would destroy, they first make mad."

"Love what you've done with the place." Hughes shuts himself away in a deep depression until Ava Gardner (Kate Beckinsale) discovers him and pulls him back in shape.

differing parts of one another's oeuvre—and it happened to be the very part the other was trying to put behind him. For DiCaprio, still eager to shed his *Titanic* puppy fat, *The Aviator* was a classic journey to the Scorsesean heart of darkness. The director, on the other hand, was trying, if not to put his earlier, more personal work behind him, to put on a show of professionalism and conjure the spirit of Hollywood crowd-pleasers past. With his pomaded hair, flashing blue eyes, and constant motion, DiCaprio gives us a portrait of the fast-talking rogue, a capitalist prince barking orders, hiring and firing on the spot—a rooster mid-crow.

"See, I wonder what gives a beautiful woman like you pleasure," purrs Hughes to a cigarette girl at the Cocoanut Grove, slipping his hand under her spangled tutu. But Hughes was a curiously sterile hedonist, which may be why Scorsese cannot connect with him, and his psychological disintegration—which many would have thought played to Scorsese's strengths—is curiously the film's weakest point.

DiCaprio commits wholeheartedly, as Hughes holes up in his private screening room naked and unshaven, filling hundreds of empty milk bottles with urine, keeping up a steady babble under his breath. Scorsese plies him with licks of hellfire—flames, sparks, haloes, scenes from *Hell's Angels* playing across his writhing back—but the intensity is dispelled by the very next scene, in which Ava Gardner (Kate Beckinsale) rolls up at Hughes's house. "Nice of you to dress for me," she says at the sight of his bedraggled form, looking around to see his apartment taped up like a spider's web, to keep the germs at bay. "Love what you've done with the place."

It gets a laugh, but the director who made *Taxi Driver* would never have allowed Travis Bickle to be so upstaged. Truth be told, Scorsese didn't have Bickle's solipsism in him anymore—or his taste for damnation. Pulling back from the brink of Hughes's mania, the last forty minutes of the film instead conjure a couple of pyrrhic victories for him as he defends himself against trumped-up charges

"It was scary to do a picture on Howard Hughes because many people asked why I wanted to make a film on him. He represents certain things that aren't the best in the world, and about our country, and about what it is to be a human being. But I thought all that was fascinating, because of the relationship that Hughes had in my mind to the country itself—about power and the corruption of power."

"The way of the future." Although the film climaxes with the successful test flight of the H-4 Hercules, any sense of triumph is undermined by the return of Hughes's obsessive behavior.

of war profiteering and finally gets his H-4 Hercules plane airborne. The Hercules's lumbering bulk is a far cry from the airy dynamism of the opening reel, and any suspicion that Scorsese might be on course to land an unambiguously triumphant ending is swiftly undercut by DiCaprio's neurotic coda, muttering "The way of the future, the way of the future," over and over to a mirror, as if in homage to previous Scorsese antiheroes. In another life, that scene would have provided the starting point for a Martin Scorsese picture about Howard Hughes, not its end.

This bifurcation of tone was borne out at the Academy Awards the following year, where *The Aviator* was nominated for eleven Oscars, including Best Picture, Best Director, Best Original Screenplay, Best Actor (for DiCaprio), and Best Supporting Actor (for Alan Alda). It won five—for Best Cinematography, Best Film Editing, Best Costume Design, Best Art Direction, and Best Supporting Actress (for Blanchett)—which seems about right: Ravishing surfaces and stellar supporting cast, but the center does not hold.

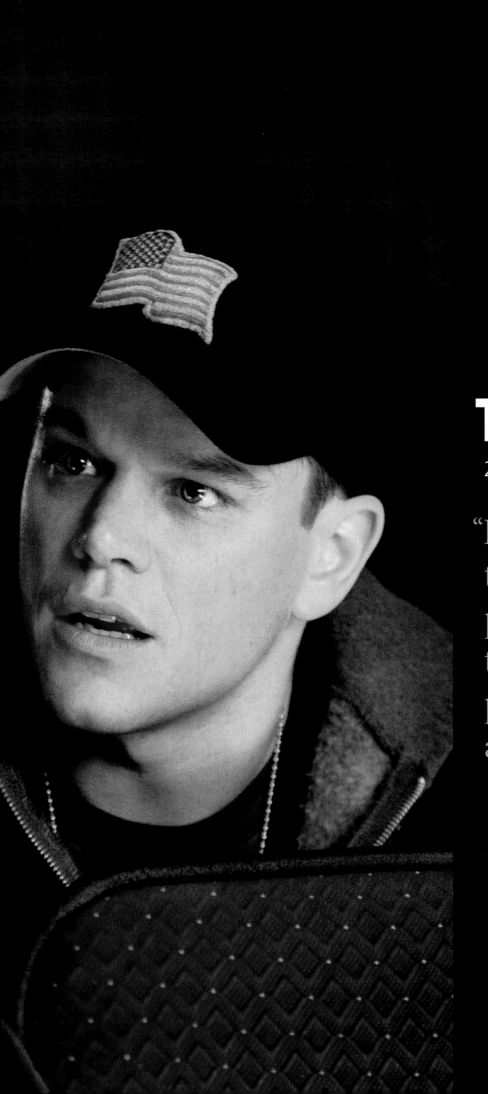

The Departed

2006

"It's the old story: In order to know you have a problem, first you have to know you have a problem. You really do, and this is my own take."

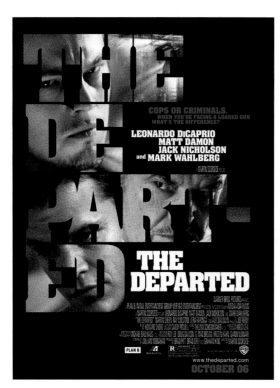

Pages 220–21: Corrupt cop Colin
Sullivan (Matt Damon) meets gang
leader Frank Costello (Jack Nicholson)
in a porno theater.

Above and opposite: "I've got ideas,
I've got ideas!" *The Departed* gave
Scorsese a long-awaited opportunity
to work with Nicholson.

Everyone came away with their own Jack stories. The evening before his first scene with Nicholson, Matt Damon was looking over the script. The phone rang.

"Hi, Matt? Marty. The director."

It always amused Damon that Scorsese announced himself this way. "Yeah, I know who you are," he said.

"Well, a funny thing has happened. Jack had some ideas for your scene tomorrow … Okay, I'll just get to it. Jack's going to wear a dildo."

Damon thought: *Uh, ok, so I'll see you at seven?* The next day, he went into rehearsal. The scene they were due to shoot was the one in which his character, Colin Sullivan, a cop on the payroll of Nicholson's gangster, Frank Costello, meets with him in a porno theater. "Here's the deal," Nicholson told him. "I'm gonna come in. I'm gonna sit there, in the overcoat, and I'm gonna pull out the big dildo and we're gonna laugh." Damon realized it was actually a really good way to get into the scene. It felt like these guys really *would* sublimate sex into violence and violence into sex. Nicholson wanted a direct line between Costello's sadism and his sexuality, and suggested that after breaking Leonardo

DiCaprio's hand in one scene, there should be an exchange between Costello and his girlfriend—"What's got you all hot and bothered?" "Come in the car, I'll show you …"

"When Jack came on the set he would do things that were just nuts," said Damon. "If you look at Leo and me in all our scenes with Jack, we are like deer caught in the headlights." It was DiCaprio's first time working with Nicholson, too. After filming a bar scene in which DiCaprio's character, Billy Costigan, has to convince Costello that he's not a mole, Nicholson turned to Scorsese and said, "I don't think he's scared enough of me—I have to be scarier." Scorsese replied, "Anything you can think of, come in and we'll just do a couple of takes tomorrow, and that'll be it. And then you can go home." The next day, he arrived on set to find himself accosted by Nicholson, proclaiming giddily, "I've got ideas, I've got ideas!"

Nobody told DiCaprio what was going on exactly, but the prop guy took him aside and warned him, "Be careful, he's got a fire extinguisher, a gun, some matches, and a bottle of whiskey." The actor sat down at the table, opposite Nicholson. The cameras rolled. Suddenly, Nicholson

"With Jack you have got to be prepared for anything. You have to remain totally open-minded … He re-wrote his dialogue and made it even dirtier. I think he got right to the heart of the character."

started sniffing his whiskey—"I smell a rat," he said and screwed up his nose like a rat smelling the air. Then he pulled out a gun and started waving it lazily in DiCaprio's face. It was a prop gun, but still dangerous. Nobody, not even Scorsese, knew if he was going to fire or not. "There was tons of improvisation with him," said DiCaprio. "I was never sure which side of Costello he was going to be playing on any particular day. It makes you terrified as an actor, and it ups the stakes."

They did four more takes that were even more extreme—in one, Nicholson doused the table in whiskey and set light to it—but Scorsese chose the earlier version. The scene took him months to edit, and it raised many questions—What is Costello's relationship with Costigan? What's his relationship with Sullivan? Might he be his father?—"and in a way, that was the moment when the picture came together for me,"

said the director. "He had to be God the father gone mad, you know, and the whole world coming down around him. And it did."

Scorsese didn't initially want to do the film. He loved the freedom of the language in William Monahan's script, a remake of the 2002 Hong Kong thriller *Infernal Affairs* transplanted to Boston, but he didn't know what he could do with the story. He'd got his fingers burned trying to please his studio masters with genre thrillers before, but Warner Bros. was extremely keen on him and DiCaprio working together again. The part of Frank Costello was intended for Robert De Niro, with Brad Pitt, who had first obtained the rights to remake the film, tentatively attached to the role of Colin Sullivan, but *Gangs of New York* co-writer Kenneth Lonergan suggested Boston native Matt Damon instead. For Costello, Scorsese went to Nicholson, an actor he

"There was a point with *The Departed* where I was ready to throw in the towel. I wanted to make the movie I thought the script was about, and I thought the studio wanted something else. I figured, jeez, at this point in my career, I just want to make films where, granted I'll stay within budget, but I just wanna make the movie I wanna make. You're gonna come to me, especially on a project like this, my home turf sort of, and then you're asking for these actors and this kind of movie? I thought this might be the end, just let me out of here and I'm going to shoot the Rolling Stones on stage, that's it."

Setting up and shooting a scene in which Costello's henchman Mr. French (Ray Winstone) pulls Billy Costigan (Leonardo DiCaprio) away from a man who mocks his request for cranberry juice.

had known for thirty years, but had never connected with on a movie, despite looking out for one.

"I wanted something iconic from Nicholson," he said. "I wanted a real presence to carry over the whole picture so that even if he was only in three scenes you would still feel the presence of this larger-than-life, almost God-like figure." The world depicted in the film was "a world where morality no longer exists. Costello knows this. I think he's almost above it. He knows that God doesn't exist anymore in the world that they're in … I think for me it just is a sadness and a sense of despair since we've been in this situation since September 11. Somehow this all came together and that's what kept me going in depicting this world sort of like a moral Ground Zero."

The first Scorsese film in twenty years to be set in the present day, *The Departed* began shooting in the spring of 2005 in locations around Boston, and New York (for its higher tax credit). He prepared his cast with the usual film class, screening Anthony Mann's noir thrillers *T-Men* (1947) and *Raw Deal* (1948), William Wellman's *The Public*

Enemy (1931), and Howard Hawks's classic *Scarface* (1932), whose iconic "X" scorings, to indicate when someone was doomed, Scorsese wanted to mimic throughout his movie. "Everyone has the same fate in this picture," he pointed out, "that's why we call them the departed." Depicting at least ten executions, one garroting, the graphic splattering of a body that has fallen from a great height, as well as more than 230 f-bombs, the film's progress through the preview process Warner Bros. insisted on was agonizingly protracted.

"It cost a lot of money, and there were big-name stars in it, and therefore I had to work with the studio very closely," said Scorsese. "Screen it, argue, discuss it, you know. We stuck to our guns. We got pretty much what we wanted, though there were a couple of things here and there we didn't get. That doesn't really matter. The thing is, I don't know if it's worth going through the process again." As the editing and reediting inched along, Scorsese grew increasingly anxious to make sure he was in New York to shoot the Rolling Stones performing for his concert film *Shine a Light*. He was supposed to spend another week

Damon (above) and DiCaprio (right) could easily have swapped their
parts as opposing moles, each infiltrating the other's organization.

"What fascinated me was that it wasn't only about
treachery in business or infidelity in love but also
duplicity through and through."

in Los Angeles to oversee the answer print of the film—the last part of
the conversion process, which can take days—so when a computer in
the lab malfunctioned, setting them back another two days, Scorsese's
patience finally snapped.

"I said, I'm out of here. I barely saw the finished print." The day of
the premiere at the Ziegfeld in Manhattan was the first time he saw the
finished film.

It is inconceivable that Scorsese would have abandoned *Taxi Driver* or
Raging Bull in such a manner—like leaving a child that is coming out
of anesthesia. A sign of Scorsese's impatience with the interminable
process of reediting the picture? Annoyance with his studio bosses
mixed in with contempt for the preview process? A little of each,

perhaps, but it also tells you how little Scorsese was thinking about
awards: Those are not the actions of someone putting the finishing
touch to his masterpiece. It's something of an irony that after the best
part of a decade making A-pictures for Harvey Weinstein to truss
up as awards horses, Scorsese should finally win his Oscar with *The
Departed*, a real cougar of a picture, as low and snarling as anything he
has made. But *of course* it didn't deserve the Oscar. It's far too good for
the Academy Awards—a hard, fast, mean B-movie in which everyone
is damned to hell, and nobody survives the final reel except a rat and
Scorsese's best curser since Joe Pesci, it has the inflamed urgency of
someone falling off the wagon.

It also has the best beginning to any Scorsese film since *Goodfellas*—
a master class of editing, exposition, shot-making, and music, all

drawn together like a slipknot. First we have Colin Sullivan, a slick opportunist rising fast through the ranks of the Massachusetts State Police Department, where he has for years acted as a mole for Frank Costello, the head of the Irish mob, who has known Sullivan since he was a boy. Then there is Billy Costigan, a police-academy misfit from the same neighborhood who is picked by his captain, Queenan (Martin Sheen), to infiltrate Costello's mob as *their* mole, even spending a few years in prison to flesh out his criminal bona fides. All this, including boyhood and prison time, is relayed in the first twenty minutes, with Thelma Schoonmaker cutting back and forth between the two men, sometimes located in the exact same position in the frame, while a guitar picks out the triplets of a tango—one of Robbie Robertson's most inspired musical cues. We *are* watching a tango, a dance, a *pas de deux*

between these two sons of Southie, raised in the same neighborhood but unaware of each other, who are to be drawn into an ever tighter embrace until finally they crack skulls.

Needless to say, Damon and DiCaprio could easily have swapped parts. Too callow for his roles in *Gangs of New York* and *The Aviator*, DiCaprio and his touch of vulnerability are an asset here; listen to the animal whimper he lets out as Queenan goes splat in front of him. He unravels feverishly as the film progresses, although it was unnecessary to have him wired on drugs: The noose is tight enough. (Drugs, as they did in *Bringing Out the Dead*, seem to function more as thematic embellishment than physiological reality.) Damon's full-beam smile masks twitches of rat cunning, the performance a kind of sequel to his Tom Ripley in Anthony Minghella's *The Talented Mr. Ripley*.

There was no camouflaging Nicholson's impact on *The Departed*. His prowling presence in the movie helped Scorsese finally win his first Oscar.

But neither man is designed to hold our attention for long and you may find yourself surprised at how little you feel when both men are rubbed out in the final reel, a blowout that leaves brain matter spattered on walls and floors like Jell-O and makes the ending of *Goodfellas* look like *What's Eating Gilbert Grape*.

Even Scorsese can't wipe the smirk from his face, arranging for a rat to tiptoe across Sullivan's window ledge, like the robin in *Blue Velvet*. The sunshine looks fake, as if the outside world were yet another ruse. (Guess what? It's not even Boston out there.) Easily Scorsese's most nihilistic picture, *The Departed* is a Rubik's Cube of assailants and backstabbers—a Gordian knot of betrayers, as tight and godless as Jacobean tragedy, with everyone competing to see who can bite off more of Monahan's filthy, funny dialogue. Top honors go to Mark Wahlberg who almost steals the picture as Queenan's bullying aide

Sergeant Dignam: "Who the fuck are you? I'm the guy who does his job. You must be the other guy." You wish he had been let loose on some of Monahan's fruitier passages, with their name-drops of Joyce, Shakespeare, and Freud. As Dignam might say: woop-de-fucking-do.

The picture is Jack's. Moving through the shadows of the film's opening minutes, Nicholson emerges into the light sporting a Satanic goatee, eyes burning, to dispense Sun Tzu–like truths and cavort with an arsenal of gaudy props: a leopard-print robe, a severed hand, that fake phallus. It's a large, showy performance on a very slow burn—Costello is a man formed by his own monstrous appetites, for sex, power, drugs—but then the reassuring feel of Jack Nicholson grandstanding may have been what secured Scorsese his Oscar.

"Could you double-check the envelope?" the director quipped when his name was read out on February 25, 2007, some twenty-six

"I look at you and I think 'what could I use you for?'" Costello calculates out loud.

"Jack I know. He has the history of Hollywood. He goes back to the late fifties. He went through Roger Corman. He understands genre. He understands different types of genre coming out of the American cinema and also European cinema and Asian cinema and all that sort of thing. I've always wanted to work with Jack."

years and seven snubs after his first Academy Award nomination, for *Raging Bull*. "That's when I realized what my place in the system would be, if I survived at all: on the outside looking in," he said when *Raging Bull* lost to Robert Redford's *Ordinary People*. His victory for *The Departed* would open a new chapter, with its own challenges for a filmmaker long accustomed to being shut out in the cold: acceptance, lionization, renewed bankability. The patron saint of blood and pasta, too mired in the reality of America to win favor in the dream factory, was now beloved. "The temperature *did* change," he says. "I was just trying to continue working. I didn't expect it. Everyone teases me 'Scorsese did not expect the Oscar.' I did not. Because the real success and satisfaction was having made all these movies *without* having major box office, *without* having Academy Awards. That was the thing."

"Everyone has the same fate in this picture. That's why we call them the departed." The body count is high, even by Scorsese's standards.

"It's harder now to make a film like *Departed*, which is insulting to a lot of people. It uses language that's offensive. And it's violent. Maybe ten or twelve years before … it wasn't that way. Maybe we were a little closer to something like a brutal reality."

Shutter Island

2010

"I've always been drawn to this sort of story. What's interesting to me is how the story keeps changing, and the reality of what's happening keeps changing, and how up until the very final scene, it's all about how the truth is perceived."

"With Leo it's always an interesting process of discovery. And I don't say that in a facile way, either, because we never know what that process is going to be, and it's always intimidating at first. And then Leo really gets into it and we start unraveling all these layers. And with *Shutter Island* the story really lent itself to that. I think this was something that surprised him a great deal by the time we'd finished the film—how far psychologically and emotionally he'd had to travel. It's probably the toughest film he's ever done."

Pages 232–3: On set with
Ben Kingsley (Dr. Cawley),
Leonardo DiCaprio (Teddy Daniels),
and Mark Ruffalo (Chuck Aule).

Scorsese picked up Laeta Kalogridis's script of Dennis Lehane's 2003 mystery novel *Shutter Island* at 10.30 p.m. one night and could not put it down. "Once I read it, I had to do it," he said. "It was like a moth to the flame." The story of two federal marshals on the hunt for a mental patient who has vanished from her cell in an asylum for the criminally insane in Boston Harbor, the book was conceived by Lehane as "a homage to B-movies and pulp"—manna from heaven for Scorsese, who has always prepped his cast and crew by screening classic films. But perhaps more than any other Scorsese film, *Shutter Island* came together in the screening room.

The first film Scorsese showed his actors—Leonardo DiCaprio, Ben Kingsley, Mark Ruffalo—was Otto Preminger's *Laura*, about a detective (Dana Andrews), who falls in love with a murder victim (Gene Tierney). Scorsese was fascinated by Andrews's body language in the film, "the way he moved through the frame, the shoulders were down, he never looked anybody in the eye."

Then he showed them Jacques Tourneur's classic noir *Out of the Past*, starring Robert Mitchum, Jane Greer, and Kirk Douglas. He wanted DiCaprio again to pay attention to the way Mitchum moved, "never seeming to really focus on anyone, always looking around because he suspects everybody." When it was over, DiCaprio applauded and told Scorsese, "That's the coolest movie I ever saw in my life."

There followed screenings of Alfred Hitchcock's *Vertigo*, John Huston's wartime documentary about shell shock *Let There Be Light*, Samuel Fuller's Korean War picture *The Steel Helmet*, and a raft of lower-than-low-budget schlockers produced in the 1940s by Val Lewton when he was the head of the horror department at RKO— *Cat People*, *I Walked with a Zombie*, *The Seventh Victim*, and *Isle of the Dead*. Scorsese remembered seeing the last of these when he was ten or eleven and walking out, he was so terrified. "It's almost like he's accessing his dreams or something, the dreams being all those movies," said DiCaprio, "They're like memories coming back to him."

DiCaprio described his character as a "giant jigsaw puzzle."

Such are the prerogatives of America's premiere film artist, nearing the end of his seventh decade. "The past in one sense recedes but in another gains in interest as [one] ages and the stage of the present empties of decisive action," wrote John Updike of the late fiction of Henry James, and so, too, with *Shutter Island*, a mazy palimpsest as haunted by the past as anything in late James. It is one of the unfortunate rules of thumb of Scorsese's late career, however, that the number of films he invokes in the run-up to making a movie is directly related to his lack of involvement with the material. If his early work felt electrified by its contact with red-hot reality, his later work can feel too cozily cocooned in film-buffery. Making movies, once a way of engaging with the world, becomes a form of retreat.

The complexity of Lehane's plot escaped just about everybody. Scorsese read a lot of Kafka while they were shooting, particularly "The Burrow," his last unfinished story about a mole-like creature scurrying through an elaborate system of tunnels it has built over the course of its life. "Teddy was like a giant jigsaw puzzle," said DiCaprio of his character, whom he called "that poor bastard" for the succession of hells they put him through—hanging from cliff tops, falling down hills—as he is violently shunted from one reality to the next. "There were a few weeks there that were some of the most hardcore filming experiences I've ever had. It was pretty intense. It got darker and darker and more emotionally intense than we had expected." At one point he turned to Scorsese, and said to him, "I have no idea where I am. What am I doing now? What's going on?"

"Don't worry," replied Scorsese. "Just do the scene again, do the take again, take it one more time, and keep pushing it." In the end, they worked out a simple numeric code—one, two, three—to indicate how extreme his character would be in each scene. Even editing the picture, coherence was elusive, the plot coming together in fits and starts, Scorsese and Thelma Schoonmaker feeling the form as they went along. "It was a process of discovery throughout, including the

"I thought it would be a fun picture to make. But it turned out to be rather disturbing. Because of the subject matter. And the nature of the different levels we have to go through. But that's the nature of filmmaking."

Left: "Storm's coming." DiCaprio and Ruffalo set the scene.

Opposite: Teddy and Chuck take shelter from the storm inside a cemetery crypt.

edit," said Scorsese. The film "started out as an entertainment, though I guess I don't really know how to do that. It always seems to become something else."

Just what that "something else" is remains the great unanswered question of Scorsese's career. Are his B-pictures to be judged against the standards of the genre to which they belong, and which he soaked up in his youth, or are they to be judged as expressions of his own singular sensibility? It's not just his virtues that are singular: Scorsese's faults are almost the opposite of the typical Hollywood filmmaker. Put through the grindhouse of the development process, tested, prescreened, and prepped to within an inch of its life, the average studio film tends, at the least, to start well. Hollywood is all about beginnings—anticipation, possibility, promise—and the studio system has grown awfully adept at getting an audience to take their seats. What it is bad at is follow-through, finish—what the business quaintly calls "third-act problems." In modern Hollywood, all's well that ends badly.

Shutter Island is the exact opposite. It has maybe the worst beginning of Scorsese's career, abrupt and overblown; a second act so berserk with twists the audience is forced to enter a state of pure, associative free fall; and then, just as you're growing convinced that what you're watching is another *Cape Fear*—another suffocatingly movieish take on the thriller that doesn't actually thrill—it resolves its resolves into a denouement of great power, emotional depth, and beauty. It's like Scorsese suddenly showed up, finally managed to meld the artist and the genre-nut within him to wring some poetry from his material.

First, the beginning. Off the coast of Massachusetts in 1954, a boat emerges from the fog, bearing two US marshals, Teddy Daniels (DiCaprio) and his new sidekick, Chuck Aule (Ruffalo), to Shutter Island's asylum for the criminally insane. "Only way on—*or off*," the captain says, adding, "Storm's coming." And then, in case we missed the point, the score lets out three foghorn blasts as our heroes approach the gates. In other words: Abandon Hope All Ye Who Enter Here! The best horror directors know how to summon the abnormal from

"This is the type of picture I like to watch, the kind
of story I like to read. Over the years, I think I've stayed
away from certain kinds of pictures that emulate the
style that I find nurturing in a way, but these are
the kinds of films I go back to and view repeatedly."

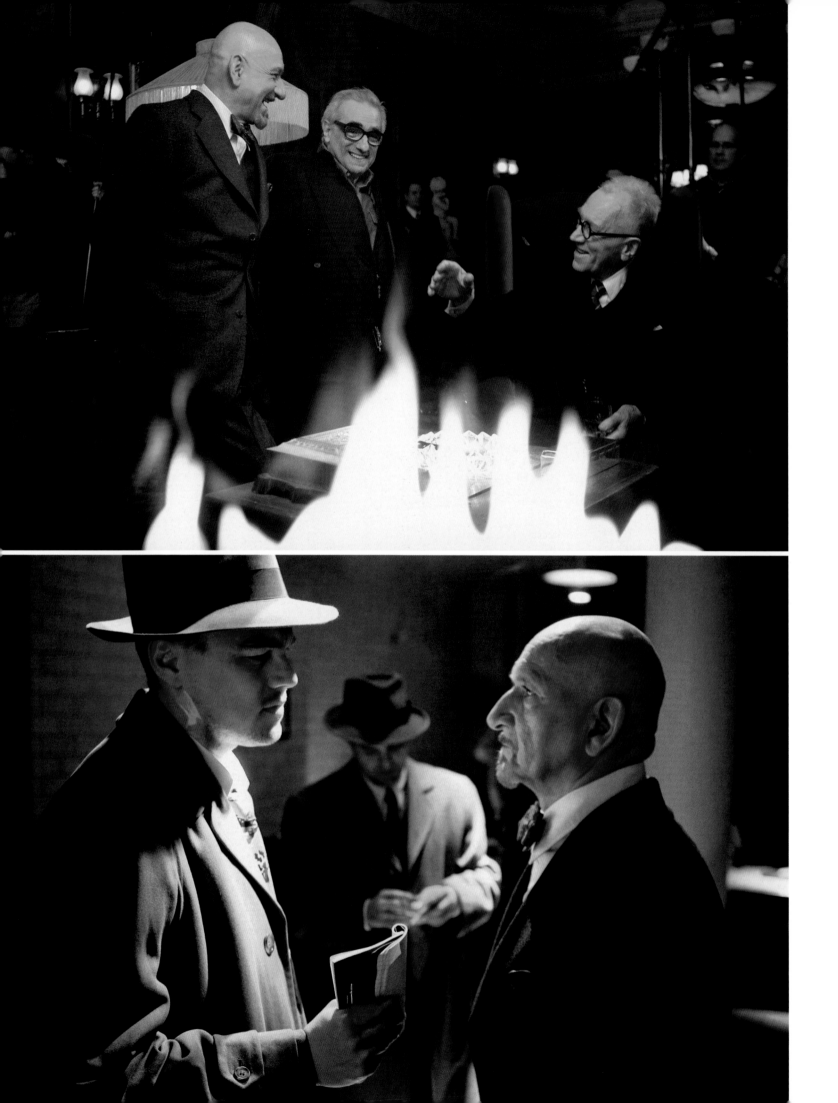

Opposite: Ben Kingsley shares a joke with Scorsese and Max von Sydow (Dr. Naehring), before going back into character as the unyielding Dr. Cawley.

Right: "You have to let me go." A disturbing dream in which Teddy's dead wife Dolores (Michelle Williams) turns to ashes in his arms.

the pond-smooth surface of normality, but Scorsese has never had the patience or coolness of temperament for suspense. He's far closer to Sam Fuller than Hitchcock. "Pull yourself together," says Teddy into a mirror, like Travis Bickle and Jake LaMotta—but they had an entire movie leading up to that breaking point. This is how *Shutter Island* begins—as intensely as most movies end.

The middle. A succession of plot twists, plus exposition, like twelve people fighting for the wheel of a car, while arguing loudly. Are the hospital's creepy top doctors, played by Ben Kingsley and Max von Sydow, involved in espionage-related psychological experimentation on their patients? Is Teddy reliving the trauma that he underwent in World War II? And what are we to make of the strange coincidence that Shutter Island apparently houses the firebug who killed Teddy's wife, Dolores (Michelle Williams)? Is Teddy himself insane? Caught in a plot which reverses direction every ten minutes, Teddy becomes a marionette, jerked this way and that, frowning throughout. The movie is shot from his point of view, ostensibly, but it's Scorsese who is finding expression here. With its eerie panopticism, hashed-about

plot, and blizzard of B-movie references—*Bedlam, Shock Corridor*—the film is an uncannily vivid rendering of how a thriller feels to its maker *as he is making it*, a report from the helter-skelter of the editing suite.

A gift all the time he and his central character are one—in *Taxi Driver*, say, or *Raging Bull*—Scorsese's expressionism overpowers the detachment required of a genre movie. Only in the final stretch do he and his protagonist become aligned, as the cause of Teddy's torment is finally revealed to us as the agony of a man forced to let go of his most sheltering illusions. Finally, Scorsese has a hold of a theme that fascinates him, the same theme that animated the ending of *The Last Temptation of Christ*. "Which would be worse—to live as a monster, or to die as a good man?" asks Teddy and for once, maybe for the first time in their collaboration, the power of DiCaprio's acting has the hallucinatory allure of Scorsese's images at his back. *Shutter Island* is that rare thing: a thriller that plays much better in retrospect than it does as you are watching it—appropriately enough, perhaps, for a film so haunted by memory. Some movies are never meant to be new. They are merely old movies in waiting.

Hugo

2011

"I loved the idea of seeing the world through a boy's eyes. Hugo is twelve years old. I was particularly drawn to him because he is a vulnerable child."

Pages 240–41 and right: *Hugo*'s spectacular set, based on a 1930s Paris train station, gave Scorsese plenty of scope to explore the possibilities of 3D for the first time.

Above: Having a twelve-year-old daughter helped Scorsese relate to child actors Chloë Grace Moretz (Isabelle) and Asa Butterfield (Hugo).

Opposite: He also worked again with his contemporary Ben Kingsley, who played pioneer filmmaker Georges Méliès.

A t a relatively late age, Scorsese found himself again living with a young daughter under his heels. In 1997, he met his fifth wife, book editor Helen Morris, after she began working on a companion book to *Kundun*. After their wedding in 1999, she moved into his Upper East Side brownstone, and within months bore him a daughter, Francesca. "It changes things," he says. "It was different from when I had my other daughters. I was much younger, you had the future ahead of you. Now it's different. So now I'm seeing the future through the eyes of my child. She is perceiving the world around her: 'What does that mean? What is this? Who's that? I believe this, I don't believe that …' All this goes on, you talk and talk and talk and before you know it you're living with this, you're dealing with it every day, even if you're shooting."

There were many times during the making of *Hugo* when he would get home late at night, shattered from the logistics of shooting his first 3D movie, to find twelve-year-old Francesca eager to conduct a conversation about, say, armadillos. "The child doesn't know what's

going on, you're exhausted," he recalls. "She goes 'look at this, I need you to see this—is that a horse to you, or is it an armadillo?' There was a time when I would have walked right by. But now you say, '*Waidaminute, waidaminute*, are you trying to tell me that's an armadillo? Because that's not an armadillo. That is an anteater.' 'No it's not.' Suddenly there's a hole in the world that you've gotta fill." His voice lowers to an imploring whisper. "'*But look I gotta get to sleep, honey, I gotta get to sleep. I'm going to go into the room upstairs,*'—there's a little room—'*I'm going to go lock myself in, I want you to be quiet.*' 'Oh, I'll be quiet …' '*Because I've got to get up tomorrow morning at five o'clock …*' This is my life."

The project came to him from Graham King, his producer on *Gangs of New York*, *The Aviator*, and *The Departed*, who told him "Marty, this is so you, you have to do it." Brian Selznick's 2007 children's book *The Invention of Hugo Cabret* tells the story of a twelve-year-old orphan who lives inside the walls of a 1930s Paris train station and who befriends the aged Georges Méliès, the great illusionist of the silent

era who fell into neglect in his later years, unaware of how much his films had changed the course of cinematic history. Scorsese's love of Méliès went back to the first time he saw *A Trip to the Moon* in 1956. "It was part of the prologue of a big roadshow of *Around the World in Eighty Days*," he says. "They showed the entire film in black and white. The action was amazing. Later on I saw it in Greenwich Village along with all these avant-garde films: Pennebaker, Cassavetes's *Faces*, they were always showing Méliès. The way the figures moved, they had a kind of primal impulse I was always drawn to, compelled by. With my asthma, I went to the movies a great deal because they couldn't do much else with me. At one point, in the late 1940s, my mother took me to visit someone, and they happened to have a 16 mm projector and they showed a black-and-white cartoon of Felix the Cat and I could see the film going through the projector, I could see the pictures moving, the beam of light. I saw it. That's something that Méliès connects me back to."

Shooting on a magnificent set at London's Shepperton Studios, on which was re-created an entire train station—a composite of the

Gare du Nord, the Gare de Lyon, and the old Gare Montparnasse, which no longer exists—Scorsese was in his element. He took inspiration from not just Méliès, but the surrealist-influenced films of the 1920s and 1930s—René Clair's *Le Million*, *Under the Roofs of Paris*, and *À Nous la Liberté*, and the beautiful Jean Vigo films *Zéro de Conduite* and *L'Atalante*. During an interview to promote the film, he name-checked no fewer than eighty-five movies, from Billy Wilder's *Ace in the Hole* to Vincente Minnelli's *Two Weeks in Another Town*. "He was the happiest I've ever seen him," says King. "He had new toys to play with. He saw a whole new way of filmmaking. He was loving it, loving the process, the hair, the makeup. He would come on set and you would hear that great laugh he has rippling through the train station. His daughter was on set quite a lot. I could see how happy he was to do a movie where she could sit next to him and watch."

The highlight, for Scorsese, was production designer Dante Ferretti's re-creation of Georges Méliès's glass studio, where they restaged scenes from Méliès films shot for shot, including the

Hugo's father (Jude Law) shows Hugo
the broken automaton.

Below: Scorsese with 3D filters
attached to his trademark horn-rims.

Opposite: "I'd imagine the whole
world was one big machine."
Hugo at work in Méliès's workshop.

underwater set for *The Kingdom of the Fairies*. They shot for five or six days. Scorsese was in movie heaven. "It was one of the best times I've had shooting a picture," he says, although he had problems adjusting to the 3D technology required to make the film. "We were all learning as we went," says King. "Marty and I would look at each other and see so many technicians sitting at their computers and be like, 'What are all these people *doing*?' One time he called 'Action!' and we did a shot, and afterwards he said, 'It's very blurry. What's going on?' He didn't have the glasses on."

As Scorsese adjusted to the new technology, the production schedule started to elongate—originally planned for July to November 2010, shooting continued into December, then January, then February. As the schedule ballooned, so the budget rose. Originally capped at around $100 million, it soon climbed to $150 million, $170 million, some estimated even $180 million by the end of production. "After one hundred days, what are you going to do—call an ambulance?" said King. "Budget wise, there just wasn't enough prep time and no one

"In my film, the cinema itself is the connection—the automaton, the machine itself becomes the emotional connection between the boy, his father, Méliès, and his family."

really realized how complicated doing a 3D film was going to be. I went through three line producers because no one knew exactly what was going on. Do I still think it's a masterpiece that will be talked about in twenty years? Yes. But once the schedule started getting out of whack, things just spiraled and spiraled and that's when the avalanche began."

There are clocks ticking throughout *Hugo*, a valentine to the days of early silent cinema which marked the decisive arrival of Scorsese's late period. "Late style is what happens if art does not abdicate its rights in favor of reality," writes Edward Said in *On Late Style: Music and Literature Against the Grain*, a fascinating look at late works, from Shakespeare's romances and the final compositions of Richard Strauss, to the dream diaries of Graham Greene, and the final fictions of Henry James. Said finds in each a rich stylistic brocade, a fascination with artifice, a backward-looking and abstracted quality, a sense of veils lifting to reveal the figure of the creator-magician putting on one last show, like Prospero in *The Tempest*:

These our actors,
As I foretold you, were all spirits and
Are melted into air, into thin air:
And, like the baseless fabric of this vision,
The cloud-capp'd towers, the gorgeous palaces,
The solemn temples, the great globe itself,
Ye all which it inherit, shall dissolve
And, like this insubstantial pageant faded,
Leave not a rack behind. We are such stuff
As dreams are made on, and our little life
Is rounded with a sleep.

This could as easily be describing *Shutter Island* and *Hugo*, both haunted houses honeycombed by memory, in which the dead are brought back to life, storms summoned, illusions spun and spirits summoned. At the center of *Hugo* sits Méliès (Ben Kingsley), his days of filming dragons and mermaids behind him, now a cranky

Left: Sacha Baron Cohen swaps his unitard for a uniform to play Hugo's nemesis, the station inspector.

Opposite: Bookstore owner Monsieur Labisse (Christopher Lee) enables Hugo to discover Méliès's past achievements.

old toy-store owner in the Gare Montparnasse. Up inside the clock tower crouches Hugo (Asa Butterfield), who runs the clocks and spends his time dodging the clutches of the station inspector (Sacha Baron Cohen) and his massive Doberman. The film opens with a chase sequence, shot in a single, pantherlike Steadicam take—a curious choice. Cross-cutting would have increased the suspense, allowing us to feel the inspector's fingers on Hugo's lapels. The effect is dreamy but muffled, Scorsese's exuberance trumping the audience's excitement, or Hugo's fear. *Hugo* lacks the emotional simplicity and directness of the genuine children's classics—*The Black Stallion, E.T., Toy Story, Fly Away Home, Spirited Away*—films with an unfakeable feel for the world seen through the eyes of a child.

Scorsese gets behind Hugo's eyes, to be sure, but I'm not sure he feels much for his boy except as a pair of eyes onto that magnificent set. And the movie does not lack for magnificence. Scorsese fills the screen with gears, springs, shutters, and wheels within wheels, then whirls his camera up walkways and down gangplanks: The whole

"These special effects are hard! Some take eighty-nine days to render— eighty-nine days to render! And what if you don't like it when it comes back? I tell them at a certain point, you've gotta tell me, you've got to say: 'This is the point of no return, Marty; you've got to make up your mind right now about this facet of the shot!' So you know that's when you've got to make up your mind."

Left: Scorsese still behind the camera even in a cameo role.

Opposite: "Happy endings only happen in the movies." Even cranky Papa Georges has to concede that things turn out well for him.

thing could be taking place inside a movie camera. "Marty the film freak has built his own Matrix," noted *New York's* David Edelstein. But we never feel Hugo's hunger, or impoverishment, or loneliness, or longing to connect. The material may have needed someone a little more shameless at the helm—although for some critics the film's lack of sentimentality was a sign of Scorsese's higher artistry. In the *New York Times*, Manohla Dargis praised *Hugo* for keeping "the treacle at bay," while Fran Lebowitz, the subject of Scorsese's 2010 documentary *Public Speaking*, proclaimed "this movie is too good for children."

Only when approaching the figure of Méliès does the stiffness depart. Scorsese is in his element restaging some of the landmarks in early film: the moment in 1896 when, according to legend, the Lumière brothers showed a film of a train rushing toward the camera and sent the audience scrambling; the shooting of Méliès's *Trip to the Moon* and *Kingdom of the Fairies*. As Scorsese's excitement levels pick up, Thelma Schoonmaker's editing rhythms quicken, and the movie's pulse flutters

into life, the embers of one filmmaker's work glowing with the breath of another. *Hugo* is a curious creature indeed: a children's film that was more beloved by film buffs than by children, a dazzling revivification of the earliest days of film, but something of a cold marvel, whose view of the human heart is as mechanical as the automaton that sits at its center. Nominated for eleven Academy Awards, winning five, *Hugo* nonetheless struggled at the box office, where it took just $74 million domestically and $112 million internationally for a worldwide gross of $186 million. Half of that money going to theater owners, King's production company was forced to absorb a loss of $80 million. Relations between the producer and director grew strained.

"Let's just say that it hasn't been an easy few months for me," said King. "There's been a lot of Ambien involved." For the moment, this put the brakes on Scorsese's next project, an adaptation of Shusaku Endo's novel *Silence* about two Jesuit priests in seventeenth-century Japan. Scorsese had been wanting to make it for years. King owned the rights.

The Wolf of Wall Street
2013

"Yeah, it's another look at America, another look at who we are. And a look at human nature—it doesn't happen just in this country. I was hoping that I could develop the style, and push it further."

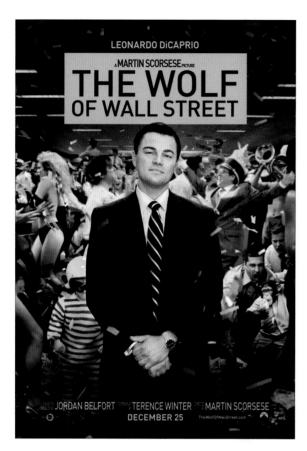

LEONARDO DiCAPRIO

A MARTIN SCORSESE PICTURE

THE WOLF
OF WALL STREET

JORDAN BELFORT · TERENCE WINTER · MARTIN SCORSESE

DECEMBER 25   TheWolfOfWallStreet.com

Pages 252–3: Conspicuous
consumption—Jordan Belfort
(Leonardo DiCaprio) welcomes FBI
agents on board his 150-foot yacht.

"The comedy in films I directed comes out of human nature. It comes out of misunderstanding, which happens every day, and with enjoyment of the humor that comes out a situation … But in the case of *The Wolf of Wall Street*, the humor comes out of their enjoyment. They're doing bad things, and there's a tension that I hope to get with the audience itself, as they find themselves maybe enjoying some of what these guys are doing and checking themselves for that. What's in us that makes us enjoy this?"

t's a modern-day *Caligula*," said Leonardo DiCaprio of Jordan Belfort's memoir *The Wolf of Wall Street*, to which the actor won the rights after a bidding war against Brad Pitt in 2007. Warner Bros. quickly optioned it as a project for him and Scorsese, but then dropped out in 2008; the two went on to make *Shutter Island*, then separated to make their own projects—for DiCaprio *Inception*, *Django Unchained*, *The Great Gatsby*, for Scorsese *Hugo*—but the pair kept talking. "I was fixated on him," said DiCaprio, who tried to set it up with other directors but couldn't bring himself to pull the trigger. "There wasn't anybody else who could bring the rawness and toughness, the music, and particularly the humor required to convey the excitement of these young punks—these robber barons—taking on the Wall Street system."

Chronicling the wild ride of an unscrupulous stockbroker who, in the late eighties, took over a Long Island brokerage house—or "boiler room"—renamed it Stratton Oakmont, and bamboozled small investors out of roughly $100 million before being arrested by the FBI, the book was a nonstop bacchanalia of sex, drugs, and conspicuous consumption. DiCaprio and Scorsese had an early conversation about how despicable the characters were. The director told him, "Look, the thing that I've learned about doing movies is, if you make these people as authentic as possible, and you don't sugarcoat that, people will forgive anything, and they will like those characters—not what they're doing, but they will be invested in them."

The pair took the book to Terence Winter, creator of HBO's *Boardwalk Empire* (for which Scorsese directed the pilot) and an ex-equity trader for Merrill Lynch. Winter immediately sensed a story in the form of the director's Mob movies, *Goodfellas* and *Casino*: a three-hour rise-and-fall epic, with lots of voiceover. He turned out a dark, snickering script—a pitch-black comedy of excess—that drew no financiers until indie producer Red Granite Pictures agreed to a budget of $100 million. When a window in Scorsese's schedule opened up in 2012, DiCaprio

The Wolf of Wall Street is certainly Scorsese's longest film—and considered by many as his funniest.

approached the director again. "I don't think we'll be able to do a movie like this too many times in the future," he told Scorsese. "It was old school, really independent filmmaking on a larger scale."

DiCaprio spent weeks with Belfort, gleaning details that he could weave into the movie—an orgy on a 747 going to Vegas, the attitude, the lingo, the type of music they listened to, the drugs they took, how they took those drugs, the effects they had. Production managers booked trained horses, scores of extras, and midgets who would be dressed in Velcro suits and thrown at targets, as described in Belfort's memoir. DiCaprio kept adding more details. "Jordan also mentioned that he had a chimpanzee on roller skates in a diaper that was handing out tickets to all the stockbrokers," he told Scorsese. "That's great, how do we get a chimpanzee?" "I don't know." "All right, somebody get on it." Scorsese called his longtime producer Emma Tillinger who told him, "Well, there's a chimpanzee who can roller-skate, but it's in Florida."

The next thing DiCaprio knew: "There's a chimpanzee, and I'm toting him around the salesroom."

There was more improvisation during production than on any other Scorsese film since *Goodfellas*, much of it from Jonah Hill, who played Donnie Azoff, a fictionalized version of Danny Porush, Stratton Oakmont's co-founder. As had been the director's method since *Mean Streets*, the actors would improvise, then the improvisation would be typed up and incorporated into the script. "I kept saying, 'Where are we?'" said Scorsese. On set, the riffing continued. Matthew McConaughey, playing the boozy Mephistopheles who instructs Belfort in the ways of Wall Street, invented the scene in which his character delivers a deranged Tuvan throat hum while beating his chest.

Below: Scorsese rams his point home to Jonah Hill (Donnie Azoff).

Right, top: Friday drinks after work, Stratton Oakmont style.

Right, bottom: "Stop flexing your muscles, Jordan, you look like a fuckin' imbecile." Unlike his clients, Jordan's wife, Naomi (Margot Robbie), sees through the front.

DiCaprio came up with the idea of throwing lobsters at his FBI nemesis, played by Kyle Chandler, as he disembarks his yacht. In an instantly infamous set piece, the point of which was originally to have Belfort finally understand what a screw-up Azoff is, DiCaprio and Scorsese had the idea of the two brokers dropping some vintage-strength Quaaludes to muffle the shock, and render Belfort's realization darkly comic. Scorsese told the actors what taking Quaaludes involves. "You try to form the word, but it isn't there," he told them. DiCaprio spent days crawling around on the set, trying to get to his Lamborghini. Scorsese was delighted. "What he did was almost like Jacques Tati or Jerry Lewis," he said.

Partly because of the departures from the script, the film took a lot of shaping in the editing room. The release date was put back as Scorsese and Thelma Schoonmaker worked day and night, seven days a week, mixing, cutting, and recutting the picture down from

four hours to a more manageable two hours fifty-nine minutes—still Scorsese's longest film to date—and to incorporate the multiple rounds of cuts from the MPAA to qualify for an R rating. The trims included the removal of many f-bombs and the tightening of the airplane orgy scene. "It was problematic, but there wasn't anything I was forced to take out or I felt uncomfortable taking out of the picture," said Scorsese, for whom the movie's sex scenes weren't really about sex: They were about obscenity.

The former altar boy had a tough time shooting some of them. His assistant director, Adam Somner, helped a great deal with the arrangement and choreography of some of the more explicit sequences, but before one such scene, Scorsese instructed Margot Robbie, the Australian actress who plays Belfort's second wife, "OK, so when you're making love …" She thought to herself: "*Making love? I wouldn't really call it that.* It was quite sweet and funny."

A roiling late-career saturnalia to set beside Picasso's *Minotaur and the Woman*, and Philip Roth's *Sabbath's Theater*, *The Wolf of Wall Street* is by turns repellent, mesmerizing, loathsome, outlandish, uproarious, exhilarating, and exhausting, and frequently all those things at once. Its release sparked a furious argument as to whether the film satirized or celebrated its characters. "Does *The Wolf of Wall Street* condemn or celebrate?" asked A. O. Scott in the *New York Times*. "Is it meant to provoke disgust or envy?" The correct response, of course, is both. Scorsese's sense of sin, from *Who's That Knocking at My Door* on, has always been tactile, sensate. It's not enough to show us sin. Nor is it enough to tell the audience that sin is sinful. Scorsese wants us to feel as if *we have sinned*—wants us to feel sheepish with our own enjoyment—and so he frontloads his picture with guilty pleasure after guilty pleasure, scene after scene of outrageous, rapacious excess. Greed is not good. Greed is *fun*.

"Given the nature of free-market capitalism—where the rule is to rise to the top at all costs—is it possible to have a financial-industry hero? And by the way,

Jordan invites his employees to a
pool party to celebrate the company's

"To present characters like this on the screen, have them reach some emotional crisis, and to see them punished for what they've done, all it does is make us feel better. And we're the victims, the people watching on screen."

"Mommy is so sick and tired of wearing panties." Naomi's tantalizing punishment for her wayward husband backfires when Jordan points out the security cameras.

"It was like mainlining adrenaline," Belfort tells us in one of his long, self-aggrandizing odes to sex, drugs, and real estate, delivered to camera. "A madhouse, a greed fest." Just as he was in *Goodfellas*, Scorsese seems fascinated by characters as spiritually dead as they are galvanically alive, rotten with their own ripeness, like apples in Dutch still lives. But Belfort's book is more boastful than Nicholas Pileggi's, narrated in the supercharged style of someone forever selling himself as the liberated id of his poor schlub readers, and the screenplay reproduces his tone exactly. "This is Ellis Island, people," he rages, as he urges the faithful to stay strong in the face of an FBI investigation. "Stratton Oakmont *is* America." DiCaprio's Belfort is like a Neanderthal Gatsby—Gatsby devolved back into his constituent elements, DNA spirals, enzymes. Standing in front of his brokers, mic in hand, back arched, forehead shiny with sweat, Belfort turns himself inside out again and again as he preaches the gospel of making a killing.

There's no Ray Liotta to charm us here, no boyish dream of inclusion. Fired after Black Monday, Belfort starts over, selling penny stock to suckers from a Long Island boiler room, and soon takes over the place. He collects together a team of eager acolytes. As well as Azoff (Jonah Hill), his manic, tubby second-in-command with gleaming white teeth, there's Robbie Feinberg, aka "Pinhead" (Brian Sacca), Alden Kupferberg, aka "Sea Otter" (Henry Zebrowski), the toupee-wearing "Rugrat" Nicky Koskoff (P. J. Byrne), "The Depraved Chinaman" Chester Ming (Kenneth Choi), and Brad Bodnick (Jon Bernthal), a tattooed toughie who's known as the Quaalude King of Bayside. Bedecked in their shiny velour clothes, frequently filmed in wide shot against lushly decorated nouveau-riche man caves, these guys make the Mob look like princes among men. They are the runts of the litter, human crud, wannabes, and they want in—into your wallets, your bank accounts, your heads, your beds.

For just under three hours, they get in: scene after scene in which asses are grabbed, money scammed, yachts crashed, Quaaludes ingested. Hundred-dollar bills flutter through the air like snowflakes—an echo of the ash and scattered paperwork that rained down in

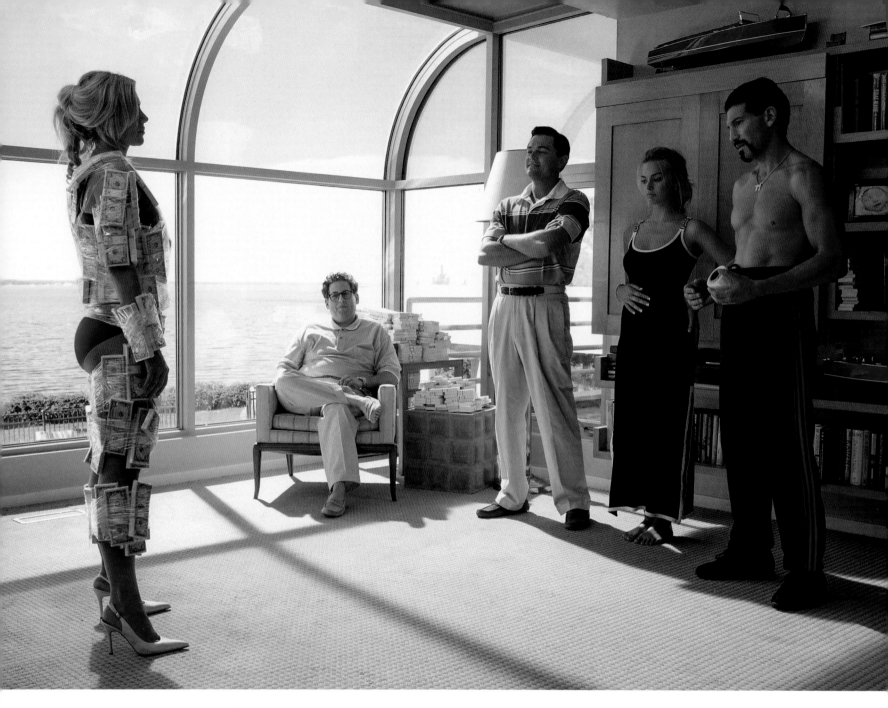

Above: Using Brad's wife, Chantalle (Katarina Cas), as a cash mule.

Right: "Fun coupons!" Jordan taunts the underpaid FBI agents who are investigating his business dealings.

"I was interested in the canvas itself—the sheer span of the action, the ground covered, the many different activities, the places, and the interactions. And then, there's the side area, the no-man's land where you shift into genuinely criminal behavior that results in great harm to many, many other people, without necessarily realizing it. It's a rise-and-fall story."

"Geddo' the pho'." With the high-grade Quaaludes in full effect, Jordan struggles to stop Donnie incriminating the pair of them.

Shutter Island and *Hugo*. Scorsese is not nearly as interested in the details of money laundering, or money skimming, as he was in *Goodfellas* and *Casino*. Terence Winter's script makes no serious attempt to explain the scams to us—several times Belfort tries, and then gives up with a wave of his hand, "You don't give a shit, do you?"—and the line gets at what is so shallow about *The Wolf of Wall Street* and so gleeful. Whatever depths the film probes do not come from the world of finance, just as *Raging Bull*'s depths do not come from the world of boxing, but from Scorsese's own brush with self-destruction in the seventies when he rose to coke-addicted, Palme d'Or–winning heights, before crashing and burning—a meteor breaking up in its own heat.

This is the arc of *Raging Bull* and *Goodfellas* and *Casino*, too. As Matt Zoller Seitz cogently observed, "those Mob films are addiction stories, too." And as every addict knows, his disease has a built-in forgetter:

The highs, in retrospect, always seem higher than they were and the lows never low enough to make a fuss over. Is there a better explanation of the moral and stylistic declension between *Raging Bull* and *The Wolf of Wall Street*? Each time Scorsese goes back to this story, his filmmaking takes off in a shower of sparks, with greater giddiness and slightly less consequence each time. *The Wolf of Wall Street* has grotesque life, like death throes, or post-mortem muscle contractions—Scorsese directs as if sucking the sap from his stripling actors. The whole movie feels spastically alive. It's one long involuntary spasm—a wet dream, a burp from the reptile brain. Both the longest film Scorsese has directed, and the funniest, it leaves you feeling—appropriately enough—spent.

Silence

2016

"How can I explain
His silence to
these people?"

ANDREW GARFIELD ADAM DRIVER and LIAM NEESON

A MARTIN SCORSESE PICTURE
SILENCE

JANUARY
Screenplay by JAY COCKS & MARTIN SCORSESE Directed by MARTIN SCORSESE

Pages 264–5: Andrew Garfield,
as Sebastião Rodrigues, and Liam
Neeson as Cristóvão Ferreira.

"We had extremely hot days and typhoons," says Prieto. "It was just the physicality of the places we were shooting, where the weather was the great complicator. Like for example the scene where they burn Kichijirō's family, very fortunately for us visually but it started raining and the wind was whipping and it was hard to keep the cameras in place and so it had a very dramatic feel. For a moment, there was talk about canceling that day because it was just really difficult. We had to slog through the mud. It was really that sort of thing all round. Or just climbing mountains to get to a spot."

When scouting for locations in Taiwan for Scorsese's long-gestating adaptation of Shūsaku Endō's novel, *Silence*, about Portuguese missionaries fighting persecution in seventeenth-century Japan, cinematographer Rodrigo Prieto realized the importance of the project to the director. "I remember looking at some of these places and thinking, from the top of that cliff there, that could be a good angle on the village. So I said, 'Marty, hold on, I'm going to go up to this cliff to take a photo and then I'll bring it just to see if the angle works.' So there I go, I start climbing the cliff, I turn around to take the photo and there's Marty climbing up the cliff as well. I'm like, 'Wow'. He came up with us. He really dove into it. It seemed to me like he was like Rodrigues and Garupe in the story because it was hard on him. Like for him it was a spiritual journey, almost penance, where the pain of the shoot was a sacrifice of some sort. It was really inspiring. Of course, that made us all work doubly hard, you know."

Appropriately enough for a book about the ultimate sacrifice, hardship defined almost every aspect of *Silence*'s development and production. Scorsese first read Shūsaku Endō's novel in 1989, when Archbishop Paul Moore sent it to him following a screening of *The Last Temptation of Christ* for New York's religious leaders. The director bought the rights to the book and assigned longtime collaborator Jay Cocks to adapt it into a screenplay, but the script wasn't to Scorsese's liking, so he went off to make *Casino* in 1995 and *Kundun* in 1997. After coming to an agreement with *Silence*'s Italian financiers, Cecchi Gori Pictures, to postpone the film further while Scorsese directed *The Departed*, *Shutter Island*, *Hugo*, and *The Wolf of Wall Street*, the Italian company finally sued, but the tale has a twist ending: *The Wolf of Wall Street*'s success at the box office—nearly $400 million globally—meant that the time, and $46 million financing, was finally right for *Silence*.

After two decades of false starts, near misses and legal wrangling, principal photography on *Silence* began in Taiwan on January 30, 2015,

Scorsese in tough filming conditions: hardship defined nearly all aspects of the production.

with Andrew Garfield, Adam Driver, and Liam Neeson starring alongside Japanese actors Tadanobu Asano, Shinya Tsukamoto, Issey Ogata, Yoshi Oida, Yōsuke Kubozuka, Nana Komatsu, and Ryo Kase, on location along the rocky coastlines, mist-laden forests and magisterially jagged mountains of Taiwan. For the film's color palette, cinematographer Prieto drew inspiration from painters like Velazquez and other Spanish and Portuguese baroque painters—blue and cyan tones at the beginning and later a golden-yellow hue. "At the beginning of the movie we're in the point of view of these Portuguese priests and what's their world view, what's their visual influence, well, it's all painters, you know religious baroque painting that's within their minds," says Prieto. "And as the movie progresses I tried to do a more Japanese style in the coloration. We then add a little more gold onto the feel of it, reminiscent of the Ming dynasty, the screens of that era in Japan that had a lot of gold plate on it. They were very beautiful. It was actually very moving too. It was a very good crystallization of their

faith. The good thing is that the light sources were allowed for that style as well, with the light emanating from the center."

More troublesome was matching the barrage of different weather conditions they encountered. "We had extremely hot days and typhoons," says Prieto. "It was just the physicality of the places we were shooting, where the weather was the great complicator. Like for example the scene where they burn Kichijirō's family, very fortunately for us visually but it started raining and the wind was whipping and it was hard to keep the cameras in place and so it had a very dramatic feel. For a moment, there was talk about canceling that day because it was just really difficult. We had to slog through the mud. It was really that sort of thing all round. Or just climbing mountains to get to a spot."

Advising the actors was Jesuit priest and writer James Martin who worked closely with Andrew Garfield in particular, leading him through the Jesuits' 30 days of spiritual exercises before filming started. When Scorsese later met Pope Francis at the Vatican's Apostolic

Left: Before filming commenced, Andrew Garfield spent seven intense days learning the Jesuits' spiritual exercises.

Left: Adam Driver as Francisco Garupe. The actor lost nearly 50 pounds in preparation for his role.

Below: Scorsese takes a moment on-set in Taiwan.

Palace before a screening of the film for 300 or so Jesuit priests, at the Pontifical Oriental Institute in Rome, he pointed out the training Garfield had undergone. "The next thing for Andrew to do is to be ordained," said Pope Francis. Scorsese looked at him and said, "Instead he got me," and roared with laughter. It turned out Francis, who had joined a Jesuit order with the aim of becoming a missionary in Asia, had read Shūsaku Endō's novel on which the film was based, and after they exchanged gifts—some framed images depicting hidden Christians in Japan for Francis, some rosaries for Scorsese—he told the director, "I hope the story of the film bears much fruit."

Silence opens in Lisbon in 1643. Two devout Jesuit missionaries, Sebastião Rodrigues (Andrew Garfield) and Francisco Garupe (Adam Driver), are told that their mentor Ferreira (Liam Neeson), who was bringing aid to the persecuted Christians of Japan, has been tortured and recanted his faith. Refusing to believe this, they demand to be allowed to travel to Japan to find him. Making furtive landfall on a

section of the Japanese coast near Nagasaki, they find their way to a small settlement where Christian villagers are secretly practicing their faith. Praying under cover of darkness, they are in mortal fear of being discovered by the feudal lords and their samurai, their very lives put at risk by the priests' presence. Often shot in guttering candle-light, shrouded in mist and shadow, the film displays muddy but hopeful faces rendered beautiful by the simple quality of their devotion, hands clasping, exchanging crosses: the images are as simple and beautiful as an Albrecht Dürer painting.

Of the two lead actors, it is Driver who seems more the natural Scorsese player—lean, intense, like a strung-out Byron—but it is Garfield, with his tremulous, shy nature, whose trials of conscience form the narrative focal point. After Rodrigues and Garupe part ways, Rodrigues forges ahead alone, coming upon another Christian enclave in a remote fishing village, where he ministers to the isolated Christians. He is soon betrayed, arrested, and falls into the hands of a sly inquisitor named Inoue (Issey Ogata) who engages Rodrigues in

Above: Under torture, Cristóvão Ferreira recants his faith.

Right and opposite: Scorsese's vision was uncompromising and, sometimes, a tough watch.

There's little soundtrack, much mud and squalor, and the scenes of torture are almost unwatchable in their cruelty, but what is perhaps most remarkable is the simplicity and stillness of Scorsese's shooting style.

extended intellectual debates about religious doctrine, while devising elaborate tortures to break his spirit—people are crucified amid crashing waves, burned alive or bled out like butchered pigs. Fanning himself like Madam Butterfly and boasting the most deceptive bucktoothed smile since John Huston in *Chinatown*, Ogata plays this subtle beast with blithe insolence. "Why do you make life so difficult for me?" he wheedles, as if the act of torture was hardest on the torturer—a complaint last heard from Joe Pesci in *Casino*, while squeezing a man's head in a vice. The simple act of apostasy that Inoue demands is painfully simple: he places them before a small embossed-metal portrait of Jesus and orders them to step on it but even this is too much for Rodrigues. "I will not abandon you," he vows.

A story of dogged endurance and unfathomable suffering that would test even the most tenacious of faiths, *Silence* is also something of a test for the cinematic faithful. Like his Jesuits, Scorsese doesn't shy from the stony path. His film boasts few enticements: there's

little soundtrack, much mud and squalor, and the scenes of torture are almost unwatchable in their cruelty, but what is perhaps most remarkable is the simplicity and stillness of Scorsese's shooting style. For the first time dispensing with the kinetic camera movements that he first evolved on *The Last Waltz* and perfected on *Raging Bull*, the violence in *Silence* is drained of all excitement—it is flat, unkinetic, almost an act of renunciation in itself, as if Scorsese has repudiated his own jittery hang-ups and peccadilloes. It could easily have been called *Stillness*. The silence of the title is God's—a silence that is the subject of Rodrigues's anguished lament at His apparent impassivity in the face of human suffering. "How can I explain His silence to these people?" asks an increasingly doubt-wracked Rodrigues. For all that Hollywood specializes in flimsy bromides about the "triumph of the human spirit," the genuine article is much more elusive. Yet here it is—stubborn, wily, unbeautiful—running right through the film like piano wire. It's a tough watch, but the mere existence of the film at all feels like some sort of miracle.

It also pointed the way forward—stylistically, technologically—towards his next film, in just the same way that *The Last Temptation of Christ* heralded *Goodfellas*. During the first week of shooting in Taiwan, they were shooting a scene in which Garfield and Driver descend the steps of the sixteenth-century Jesuit college in Macau at CMPC Studios in Taipei. The backdrop of the harbor was to be filled in later by the digital artists at Industrial Light & Magic, headed up by visual effects supervisor Pablo Helman. In between takes, Helman and Scorsese got to talking about the new performance-capture technology he was developing that was marker-less, making it more actor- and director-friendly. "At the time, I thought that he was doing *Sinatra*, so I pitched to him, maybe we could do a young Sinatra for him," says Helman. "He said, 'Well, that sounds like it could work for another project that I've been thinking about. It's called *The Irishman*'. He said, 'No markers, no helmet, no nothing. You develop the technology. When you're finished, give me a call'. So, I just kind of took a breath and I said, 'You know, we'll develop the technology'."

It took about eight weeks to develop a prototype and when post-production on *Silence* ended in the fall of 2015, Helman dropped by the set of HBO's *Vinyl*, using one of the sets to recreate the scene where De Niro's Jimmy explodes over the all-pink Cadillac Coup DeVille bought by Johnny Roast Beef with the money from the Lufthansa heist. Helman selected ten seconds of the clip, and took it back to the headquarters of Industrial Light & Magic, just outside San Francisco, where he worked on it for three months. Near the end of December, he showed the filmmakers two clips, one with a de-aged De Niro, one from the original *Goodfellas*, side-by-side, at Scorsese's offices on 57th Street. "We're looking at a monitor and Marty's face just lit up, going, 'Oh my God. This is incredible'," recalls Helman. "Right there he was like, 'Yeah, this is going to be my next movie'. It was a great feeling. I mean, you could see it in his face. Bob just looked at me and says, 'You've extended my career by 30 years'. It was an incredible feeling of accomplishment, but also of panic because it's a combination of things. 'Yeah, we're going to do this … But now we have to do it'."

The Irishman

2018

"It's the human dilemma,
how to come to any kind of
term with your extinction.
So, that's what it's all come
down to. We had to take it
down that road, face it
and play it out."

"I mean, there were a lot of times I thought the movie itself wasn't going to happen, but I always knew if Bob was going to ask Joe, he was going to do it, and that was that. We knew we'd be able to get the band back together."

Pages 272–3: Robert De Niro as Frank Sheeran and Joe Pesci as Russell Bufalino.

Right: Stephen Graham as rising Teamster, Anthony "Tony Pro" Provenzano.

Robert De Niro and Scorsese were on a call to the late Brad Grey, the head of Paramount, in July of 2009, talking about a planned adaption of Don Winslow's 2006 novel about an ageing hitman, *The Winter of Frankie Machine*, when De Niro suddenly introduced James Brandt's memoir, *I Hear You Paint Houses* into the conversation. "We were literally on a call," recalls *Irishman* producer Jane Rosenthal. "It was Brad Grey, Marty, Bob, Me, Emma [Koskoff] all on this call talking about going to make *Frankie Machine*. We wanted to do some rewriting. As we were on this call it was literally Bob who said, 'Well, there's this other book, and maybe we option that too, and maybe we should do more this other book.' Everybody's in different places, and you hear Brad Grey say, 'Let me get this straight, you want to take a green-light movie, and turn it into a development deal … Is that right?' You could hear everybody go, '*Mm-hmm. Mm-hmm. Mm-hmm …*'. But then Brad said, 'Okay, I'm fine with that. That's easier.' On one hand, you felt like, 'Okay, well this is depressing, it's not going forward, but Bob felt that his next collaboration with Marty, whatever it was going to be, had to be very special, and it's hard for anyone outside of the two of them to define what that 'special' is."

De Niro first read Brandt's book at the recommendation of screenwriter Eric Roth, who had written *The Good Shepherd* for him. Based on thousands of hours of interviews conducted by James Brandt, a former prosecutor, with alleged hitman Frank Sheeran before his death in 2003, the book told the story of Sheeran's war years on the battlefield at Anzio, his return to Philly to find what work he could: first truck driver, then small-time crook, then union organizer and trusted mob confederate, one of the few non-Italians to make the FBI's list of Cosa Nostra criminals. A granular portrait of a post-war American working man—tough, taciturn, loyal—the book also offered a window into a soul tortured in his later years over his part in the disappearance of Teamsters union boss Jimmy Hoffa. De Niro was rapt.

"When I read it, I said, 'God, Marty, you have to read this book, I think this is much more what we would want to do'," says De Niro. "It just seemed so real to me, with all the dialogue, and this and that. I knew Marty would understand right away, as soon as he read it, that this was more something that we should do." Scorsese was in no hurry to get back to the mob. After making four films with De Niro touching on organized crime, either directly or indirectly—*Mean Streets* (1973), *Raging Bull* (1980), *Goodfellas* (1990), and *Casino* (1995)—it felt like the subject was all played out. "After *Casino*, I felt that was it," he says. "*Goodfellas* was at that point in time for me, a kind of final statement. *Casino* became an

extension of that, that did it on a bigger scale, about excess and America, really. But, in any event, I didn't want to make another. Meaning where else do we go together? What do we explore?" As De Niro started to describe the character of Sheeran—a man who is left no choice but to betray the man he loves like a father—Scorsese "saw something happen that you can't create. It was inherent in him, there was an emotional reaction. When I saw that, I said, 'There's something here, if he feels this way'. At the time, I was playing around with the ideas of the Jean-Pierre Melville films and the Jacques Becker films about the aging wise guy, the aging underworld figure who isn't necessarily a monster, who has to sort of make do with his life, count the blessings around him, and fades away. I thought, if he could tap into that character that way, I know I could go there because it's genuine and it's real, and however it turns out, it needs to be done—it has to be done."

It was De Niro's idea to approach Al Pacino and Joe Pesci to co-star. After being approached by De Niro to gauge his enthusiasm, Pacino met with Scorsese in one of the cabins at the Beverly Hills hotel, during the awards-season build-up for *The Departed*. "The only thing he said that I remember was 'You're going to do this? It's going to happen?'" says Scorsese. "Because the question is real, we're all getting older and sure enough it took some years to pull together." Pesci was trickier. In 1999, the actor

had announced his retirement from movies in order to record music and play golf, and while he had returned to take a small part in De Niro's 2006 film about the CIA, *The Good Shepherd*, was initially reluctant to return to make another film with Scorsese and De Niro about the mob. What De Niro's phlegmatic longtime producing partner, Jane Rosenthal, calls "the Question of Joe" hung over the first few years of the film's development. He turned them down literally dozens of times before relenting, remembers Rosenthal. "'What's the offer? How much?' And then, 'I'm playing golf, I'm doing this, I don't want to be bothered'. Joe could say no, and no, and no. Bob would say, 'Joe's going to do it. Joe will do it. Let me talk to Joe and he'll do it'. I never in a million years thought Joe wouldn't do it if Bob asked him. I mean, there were a lot of times I thought the movie itself wasn't going to happen, but I always knew if Bob was going to ask Joe, he was going to do it, and that was that. We knew we'd be able to get the band back together."

Finally, on September 18th, 2017, ten years after De Niro first read Charles Brandt's book, with locations locked, sets built, and casting completed, principal photography on *The Irishman* began at Randall's Island in Manhattan. If the hardships endured while shooting *Silence*— typhoons, legal battles, endless mud—had been, in some sense, the point of the production for Scorsese, *The Irishman* represented a kind of

homecoming. "*Silence* was hard on him, almost penance, where the pain of the shoot was a sacrifice on his part," says cinematographer Rodrigo Prieto. "I found Marty to be much more joyful on this one, just to be back with all his friends. Every day he comes in a little nervous, and everybody has to be very quiet, so he can concentrate—it's all about 'okay, what are we doing? This is a shot we talked about. Do you like it like this? Do you want to adjust it?' It's also for the actors. There's a big crew and they're all on their walkie-talkies and he tries to make all that disappear. But once the camera starts rolling and he sees the first performance, that nervousness melts away. That's when the joy comes in."

The cameras required to shoot all the information that Industrial Light & Magic needed were huge. Weighing about 64 pounds, with three lenses, sprouting so many cables they looked like a Medusa. Everyone called it the "three-headed monster." For dialogue scenes, which Scorsese liked to shoot using two cameras, that meant a total of six cameras trained on the actors at any one time. "We had to work for nine million cameras," says Pesci. "It was all new to me. Working with two cameras, I was learning so much from Marty and from Bob on this. I'd be like 'which camera? You got 12 cameras out here. Which lens?' I remember I was walking down the hall on one thing, and Marty said, 'You look like you're looking all around.' I said,

'Well, I don't know where to look. I'm walking! I don't want to look at any of those lenses!'"

On *Goodfellas*, Pesci had helped improvise many of the film's funniest riffs—the impromptu art appreciation session at his mother's dining table ("One dog goes one way, and the other dog goes the other way. And this guy's saying, 'waddaya want from me?'"), the interaction with Spider, only one line of which was scripted ("Why don't you go fuck yourself, Tommy") and the infamous "Do you think I'm funny?" exchange between Tommy and Henry. *The Irishman* called for something different. The so-called "quiet don" who conducted mob business behind the lace curtains of a nondescript Drapers in downtown Philly, Russell Bufalino is a man who utters, in the course of the film, only a single expletive. In the script it was two. Pesci got it down to one. "What Joe needed to do, and he did it brilliantly, was to pull back and have an inner power and inner control, an inner strength and people could shout, scream, run around the room, turn tables over, whatever, he would stand there," says Scorsese. "Joe is tapped into a certain authenticity of that street life in a way that other actors are not. They just aren't. And he has an instinctive reaction against anything that is slightly off. Like, 'He would never look at me that way,' or 'I can't seem to get my . . .'. He wouldn't touch the doorknob, like Howard Hughes.

Left: Martin Scorsese directing a scene with Robert De Niro and Joe Pesci.

Right: Russell Bufalino (Pesci) at the climatic Teamster dinner in New Jersey.

I said, 'Okay, what is it?' And we'd find it. It was quite a process, during the shoot."

Despite having been introduced to Pacino in the early 1970s by Francis Ford Coppola, Scorsese had never worked with Pacino, although he had been briefly in the frame to direct *Serpico*. The actor described himself as being "in paradise." He prepped each scene by listening to Hoffa's original speeches on headphones to capture his distinctive, propulsive rhythm, and sometimes asked to improvise a little, just to feel the blood running through his veins. "Sometimes when I have a pretty heavy scene, I try to put some music on before," says Ray Romano, who plays Teamster lawyer Bill Bufalino. "So I asked him—'is it music?' And no, he had all different speeches of Hoffa. He was listening to Jimmy Hoffa's speech right up, right up to 'action."

One of the longest and hardest sequences to shoot was the climactic dinner thrown by the Teamsters at a New Jersey casino in appreciation of Sheeran's years of service to the union—featuring all the major actors in the film, together with hundreds of extras, a small orchestra, and a troupe of dancing girls, all together for hours upon hours in the smoke and haze of an abandoned Harlem club, the Alhambra Ballroom on 126th Street. "It was thrilling but hard on everyone because of the scope and volume of material that needed to be committed to film," remembers Stephanie Kurtzuba, who played Sheeran's second wife Irene. At one point she looked around at the actors at the tables around them—De Niro, Pacino, Pesci,

Harvey Keitel, as well as Scorsese, shuttling back and forth between the tables—turned to Anna Paquin and said, "'Are we here right now?' And she was like, 'Yup'. It was almost ridiculous." Watching it all unfold from the balcony was producer Jane Rosenthal who found herself watching take after take. "When you watch all those guys play at the top of their game, it's the most exhilarating thing," she says. "It's those very little, subtle things that they do, and that's when you go back to where all these guys grew up and what they observed growing up, that they can trigger certain things and bring out the best of the best that they have. There isn't anything like it. I don't like saying things are 'the end of an era' but you talk about how business changed, how politics changed, how communications changed. This movie captures that moment."

If *Mean Streets* was a firecracker tossed into the audience's lap and *Goodfellas* was a meteor burning up in its own heat, then *The Irishman* is a reminder that nothing is as dangerous as a fire you think has gone out: the embers of memory are still scalding hot coals. Both an elegy for the gangster genre Scorsese has made his own and a last hurrah for acting legends eager to feel the blood pumping through their veins once more, the film is remarkable for the sobriety of Scorsese's shooting style, bringing to a head all the elements of Scorsese's late period, from the increased use of flashbacks in *Shutter Island* and *Hugo*; to the imagery of ash and scattered papers in both films; the deepening delight in cinema's powers of illusion

in *Hugo* and *Rolling Thunder Revue: A Bob Dylan Story*, the attenuated, filament-wire shooting style he evolved with Prieto while making *Silence*. Gone are the ritzy suits, Keith Richards riffs and kinetic camera workouts that turned *Goodfellas* into such a giddy free-for-all. In their place a nested structure of flashbacks, the strains of early doo-wop, and a shooting style leisurely and coiled where once it was exuberant and surging, summoning the vanished world of abandoned garages and auto-shops, bowling alleys, soda fountains and roadside motels. Here are De Niro and Al Pacino cracking a quiet joke over the Watergate hearings, their faces as familiar to us as our own fathers, the weight of years lifted from their faces by digital artistry. Here are Joe Pesci and De Niro determining a man's fate with an exchange of looks. One beat. Two beats. The guy's as good as gone.

At its center is a road trip taken from Philly to Detroit in 1975 by mob boss Russell Bufalino (Pesci) and his favored hitman, Frank Sheeran (De Niro), to a Bufalino family wedding. Driving in a Lincoln continental with their wives, they make their way from Philly to Detroit to attend a wedding of one of their cousins. "Wake me up when we get to Lewisberg," he says, pushing back in his seat. You know you're in for something different when the first thing Joe Pesci does in a movie is take a nap. Bufalino is quite unlike any of the motormouths we have seen Pesci play for Scorsese in the past. The highest-ranking mafia member we have seen head up a Scorsese picture, Bufalino is also the quietest, "the quiet don", in whose eyes ruthlessness mixes with an avuncular twinkle—"the kid" he calls Frank— and the entire film seems to find its rhythm in the actor's mixture of the leisurely and the lethal. Between stops for gas, cigarette breaks and to buy wedding presents, Pesci also finds time to collect money and issue a quiet threat to a jeweler. Only once we get to Detroit is the true nature of their trip apparent. The wedding is also a funeral.

Like *Mean Streets* and *Goodfellas*, the film draws a stark triangle between Bufalino, Sheeran and the man he was assigned to protect, the head of the Teamsters, Jimmy Hoffa—in Pacino's powerful performance, a bellicose but charming rogue who likes to puff his chest as much as he loves devouring ice-cream sundaes with Frank's daughter Peggy. He is a familiar figure in Scorsese's demonology, the film's wild card, who will cause no end of heartbreak for the well-intentioned Frank. Between these two men, he shuttles, a peacemaker trying to keep everyone happy and make things right, caught in one corner of a triangle that will slowly crush him like a vice. What we have, essentially, is a love triangle between men who pay the ultimate price for their fondness for one another, with the mob in the role of the avenging Furies. But while we have seen many deaths in Scorsese's films, *The Irishman* is the first of his works to feel properly death-haunted. Drained of excitement, Sheeran's hits are shockingly abrupt, performed with the diligence of a plumber. Freeze-frames, once a way for Scorsese to slow down and savor a too-vivid present (an explosion, a knife attack) became instead a way of flashing forward to the end that waits us all: "*Allen Dorfman, shot eight times in the head in a Chicago parking lot, 1979*", "*Roofers Union President John McCullough, shot six times in the head in his kitchen, 1980*" or "*well-liked by everyone. Died of natural causes.*" By the end, when Sheeran is told by FBI agents that everyone he is protecting has died, including his lawyer, he asks, suspiciously, "Who did it?"

"Cancer" comes the reply.

This time, the mob have competition.

Far left: The Hoffa hit: Bufalino (Pesci) takes a nap, Sheeran (De Niro) drives.

Left: Scorsese and Pacino (Hoffa) on-set and in court.

Above: Most of the people in Sheeran's life are now gone, but Hoffa still haunts him.

By the end, the euphemism that gave Brandt's book its title—"paint houses" for "redecorate the walls with blood"—seems no euphemism. This is work. A lifetime of it. Unlike *Goodfellas* and *Casino*, in which the Feds come down like a curtain on the final act, *The Irishman* shows what happens when a man quite literally gets away with murder. The last twenty minutes have no equal in Scorsese's work. As time gets more precious, an awful clarity descends. Most of the people Sheeran was protecting are gone and the secrets seem to be forcing their way out of him. The memory of Hoffa eats at him like the arthritis eating away at his lower back. The nurse leaves him, and the camera does, too, following her down a corridor where she hands in her notes, but as she prepares to go, the camera doubles back on itself, turns through 180 degrees and returns to the room. Except this time it is night and a priest is at his side, delivering an absolution. Whatever has this man in its grip is not about to let go of him so easily.

"Al Pacino said, when he saw the picture, 'You have had to have gone through the 76 years in order to make this film," says Scorsese. "It's the human dilemma, how to come to any kind of term with your extinction. So, that's what it's all come down to. We had to take it down that road, face it and play it out. There's that great line in a crazy book, *Journey to the End of the Night*, by Louis-Ferdinand Céline, from the 1930s, in which this woman shoots the main character at the end, and he says, 'I don't understand why you feel this way. What has happened with you?' She says, 'What's happened to me is a whole life has happened.' Bang! She shoots him. A whole life has happened . . . So many different stories occur in that world, and still do even now, right? There's always something. There's always so much material, but this strips it down to the heart, for me. This is basically what I've been trying to get to all these years. I can't sit and say I'm any wiser but on the other hand you've been through a great deal and it doesn't feel natural to resist what I know as basic truths. And when I say that I have an image of a dark hallway and some old woman sitting in a wooden chair in the front of the building, like an old apartment on Elizabeth Street. You know, seeing the old people sitting there wearing black. Or an old man getting up, making the espresso. That's really it. Speaking Sicilian and I'm the kid down the hall and I see them and that afternoon light is shining on the wooden floors. You could still smell the coffee. It's that kind of thing. They would put these peppers, red peppers and green peppers, they'd put them on the stove and they'd, it's an incredible image, the flame below it the skin would just burn off and that's how they'd start working and it was fascinating to watch. My mother used to do it too. So it's a very important image. And that's something that's in you."

The Documentaries

"Whenever I hear people ... make a hard distinction between film and life, I think to myself that it's just a way of avoiding the power of cinema. Of course it's not life—it's the invocation of life, it's an ongoing dialogue with life."

Scorsese's documentaries are not, for him, a sideline. He was schooled in documentaries, found paid work making them upon leaving NYU, and his collaborations with Thelma Schoonmaker later informed the rough, on-the-fly aesthetic of *Mean Streets*, *Raging Bull*, *Goodfellas*, and *Casino*. Scorsese's portraits of the Mob, and the streets, all the things he is famous for, are unimaginable without his documentary work. "I don't make the distinction between my documentaries and my dramatic films," he has said. "How can I distinguish between them?" If his feature films aspire to the immediacy of documentary, his documentaries sometimes come with the production values and polish of features. *The Last Waltz*, his elegiac 1978 movie of The Band's farewell concert, was storyboarded down to the last frame. For his 2008 Rolling Stones concert film *Shine a Light*, Scorsese employed nine cinematographers, operating no fewer than eighteen cameras, with so many lights on Mick Jagger at one point that he posed a fire hazard. "Frankly, I was afraid he'd go up in smoke," Scorsese only half-joked.

At NYU, documentaries were the passion of Haig Manoogian, Scorsese's mentor, who eulogized the work of the Maysles brothers, Leacock and Pennebaker, Chris Marker, also the narrative films that came out of Italian neorealism and the French New Wave—both documentary influenced. The neorealist films, especially Roberto Rossellini's *Paisan* and *Journey to Italy*, made a big impact on Scorsese. "That was my universe, those were my aunts and my uncles and my parents," he said. "No matter how many Westerns I liked, whenever I went to make a film it would have elements of documentary, like the neorealist films. I always feel that if I can, at times, get something on film that has the truthfulness and power that seem to come from the documentary—to me that's the ultimate quest, really."

While still trying to complete *Who's That Knocking at My Door*, he supplemented his $55-a-week NYU teaching paycheck by editing documentaries with Thelma Schoonmaker over at Michael Wadleigh's Paradigm Pictures, on West 86th Street. They would work for PBS and *The Merv Griffin Show* by day and work through the night to finish

"It's good to see you all. It's good to see *anybody*!" Keith Richards counts his blessings in *Shine a Light* (2008).

Above: Not all peace and love, director Mike Wadleigh remonstrates with Scorsese and Thelma Schoonmaker during the making of *Woodstock* (1970).

Right: The thrill may have gone for B. B. King, but *Medicine Ball Caravan* (1971) was just the beginning for Scorsese.

Knocking in the tiny editing suite on the ground floor. Out of this creative hive came Scorsese's first screen credit, as first assistant director on Wadleigh's documentary of the 1969 Woodstock music festival. "An extraordinary, life-changing experience," Scorsese later called the festival. "It was wonderful because coming from where I come from, boy, I like seeing people happy." They came away with 120 miles of footage, which he and Schoonmaker assembled into a three-hour film, working out of another room on the second floor at 86th Street that used to be a pool hall, using seven projectors, three or four of them projecting in sync onto a white wall. It was from this that they got the idea of using split screens. "There was something about the visceral quality of all the film going through the projectors simultaneously," said Scorsese. "And we agreed that was the way it should be cut."

Eventually, he and Wadleigh butted heads and Scorsese was fired. However, *Woodstock* (1970) was a huge commercial and critical success, received an Academy Award for Best Documentary Feature, and led to Scorsese's job editing *Medicine Ball Caravan* (later called

We Have Come for Your Daughters) for Fred Weintraub—the job that first drew him to Los Angeles. It was the height of Scorsese's own hippie phase. Wearing jeans and cowboy shirts purchased on Melrose Avenue, he grew his hair long and a thick beard. "At that point there was a part of me that wanted to erase everything of where I came from," he said. "I had a feeling that I had escaped." It was out of this feeling that *Alice Doesn't Live Here Anymore* grew, but *Alice* also stoked memories of his mother—"she was more old world but she had that kind of humor, and irony"—and as filming wound down, he shot a small documentary about his parents for the National Endowment for the Humanities in Washington, one of a series of films about immigrant groups—Jews, Italians, Irish, Greeks, etc.—to celebrate the Bicentennial.

Shot in two three-hour periods over a single weekend in his parents' living room, from a sheet of questions prepared with the help of Mardik Martin, Scorsese's old friend from NYU, *Italianamerican* (1974) marks the embracing of the director's roots, both psychologically and creatively, that would eventually lead to *Raging Bull*. It opens with

"I was able to learn things about my parents that I didn't know … I learned how they lived in the twenties and thirties, and I saw it as the story of these two people. I had seen them as parents, not as people. Then suddenly they became people and it was a love story."

Scorsese sitting down with his mother and father to break the ice before the interview starts. "Why are you sitting over there?" Catherine asks Charlie, seeing him perched at the end of the sofa. "I'm sitting over here," Charlie responds, "because this is where I want to sit." Catherine turns to the camera "This man, after forty-two years of marriage, and he sits over there!" she importunes. From that moment, any idea that the film was going to be a straightforward immigrant story or historical document goes out the window. It is those things, but first and foremost it is a portrait of a forty-two-year marriage, in all its gnarled, affectionate, passive-aggressive, harrumphing detail. "It's the best thing I've ever done," Scorsese declared recently. "It was then I realized that just one image of one person can tell a story. A world. They were better than actors, but they weren't actors."

Catherine is undoubtedly the star of the film: voluble, quick-witted, amused and amusing, with a flair for self-dramatization that makes her very much the mother of her son, and explains why she found it so easy to slip into the ensembles of *Goodfellas* and *Casino* (she ended up with thirteen acting credits, all told). Her hands, used to emphasize this point or underline that, carve out little ballet figures in the air. Scorsese's father, Charlie, is the quieter figure, at least at first, ridiculing his wife for affecting an accent for the cameras, but clearly entranced by her, his fondness for tough women going back to his first-generation immigrant mother ("a whip"), whose astringent legacy is left hanging like a question mark over the dining-room table. It's a rare moment of silence, maybe the only one: The rest of the film is a joyous, cascading overspill of talk, frequently in stereo, with Catherine and Charlie tag-teaming each anecdote, interrupting and correcting one another. For anyone who wonders where the torrents of talk in Scorsese's pictures come from, here is the mother (and father) lode. The film ends with Catherine asking if she can put all her furniture back the way it was, still telling stories as she does it. "Are you still shooting this thing?" she asks, to laughter. "I'll murder you! You'll never get out of this house alive!" Scorsese leaves the footage in place as ironic testimonial to the power of families.

If *Italianamerican* constituted an embrace of his parents, an extension of the autobiographical urge undergirding *Mean Streets*, *American Boy* (1978), a piece about wayward sons, acknowledged the more destructive urges running through *Taxi Driver*. A profile of Scorsese's friend Steven Prince, who had taken the role of the gun salesman in *Taxi Driver*—once a road manager for Neil Diamond and a reformed heroin junkie—the film is a tragicomic portrait of a young hustler, infused with Scorsese's tenderness and affection for his subject. Shot over two weekends, mostly in Prince's living room, the film starts with a brawl between Prince and George Memmoli (the pool-hall owner in *Mean Streets*), then settles into a series of stories, told by Prince himself, of his various japes and scrapes: the time he shot a man who stole tires from the garage he was working at, his run-in with a gorilla, his coming out, his story about injecting adrenaline into the heart of a woman who had overdosed with the help of a medical dictionary and a magic marker (an episode that later found its way into Quentin Tarantino's *Pulp Fiction*). By the final section the film has

turned, by unnoticeable degrees, into a sinewy survivor's testimonial. "Steven almost died several times and so did I," said Scorsese. "But we're still here. Steven didn't go to rehab; he pulled himself through, which is extraordinary. Survive. But how? That eats away at me."

Completed during Scorsese's most tumultuous period, coming off the production of *New York, New York*, the documentary operated as something of a life vest for its maker. Scorsese seemed unwilling to give himself a moment's rest, instead taking on a barrage of projects—not just *American Boy*, but a stage play with Liza Minnelli, and *The Last Waltz*, his documentary about The Band's farewell concert—as if sandbagging the door. "I was exhausted, but it was as though I couldn't stop filming," he said. "I was so wound up I had to carry on." Upon being retained to shoot *The Last Waltz*, his cinematographer Michael Chapman exclaimed, "Marty, you're a monster! The most dangerous person I ever met! I'm begging you, I can't go on. Let me die in peace!"

The Last Waltz (1978) was an elegy not just to The Band, but to the seventies, a way of life—"a goddam impossible way of life," as Robbie

Opposite: "He's no saint, but who is? And you yourself, who are you to cast the first stone?" Scorsese's affection for his friend Steven Prince shone through in *American Boy* (1978).

Right: Robbie Robertson, Bob Dylan, and Rick Danko in *The Last Waltz* (1978).

Below: At the 1978 Cannes Film Festival with Robertson, who has gone on to write, arrange, or supervise music for numerous Scorsese feature films, from *Raging Bull* through to *The Irishman*.

"When I finished *The Last Waltz* I thought that it was the best work I had ever done."

Robertson, the lead guitarist, puts it in one of the behind-the-scenes interviews that Scorsese interleaves into concert footage of the group's final concert, at San Francisco's Winterland Ballroom in November 1976. Filmed in 35 mm, using seven cameras, the documentary captures The Band performing with a series of famous guests—Joni Mitchell, Neil Young, Muddy Waters, Eric Clapton, Bob Dylan, and more—against an elegant stage, backed with drapes and candelabra. Scorsese trained his camera on the performers' faces much more than their instruments, catching them in states of rapt transport, and the result is as soulful as rock music gets.

Watching dailies of the concert, he hit on the idea of an opera where all the elements, musical or otherwise, would be linked and decided to shoot three numbers on a soundstage at MGM, against sets built by Boris Leven, his production designer on *New York, New York*, from a color palette based on the burning of Atlanta in *Gone with the Wind*: burnt-out bronze, reds, chocolate browns. The whole thing was storyboarded, as was the concert itself—the changes in lighting and

the camera movements matched the lyrics exactly—and took nearly two years to edit. It was as tightly controlled as *New York, New York* had been chaotic, as if Scorsese were engaged in an urgent act of self-reconstruction. "That's where I started getting back in line," he says. "[*The Last Waltz*] kept me in line, working like a person in therapy in hospital. But there is no doubt: I didn't think I'd never find it again."

Documentary filmmaking, in this instance, seems to have been much more than just a view of the world around him, but a means of staying alive—a window into his soul. It would be nearly two decades before Scorsese's next documentary work, but what started as a trickle,

with *A Personal Journey with Martin Scorsese through American Movies* (1995) and *My Voyage to Italy* (1999), had by the mid-2000s turned into a flood, with the opening episode of *The Blues* (2003), a made-for-TV documentary series about the roots of blues music, *No Direction Home* (2005), a documentary about the early life and career of Bob Dylan, *Shine a Light* (2008), his Rolling Stones concert film, *Public Speaking* (2010), about Scorsese's friend, wit and raconteur Fran Lebowitz, *A Letter to Elia* (2010), about director Elia Kazan, and *George Harrison: Living in the Material World* (2011), his unusually searching look at Harrison's career and post-Beatles search for spiritual fulfillment,

"We had to find the thread of it, which was that he was going to be himself wherever it was going to take him. Ultimately, he was going to disappoint a lot of people, make them angry by doing that, but he did it. That's important, I think, for an artist."

No Direction Home (2005) documented the early life and career of Bob Dylan, an artist who, like Scorsese, has never been afraid to swim against the tide.

and *The 50-Year-Argument*, his warm celebration of the *New York Review of Books*, weaving together archival footage of the likes of James Baldwin and Gore Vidal with interviews with the paper's founding editor, Robert Silvers. This time Scorsese seems gripped by an urge towards summation, a desire to get down all his loves and enthusiasms while he still had time—to run out the clock.

Shine a Light (2008) was his way of repaying the debt he owed the Rolling Stones—the band whose music has featured in more of his movies than any other. "The actual visualization of sequences and scenes in *Mean Streets* comes a lot from their music, from living with their music and listening to it," he said. "Not just the songs I use in the film. No, it's about the tone and the mood of their music, their attitude. I just kept listening to it. Then I kept imagining scenes in

movies. And interpreting . . . those songs inspired me to do that, to find a way to put those stories on film. So the debt is incalculable. I don't know what to say. In my mind, I did this film forty years ago. It just happened to get around to being filmed right now."

Mick Jagger had invited Scorsese to shoot one of the Stones' live shows, maybe on the beach in Rio, using 3D cameras, but Scorsese wasn't sure he could add much to such a big spectacle and suggested doing something much smaller, in a more modest venue where he could stay close to the group. Scorsese wanted to show how the band members played off each other on stage, the physical and psychic energy they exchanged. After considering New York's Radio City Music Hall, they decided on the nearby Beacon Theater. Using eighteen cameras, operated by a small army of cinematographers, headed by Robert Richardson, and including Robert Elswit, fresh from his Oscar success for *There Will Be Blood*, and Andrew Lesnie, director of photography on the *Lord of the Rings* trilogy, Scorsese directed in front of a bank of screens like a sportscaster. Even

with several cameras on each band member, keeping track of the performers was hard, so much did they move around. Beforehand, he asked Jagger if he could guarantee a duet with Keith Richards at some point. "I think I could do 'Faraway Eyes' if I get him on to the stage but I don't know where he's going to be," replied Jagger. "You'd have better luck predicting the Grand National."

The result is beautifully calibrated chaos—"madness, wonderful madness!" as Scorsese put it—led by the ever-Byronic Jagger, whirling, leaping, strutting, and wriggling, as the band powers its way through a set including "Jumpin' Jack Flash," "Some Girls," "Tumbling Dice," "Start Me Up," "(I Can't Get No) Satisfaction" and "Sympathy for the Devil," during which Jagger stands silhouetted against a wall of lights.

"Is this normal movie lighting?" asks Charlie Watts at one point. Jagger fans himself with his shirt, laughing. The three remaining founder members of the band were now in their sixties, a point underlined by excerpts from old television interviews going back to 1964, including a 1972 clip of Dick Cavett asking Jagger if he can imagine carrying on when he's sixty ("Easily"). *Shine a Light* amounts to a powerful testament to gnarly perseverance. "It's good to see you all," Richards says to the throng. "It's good to see *anybody*." Now sixty-two, his upper arms shriveled, his face as graven as an Easter Island statue, Richards resembles an old Gypsy madam, his lips dangling a cigarette as he browses his guitar strings—in one glorious shot we see him *spit* his cigarette out, in a spray of bright sparks—before

"The idea wasn't to make a documentary film, it was to capture the performance. I've always said, from when I first heard their music, 'I'm gonna get that on film some day.' It only took forty years or so, but what can I say?"

Left: "Madness, wonderful madness!" Scorsese tries out as the fifth Rolling Stone. *Shine a Light* (2008).

Right: *Rolling Thunder Revue: A Bob Dylan Story* (2019) took a playful, ludic approach to the mercurial Dylan.

ending the concert bending down, hugging his guitar, trying to catch his breath. It was one of Scorsese's favorite moments. "And then he finds the strength to get up again, to resurrect," he said—like Jesus Christ, Jake LaMotta, and Martin Scorsese before him.

Even more of an artistic statement was Scorsese's second film about Bob Dylan, *Rolling Thunder Revue: A Bob Dylan Story* (2019). As its title suggested, the documentary took a playful, ludic approach to the mercurial Dylan, interleaving archival footage of the musician's concert tour of 1974, which drew a bus-load of musicians, poets, reporters, photographers, money men and celebrity hangers-on—Joan Baez, Joni Mitchell, Sam Shepard, and Allen Ginsberg—together with a series of fictional, 'mockumentary'-style talking heads, including Martin von Haselberg as a director who is supposedly filming the footage, and Sharon Stone telling the equally fictitious story of how she attended a Dylan concert as a seventeen-year-old and was invited to join the caravan. A documentary that is also a prank, a come-on, the film opens with a clip from an 1896 film by Méliès and announces its intentions with a typically cryptic remark from Dylan: "If someone's wearing a mask he's gonna tell you the truth. If he's not wearing a mask it's highly unlikely."

The tour was a flop, financially—Dylan jokes that the tour happened so long ago that he "wasn't even born"—but the tour rejuvenated him musically, eight years after a 1966 motorcycle accident. Here is the singer on stage, his hat festooned with flowers, his face covered in white paint, along with his band, in tribute to KISS. Here is Patti Smith, at a pre-tour party in New York, making up a wild story about a meteorite crashing to earth, while Dylan nods enthusiastically; here is Joni Mitchell, jamming on her song "Coyote" in Gordon Lightfoot's Toronto apartment; here is Allen Ginsberg talking about his respect and rivalry with the singer-songwriter; and here is Dylan, ducking and deflecting the cameras at every turn: uneasy about his fame, delighted by the spectacle of his own self-immolation, which catches Scorsese's eye and admiration. The result is disjointed and over-long but also mesmerizing and carnivalesque, its jangling chaos like that of a Dylan song come to life, holding a cracked mirror up to Vietnam-era America.

Opposite: Portrait by Michael Grecco, 2006.

Overleaf: With daughter Francesca at a Giorgio Armani event, 2007.

Fast Forward

These days, on the cusp of his 80th birthday, there is only one consideration when choosing projects: the amount of time he has left. "That's really what it is now, the only consideration, really," he told me in 2011. "It's always the material. Are you attracted to the material at all? Can you find a way to say something that's in your heart or your mind? Sometimes it just doesn't play. In the case of a couple of pictures, like *The Departed*, that wasn't necessarily a picture I was planning to make, but for personal reasons I made it. That's not an excuse. Even if you have to make something, it still has to be you. You can't do that to the audience. You can't just throw something out there that you haven't tried to do the best you can on. That you haven't found something of yourself in . . . The one I'm flying out to now is a big movie. What I mean by that is that it has the elements that keep me focused, and that I want to express, it has wonderful actors, people I'm kind of—we hang together, so to speak. I feel comfortable. How am I going to do it? I have no idea what the visuals are. Maybe tomorrow I'll see something, but I know it's sky. It's country. It's small towns. So it's got to be something else, and I think I know what it is, but can I do it?"

Based on David Grann's historical book, *Killers of the Flower Moon* centers around the Osage Nation murders, during which dozens of Indians in possession of great fortunes, thanks to the discovery of oil on their land, were dispatched by poison, gunshot, and dynamite. Serving under a young J. Edgar Hoover in the infancy of the FBI, former Texas Ranger Tom White must determine who committed these crimes, as the conspiracy spreads to include lawyers, bankers, doctors, and even lawman William K. Hale, a respected former cattleman known as the 'King of the Osage Hills' who seems to run Eastern Oklahoma as his own personal fiefdom. Starring Leonardo di Caprio and De Niro, together onscreen for the first time since 1996's *This Boy's Life*, alongside many Native American actors and crew members, the $200 million Western crime drama was supposed to begin shooting in March of 2020, but then the coronavirus pandemic intervened, putting it off until February 2021, as was revealed by principal chief Geoffrey Standing Bear in an August 5 address—the first time the shooting schedule of a Martin Scorsese movie has been reported, not by *Variety*, but the 7th Osage Nation Congress.

"For me, I like to try stories that are opportunities to—what's the word? Not learn, but to spend time with themes and searches that deal with the more spiritual aspect of whatever time we have left," says Scorsese. "What we did or who we are or if we are anything. So, that's really important. I'm trying to read so much, but it's impossible. There's certain books that really connect with me, I've optioned a couple, I'm getting scripts written.

"I learned the hard way, but there is no doubt that the family unit is the key thing …"

They're small scale, you know, but it'd be interesting to try. And music. Not documentaries, films, music films. Music is the thing, it is the element that is so universal to everyone, you know. We're talking to Robbie Robertson, we're talking about doing something with Robbie and Van Morrison. I want to do a picture with him. Then, you know, he's elusive. You have to pursue him. David Johansen, too. We're planning one on David Johansen. I hope to shoot it in the first week of January, but just the New York cabaret scene that goes back to the late sixties. He has so much history in him. I learned so much from listening to his work, but also his selection of music. He does a radio show here on XM. I've learned a great deal."

In a letter written to his fourteen-year-old daughter Francesca, and published in the Italian news magazine *L'Espresso* in January 2014, Scorsese addressed the subject of protecting "the spark of connection" that leads him to make films and which, he believes, will continue to drive people to do so after he is gone:

Dearest Francesca,

I'm writing this letter to you about the future. I'm looking at it through the lens of my world. Through the lens of cinema, which has been at the center of that world.

For the last few years, I've realized that the idea of cinema that I grew up with, that's there in the movies I've been showing you since you were a child, and that was thriving when I started making pictures, is coming to a close. I'm not referring to the films that have already been made. I'm referring to the ones that are to come.

I don't mean to be despairing. I'm not writing these words in a spirit of defeat. On the contrary, I think the future is bright.

We always knew that the movies were a business, and that the art of cinema was made possible because it aligned with business conditions. None of us who started in the sixties and seventies had any illusions on that front. We knew we would have to work hard to protect what we loved. We also knew we might have to go through some rough periods. And I suppose we realized, on some level, we might face a time when every inconvenient or unpredictable element in the moviemaking process would be minimized, maybe even eliminated. The most unpredictable element of all? Cinema. And the people who make it.

I don't want to repeat what has been said and written by so many others before me, about all the changes in the business, and I'm heartened by the exceptions to the overall trend in moviemaking— Wes Anderson, Richard Linklater, David Fincher, Alexander Payne, the Coen brothers, James Gray, and Paul Thomas Anderson are all managing to get pictures made, and Paul not only got *The Master* made in 70 mm, he even got it *shown* that way in a few cities. Anyone who cares about cinema should be thankful.

And I'm also moved by the artists who are continuing to get their pictures made all over the world, in France, in South Korea, in England, in Japan, in Africa. It's getting harder all the time, but they're getting the films done.

But I don't think I'm being pessimistic when I say that the art of cinema and the movie business are now at a crossroads. Audiovisual entertainment and what we know as cinema—moving pictures conceived by individuals—appear to be headed in different directions. In the future, you'll probably see less and less of what we recognize as cinema on multiplex screens and more and more of it in smaller theaters, online, and, I suppose, in spaces and circumstances that I can't predict.

So why is the future so bright? Because for the very first time in the history of the art form, movies really can be made for very little money. This was unheard of when I was growing up, and extremely low budget movies have always been the exception rather than the rule. Now, it's the reverse. You can get beautiful images with affordable cameras. You can record sound. You can edit and mix and color-correct at home. This has all come to pass.

But with all the attention paid to the machinery of making movies and to the advances in technology that have led to this revolution in moviemaking, there is one important thing to remember: The tools don't make the movie, *you* make the movie. It's freeing to pick up a camera and start shooting and then put it together with Final Cut Pro. Making a movie—the one you *need* to make—is something else. There are no shortcuts.

If John Cassavetes, my friend and mentor, were alive today, he would certainly be using all the equipment that's available. But he would be saying the same things he always said—you have to be absolutely dedicated to the work, you have to give everything of yourself, and you have to protect the spark of connection that drove you to make the picture in the first place. You have to protect it with your life. In the past, because making movies was so expensive, we had to protect against exhaustion and compromise. In the future, you'll have to steel yourself against something else: the temptation to go with the flow, and allow the movie to drift and float away.

This isn't just a matter of cinema. There are no shortcuts to anything. I'm not saying that everything has to be difficult. I'm saying that the voice that sparks you is *your* voice—that's the inner light, as the Quakers put it.

That's you. That's the truth.

All my love,
Dad

Filmography

AS DIRECTOR

Opening dates are for the United States (general release) unless stated.

Amateur/Short films

Vesuvius VI
1959

What's a Nice Girl Like You Doing in a Place Like This?
(New York University Department of Television, Motion Picture and Radio Presentations/Summer Motion Picture Workshop)
9 minutes
Screenplay: Martin Scorsese
Cinematography: James Newman
Cast: Sarah Braveman (Psychoanalyst), Zeph Michaelis (Harry), Fred Sica (Friend), Mimi Stark (Harry's Wife), Robert Uricola (Singer)
1963

It's Not Just You, Murray!
(New York University Department of Television, Motion Pictures and Radio Presentations)
15 minutes
Screenplay: Martin Scorsese, Mardik Martin
Cinematography: Richard H. Coll
Cast: Ira Rubin (Murray), San De Fazio (Joe), Dominick Grieco (Lefty), Andrea Martin (Wife), Catherine Scorsese (Mother), Robert Uricola (Singer)
1964

The Big Shave
(New York University Film School/Belgian Cinematheque)
6 minutes
Screenplay: Martin Scorsese
Cinematography: Ares Demertzis
Cast: Peter Bernuth (Young Man)
First shown 1968 (Festival of Experimental Cinema, Belgium)

Feature films

Who's That Knocking at My Door
(Trimod Films)
90 minutes
Screenplay: Martin Scorsese
Cinematography: Richard H. Coll, Michael Wadleigh
Cast: Harvey Keitel (J.R.), Harry Northup (Harry), Zina Bethune (Girl), Anne Collette (Girl in Dream), Lennard Kuras (Joey), Catherine Scorsese (J.R.'s mother)
First shown November 15, 1967 (Chicago International Film Festival) under the title *I Call First*

Boxcar Bertha
(American International Pictures)
88 minutes
Screenplay: Joyce H. Corrington, John William Corrington
Cinematography: John Stephens
Cast: Barbara Hershey ("Boxcar" Bertha Thompson), David Carradine ("Big" Bill Shelly), Barry Primus (Rake Brown), Bernie Casey (Von Morton), John Carradine (H. Buckram Sartoris)
Opened June 14, 1972

Mean Streets
(Warner Bros./Taplin-Perry-Scorsese Productions)
112 minutes
Screenplay: Martin Scorsese, Mardik Martin
Cinematography: Kent Wakeford
Cast: Robert De Niro (Johnny Boy), Harvey Keitel (Charlie), David Proval (Tony), Amy Robinson (Teresa), Richard Romanus (Michael), Cesare Danova (Giovanni)
Opened October 14, 1973

Alice Doesn't Live Here Anymore
(Warner Bros.)
112 minutes
Screenplay: Robert Getchell
Cinematography: Kent Wakeford
Cast: Ellen Burstyn (Alice Hyatt), Alfred Lutter (Tommy), Harvey Keitel (Ben), Diane Ladd (Flo), Vic Tayback (Mel), Kris Kristofferson (David)
Opened December 9, 1974

Taxi Driver
(Columbia Pictures/Bill Phillips/Italo Judeo Productions)
113 minutes
Screenplay: Paul Schrader
Cinematography: Michael Chapman
Cast: Robert De Niro (Travis Bickle), Jodie Foster (Iris), Cybill Shepherd (Betsy), Harvey Keitel (Matthew "Sport" Higgins), Peter Boyle (Wizard), Albert Brooks (Tom)
Opened February 8, 1976

New York, New York
(Chartoff-Winkler Productions)
155 minutes (original release); 136 minutes (edited re-release); 163 minutes (DVD edition)
Screenplay: Earl Mac Rauch, Mardik Martin
Cinematography: László Kovács
Cast: Liza Minnelli (Francine Evans), Robert De Niro (Jimmy Doyle), Lionel Stander (Tony Harwell), Barry Primus (Paul Wilson), Mary Kay Place (Bernice Bennett), Georgie Auld (Frankie Harte), George Memmoli (Nicky)
Opened June 21, 1977

Raging Bull
(United Artists/Chartoff-Winkler Productions)
129 minutes
Screenplay: Paul Schrader, Mardik Martin
Cinematography: Michael Chapman
Cast: Robert De Niro (Jake LaMotta), Cathy Moriarty (Vickie LaMotta), Joe Pesci (Joey), Frank Vincent (Salvy), Nicholas Colasanto (Tommy Como)
Opened December 19, 1980

The King of Comedy
(Embassy International Pictures/Twentieth Century Fox)
109 minutes
Screenplay: Paul D. Zimmerman
Cinematography: Fred Schuler
Cast: Robert De Niro (Rupert Pupkin), Jerry Lewis (Jerry Langford), Diahnne Abbott (Rita Keane), Sandra Bernhard (Masha), Tony Randall (Himself)
Opened December 18, 1982 (Iceland), February 18, 1983 (USA)

After Hours
(The Geffen Company/Double Play)
97 minutes
Screenplay: Joseph Minion
Cinematography: Michael Ballhaus
Cast: Griffin Dunne (Paul Hackett), Rosanna Arquette (Marcy Franklin), Verna Bloom (June), Thomas Chong (Pepe), Linda Fiorentino (Kiki Bridges), Teri Garr (Julie), John Heard (Thomas "Tom" Schorr), Cheech Marin (Neil), Catherine O'Hara (Gail)
Opened October 11, 1985

The Color of Money
(Touchstone Pictures/Silver Screen Partners II)
119 minutes
Screenplay: Richard Price
Cinematography: Michael Ballhaus
Cast: Paul Newman ("Fast" Eddie Felson), Tom Cruise (Vincent Lauria), Mary Elizabeth Mastrantonio (Carmen),

Helen Shaver (Janelle), John Turturro (Julian)
Opened October 17, 1986

The Last Temptation of Christ
(Universal Pictures/Cineplex Odeon Films)
164 minutes
Screenplay: Paul Schrader
Cinematography: Michael Ballhaus
Cast: Willem Dafoe (Jesus), Harvey Keitel (Judas), Barbara Hershey (Mary Magdalene), Harry Dean Stanton (Saul/Paul), David Bowie (Pontius Pilate)
Opened August 12, 1988

New York Stories
(anthology film with segments directed by Woody Allen, Francis Ford Coppola, and Scorsese)
(Touchstone Pictures)
124 minutes
Scorsese segment: "Life Lessons"
Screenplay: Richard Price
Cinematography: Néstor Almendros
Cast: Nick Nolte (Lionel Dobie), Rosanna Arquette (Paulette), Patrick O'Neal (Phillip Fowler), Phil Harper (Businessman), Paul Herman (Detective Flynn)
Opened March 10, 1989

Goodfellas
(Warner Bros.)
146 minutes
Screenplay: Nicholas Pileggi, Martin Scorsese
Cinematography: Michael Ballhaus
Cast: Robert De Niro (James "Jimmy" Conway), Ray Liotta (Henry Hill), Joe Pesci (Tommy DeVito), Lorraine Bracco (Karen Hill), Paul Sorvino (Paul Cicero), Frank Sivero (Frankie Carbone), Tony Darrow (Sonny Bunz), Mike Starr (Frenchy), Frank Vincent (Billy Batts)
Opened September 19, 1990

Cape Fear
(Amblin Entertainment/Cappa Films/Tribeca Productions)
128 minutes
Screenplay: Wesley Strick
Cinematography: Freddie Francis
Cast: Robert De Niro (Max Cady), Nick Nolte (Sam Bowden), Jessica Lange (Leigh Bowden), Juliette Lewis (Danielle Bowden), Joe Don Baker (Claude Kersek), Robert Mitchum (Lieutenant Elgart), Gregory Peck (Lee Heller), Martin Balsam (Judge)
Opened November 13, 1991

The Age of Innocence
(Columbia Pictures/Cappa Productions)
139 minutes
Screenplay: Jay Cocks, Martin Scorsese
Cinematography: Michael Ballhaus
Cast: Daniel Day-Lewis (Newland Archer), Michelle Pfeiffer (Ellen Olenska), Winona Ryder (May Welland)
Opened October 1, 1993

Casino
(Universal Pictures/Syalis DA/Légende Entreprises/De Fina-Cappa)
178 minutes
Screenplay: Nicholas Pileggi, Martin Scorsese
Cinematography: Robert Richardson
Cast: Robert De Niro (Sam "Ace" Rothstein), Sharon Stone (Ginger McKenna), Joe Pesci (Nicky Santoro), James Woods (Lester Diamond), Don Rickles (Billy Sherbert), Kevin Pollak (Phillip Green)
Opened November 22, 1995

Accepting the Best Director Oscar for *The Departed*, February 25, 2007.

Kundun
(De Fina-Cappa/Dune Films/Refuge Productions/Touchstone Pictures)
134 minutes
Screenplay: Melissa Mathison
Cinematography: Roger Deakins
Cast: Tenzin Thuthob Tsarong (Dalai Lama, adult), Gyurme Tethong (Dalai Lama, aged 12), Tulku Jamyang Kunga Tenzin (Dalai Lama, aged 5), Tenzin Yeshi Paichang (Dalai Lama, aged 2), Tencho Gyalpo (Mother)
Opened December 25, 1997

Bringing Out the Dead
(De Fina-Cappa/Paramount Pictures/Touchstone Pictures)
121 minutes
Screenplay: Paul Schrader
Cinematography: Robert Richardson
Cast: Nicolas Cage (Frank Pierce), Patricia Arquette (Mary Burke), John Goodman (Larry), Ving Rhames (Marcus), Tom Sizemore (Tom Wolls)
Opened October 22, 1999

Gangs of New York
(Miramax Films/IEG/Alberto Grimaldi Productions)
167 minutes
Screenplay: Jay Cocks, Steven Zaillian, Kenneth Lonergan
Cinematography: Michael Ballhaus
Cast: Leonardo DiCaprio (Amsterdam Vallon), Daniel Day-Lewis (Bill "The Butcher" Cutting), Cameron Diaz (Jenny Everdeane), Jim Broadbent (William "Boss" Tweed), John C. Reilly (Happy Jack Mulraney), Henry Thomas (Johnny Sirocco), Liam Neeson ("Priest" Vallon)
Opened December 20, 2002

The Aviator
(Forward Pass/Appian Way/IMF Internationale Medien und Film GmbH & Co. 3. Produktions KG/IEG/Warner Bros./Miramax Films/Cappa Productions)
170 minutes
Screenplay: John Logan
Cinematography: Robert Richardson
Cast: Leonardo DiCaprio (Howard Hughes), Cate Blanchett (Katharine Hepburn), Kate Beckinsale (Ava Gardner), John C. Reilly (Noah Dietrich), Alec Baldwin (Juan Trippe), Alan Alda (Senator Ralph Owen Brewster), Ian Holm (Professor Fitz), Danny Huston (Jack Frye), Gwen Stefani (Jean Harlow), Jude Law (Errol Flynn)
Opened December 25, 2004

The Departed
(Warner Bros./Plan B Entertainment/IEG/Vertigo Entertainment/Media Asia Films)
151 minutes
Screenplay: William Monahan
Cinematography: Michael Ballhaus
Cast: Leonardo DiCaprio (Billy Costigan), Matt Damon (Colin Sullivan), Jack Nicholson (Frank Costello), Mark Wahlberg (Staff Sergeant Dignam), Martin Sheen (Captain Queenan), Ray Winstone (Mr. French), Vera Farmiga (Madolyn), Anthony Anderson (Brown), Alec Baldwin (Captain Ellerby)
Opened October 6, 2006

Shutter Island
(Paramount Pictures/Phoenix Pictures/Sikelia Productions/Appian Way)
138 minutes
Screenplay: Laeta Kalogridis
Cinematography: Robert Richardson
Cast: Leonard DiCaprio (Teddy Daniels), Mark Ruffalo (Chuck Aule), Ben Kingsley (Dr. Cawley), Max von Sydow (Dr. Naehring), Michelle Williams (Dolores), Emily Mortimer (Rachel 1), Patricia Clarkson (Rachel 2), Jackie Earle Haley (George Noyce)
Opened February 19, 2010

Hugo
(Paramount Pictures/GK Films/Infinitum Nihil)
126 minutes
Screenplay: John Logan
Cinematography: Robert Richardson
Cast: Ben Kingsley (Georges Méliès), Sacha Baron Cohen (Station Inspector), Asa Butterfield (Hugo Cabret),
Chloë Grace Moretz (Isabelle), Ray Winstone (Uncle Claude), Emily Mortimer (Lisette), Christopher Lee (Monsieur Labisse), Helen McCrory (Mama Jeanne), Richard Griffiths (Monsieur Frick), Jude Law (Hugo's Father)
Opened November 23, 2011

The Wolf of Wall Street
(Red Granite Pictures/Sikelia Productions/Appian Way/EMJAG Productions)
179 minutes
Screenplay: Terence Winter
Cinematography: Rodrigo Prieto
Cast: Leonardo DiCaprio (Jordan Belfort), Jonah Hill (Donnie Azoff), Margot Robbie (Naomi Lapaglia), Matthew McConaughey (Mark Hanna), Jon Bernthal (Brad)
Opened December 25, 2013

Silence
(SharpSword Films, AI Film, Emmett/Furla/Oasis Films, CatchPlay, IM Global, Verdi Productions, YLK Sikelia, Fábrica de Cine)
161 minutes
Screenplay: Jay Cocks, Martin Scorsese
Cinematography: Rodrigo Prieto
Cast: Andrew Garfield (Sebastião Rodrigues), Adam Driver (Francisco Garupe), Tadanobu Asano (The Interpreter), Ciarán Hinds (Alessandro Valignano), Liam Neeson (Cristóvão Ferreira), Shinya Tsukamoto (Mokichi)
Opened December 23, 2016

The Irishman
(TriBeCa Productions, Sikelia Productions, Winkler Films)
209 minutes
Screenplay: Steven Zaillian
Cinematography: Rodrigo Prieto
Cast: Robert De Niro (Frank Sheeran), Al Pacino (Jimmy Hoffa), Joe Pesci (Russell Bufalino), Ray Romano (Bill Bufalino), Bobby Cannavale (Skinny Razor), Anna Paquin (Older Peggy Sheeran), Lucy Gallina (Young Peggy Sheeran), Stephen Graham (Anthony "Tony Pro" Provenzano), Harvey Keitel (Angelo Bruno)
Opened November 1, 2019

Documentaries

Street Scenes
(New York Cinetracts Collective)
75 minutes
Cinematography: Nancy Bennett, John Butman, Dick Catron, Frederick Elmes, Bill Etra, Tom Famighetti, Peter Flynn, Robert Foresta, David Freeberg, Tiger Graham, Fred Hadley, Tony Janetti, Arnold Klein, Don Lenzer, Ron Levitas, Didier Loiseau, David Ludwig, Harry Peck Bolles, Bob Pitts, Laura Primakoff, Peter Rea, Danny Schneider, Gordon Stein, Oliver Stone, Ed Summer, Bruce Tabor, Nat Tripp, Stan Weiser, Bob Zahn
First shown September 14, 1970 (New York Film Festival)

Italianamerican
(National Communications Foundation)
49 minutes
Screenplay: Lawrence Cohen, Mardik Martin
Cinematography: Alec Hirschfeld
First shown October 1974 (New York Film Festival)

The Last Waltz
(FM Productions/Last Waltz Inc.)
117 minutes
Screenplay: Mardik Martin (treatment)
Cinematography: Michael Chapman
Opened April 26, 1978

American Boy: A Profile of Steven Prince
(New Empire Films/Scorsese Films)
55 minutes
Screenplay: Julia Cameron, Mardik Martin
Cinematography: Michael Chapman
First shown October 1978 (New York Film Festival)

A Personal Journey with Martin Scorsese Through American Movies
(British Film Institute/Miramax Films)
225 minutes
Screenplay: Martin Scorsese, Henry Wilson
Cinematography: Jean-Yves Escoffier, Frances Reid, Nancy Schreiber
First broadcast May 21, 1995 (UK)

My Voyage to Italy
"Il mio viaggio in Italia" (original title)
(Paso Doble Film/MediaTrade/Cappa Productions)
246 minutes
Screenplay: Suso Cecchi d'Amico, Raffaele Donato, Kent Jones, Martin Scorsese
Cinematography: Phil Abraham, William Rexer
First shown September 11, 1999 (Venice Film Festival)

The Neighborhood
(Short documentary segment for *The Concert for New York City*)
(Miramax/Double A Films)
7 minutes
Screenplay: Martin Scorsese, Kent Jones
Cinematography: Antonio Ferrara
First shown October 20, 2001

Feel like Going Home
(Opening episode of *The Blues* television documentary series)
(BBC/Cappa Productions)
110 minutes
Screenplay: Peter Guralnick
Cinematography: Arthur Jafa
First broadcast September 28, 2003

Lady by the Sea: The Statue of Liberty
(History Channel)
55 minutes
Screenplay: Kent Jones, Martin Scorsese
Cinematography: Robert Shepard
First broadcast January 14, 2004

No Direction Home: Bob Dylan
(Episode of the *American Masters* television documentary series)
(Spitfire Pictures/Grey Water Park Productions/Thirteen WNET/Cappa DeFina Productions/PBS/Vulcan Productions/BBC/NHK/Box TV)
208 minutes
Cinematography: Mustapha Barat
First broadcast September 26, 2005 (UK)

Shine a Light
(Paramount Classics/Grand Entertainment (Row)/Shine a Light/Concert Productions International/Shangri-La Entertainment)
122 minutes
Cinematography: Robert Richardson
First shown February 7, 2008 (Berlin International Film Festival)

A Letter to Elia
(Episode of the *American Masters* television documentary series)
(Far Hills Pictures/Sikelia Productions)
60 minutes
Directors: Kent Jones, Martin Scorsese
Screenplay: Kent Jones, Martin Scorsese
Cinematography: Mark Raker
First broadcast October 4, 2010

Public Speaking
(HBO/American Express/Sikelia Productions/Consolidated Documentaries)
84 minutes
Cinematography: Ellen Kuras
First shown November 22, 2010

George Harrison: Living in the Material World
(Grove Street Pictures/Spitfire Pictures/Sikelia Productions/Grove Street Productions)
208 minutes
Cinematography: Martin Kenzie, Robert Richardson
Opened September 2, 2011 (Telluride Film Festival, Colorado)

The New York Review of Books: A 50 Year Argument
(Sikelia Productions/WOWOW/HBO/BBC)
95 minutes
Directors: Martin Scorsese, David Tedeschi
Cinematography: Ellen Kuras, Lisa Rinzler
First shown (as a work in progress) February 14, 2014 (Berlin International Film Festival)

Rolling Thunder Revue: A Bob Dylan Story
(Grey Water Park Productions, Sikelia Productions)
142 minutes
Cinematography: Paul Goldsmith and Ellen Kuras
First shown June 12, 2019

Television episodes

Amazing Stories
Episode "Mirror, Mirror"
(Amblin Entertainment/Universal TV)
24 minutes
Screenplay: Steven Spielberg, Joseph Minion
Cinematography: Robert Stevens
Cast: Sam Waterston (Jordan Manmouth), Helen Shaver
(Karen), Tim Robbins (Jordan's Phantom)
First broadcast March 9, 1986

Boardwalk Empire
Pilot episode "Boardwalk Empire"
(HBO/Leverage Management/Closest to the Hole Productions/
Sikelia Productions/Cold Front Productions)
72 minutes
Screenplay: Terence Winter
Cinematography: Stuart Dryburgh
Cast: Steve Buscemi (Enoch "Nucky" Thompson),
Michael Pitt (James "Jimmy" Darmody), Kelly Macdonald
(Margaret Schroeder), Michael Shannon (Nelson Van Alden),
Shea Whigham (Elias "Eli" Thompson)
First broadcast September 19, 2010

Vinyl
Pilot episode
(Paramount Television, Jagged Productions, Sikelia Productions,
Cold Front Productions)
113 minutes
Story by: Rich Cohen, Mick Jagger, Martin Scorsese and Terence
Winter
Teleplay by: Terence Winter and George Mastras
Cinematography: Rodrigo Prieto, Reed Morano and David
Franco
Cast: Bobby Cannavale (Richie Finestra), Paul Ben-Victor
(Maury Gold), P. J. Byrne (Scott Leavitt), Max Casella (Julian
"Julie" Silver), Ato Essandoh (Lester Grimes), James Jagger (Kip
Stevens), J. C. MacKenzie (Skip Fontaine), Jack Quaid (Clark
Morelle), Ray Romano (Zak Yankovich), Birgitte Hjort Sørensen
(Ingrid), Juno Temple (Jamie Vine), Olivia Wilde (Devon
Finestra)
First broadcast February 14, 2016

Commercials, music videos, and promotional shorts

Armani commercial (I)
(Emporio Armani)
30 seconds
Screenplay: Martin Scorsese
Cinematography: Néstor Almendros
Cast: Christophe Bouquin, Cristina Marsilach
First broadcast 1986

Bad
(Extended music video for Michael Jackson's single)
(Optimum Productions)
17 minutes
Screenplay: Richard Price
Cinematography: Michael Chapman
Cast: Michael Jackson (Daryl), Adam Nathan (Tip),
Pedro Sanchez (Nelson), Wesley Snipes (Mini Max),
Roberta Flack (Daryl's Mother)
First shown August 31, 1987

Somewhere Down the Crazy River
(Promotional video for Robbie Robertson's single)
(Limelight)
5 minutes
Screenplay: Martin Scorsese
Cinematography: Mark Plummer
Cast: Robbie Robertson, Sammy BoDean, Maria McKee
First shown October 27, 1987

Armani commercial (II)
(Emporio Armani)
20 seconds
Screenplay: Martin Scorsese
Cinematography: Michael Ballhaus
Cast: Jens Peter, Elisabetta Ramella
First broadcast 1988

Made in Milan
(promotional documentary short interviewing Giorgio Armani
as he prepares for a show)
(Emporio Armani)
2 minutes
Screenplay: Jay Cocks
Cinematography: Néstor Almendros
Cast: Giorgio Armani, Ugo Armani, Maria Raimondi
First broadcast 1990

American Express commercial
(Tool of North America)
90 seconds
Cinematography: Robert Richardson
Cast: Robert De Niro, Martin Scorsese
First broadcast 2005

The Key to Reserva
(promotional short advertising Freixenet Cava)
(JWT/Ovideo TV)
10 minutes
Screenplay: Ted Griffin
Cinematography: Harris Savides
Cast: Simon Baker (Roger Thornberry), Kelli O'Hara (Grace
Thornberry), Michael Stuhlbarg (Louis Bernard), Christopher
Denham (Leonard), Richard Easton (Mr. Carroll)
First shown December 14, 2007 (Spain)

Bleu de Chanel commercial
1 minute
Cinematography: Stuart Dryburgh
Cast: Gaspard Ulliel, Ingrid Schram, Amalie Bruun
First broadcast August 2010

The Audition
(promotional short advertising Studio City Macau Resort
and Casino)
16 minutes
Screenplay: Terence Winter
Cinematography: Rodrigo Prieto
Cast: Robert De Niro (himself), Leonardo DiCaprio (himself),
Brad Pitt (himself/Aaron Cross), Martin Scorsese (himself),
Rodrigo Prieto (himself)
First shown October 3, 2015 (Busan)

AS PRODUCER

For films that Scorsese directed and produced, only producer
details are listed here.

Short films

The Big Shave
Produced by Martin Scorsese

Item 72-D: The Adventures of Spa and Fon
(Summerfilm Limited)
Director: Edward Summer
Screenplay: John Byrum, Harry Narunsky, Edward Summer
Cinematography: John Byrum, Michael Sullivan
Executive producer: Haig Manoogian
Consulting producer: Martin Scorsese
Producer: Edward Summer
Co-producer: Genise Michaile
Cast: Hervé Villechaize, Michael Sullivan, Mark Alexander,
Larry Bercowitz, William H. Boesen
First shown November 1970 (Chicago International Film Festival)

Feature films

The Grifters
(Cineplex-Odeon Films)
110 minutes
Director: Stephen Frears
Screenplay: Donald E. Westlake

Cinematography: Oliver Stapleton
Executive producer: Barbara De Fina
Producers: Robert A. Harris, Jim Painter, Martin Scorsese
Co-producer: Peggy Rajski
Cast: Anjelica Huston, John Cusack, Annette Bening,
Pat Hingle, Henry Jones, Gailard Sartain, J. T. Walsh
Opened January 4, 1991

Naked in New York
(Some Film)
95 minutes
Director: Daniel Algrant
Screenplay: Daniel Algrant, John Warren
Cinematography: Joey Forsyte
Executive producer: Martin Scorsese
Producer: Frederick Zollo
Line producer: Carol Cuddy
Cast: Eric Stoltz, Mary-Louise Parker, Ralph Macchio,
Jill Clayburgh, Tony Curtis, Timothy Dalton
First shown September 1993 (Deauville American Film
Festival, France), Opened April 13, 1994 (USA)

Mad Dog and Glory
(Universal Pictures/Mad Dog Productions)
97 minutes
Director: John McNaughton
Screenplay: Richard Price
Cinematography: Robby Müller
Executive producer: Richard Price
Producers: Barbara De Fina, Martin Scorsese
Co-producer: Steven A. Jones
Cast: Robert De Niro, Uma Thurman, Bill Murray,
David Caruso, Kathy Baker
Opened March 5, 1993

Con gli occhi chiusi
(Canal + España/Creativos Asociados de Radio y Televisión
[CARTEL]/MG Italian International Film/MG Sri/Paradis
Films/Radiotelevisione Italiana)
113 minutes
Director: Francesca Archibugi
Screenplay: Francesca Archibugi
Cinematography: Giuseppe Lanci
Executive producers: Donatella Ibba, Martin Scorsese
Producers: Guido De Laurentiis, Fulvio Lucisano,
Leo Pescarolo
Associate producer: Raffaele Donato
Cast: Stefania Sandrelli, Marco Messeri, Debora Caprioglio,
Alessia Fugardi, Fabio Modesti
Opened December 22, 1994 (Italy)

Search and Destroy
(Autumn Pictures/Nu Image Films/October Films)
90 minutes
Director: David Salle
Screenplay: Michael Almereyda
Cinematography: Bobby Bukowski, Michael Spiller
Executive producers: Danny Dimbort, Avi Lerner,
Martin Scorsese
Producers: Ruth Charny, Elie Cohn, Dan Lupovitz
Associate producers: Mark Blum, Boaz Davidson, Trevor Short
Cast: Dennis Hopper, Jason Ferraro, Robert Knepper, Griffin
Dunne, Martin Scorsese, Rosanna Arquette, David Thornton,
John Turturro, Ethan Hawke
Opened May 5, 1995

Clockers
(Universal Pictures/40 Acres & A Mule Filmworks)
128 minutes
Director: Spike Lee
Screenplay: Richard Price, Spike Lee
Cinematography: Malik Hassan Sayeed
Executive producers: Monty Ross, Rosalie Swedlin
Producers: Jon Kilik, Spike Lee, Martin Scorsese
Co-producer: Richard Price
Cast: Harvey Keitel, John Turturro, Delroy Lindo, Mekhi Phifer,
Isaiah Washington, Keith David
Opened September 13, 1995

Grace of My Heart
(Cappa Productions/Gramercy Pictures/Universal Pictures)
116 minutes

Director: Allison Anders
Screenplay: Allison Anders
Cinematography: Jean-Yves Escoffier
Executive producer: Martin Scorsese
Producers: Ruth Charny, Daniel Hassid
Co-producer: Elliot Lewis Rosenblatt
Line producers: Burtt Harris, Elliot Lewis Rosenblatt
Cast: Illeana Douglas, Matt Dillon, Eric Stoltz, John Turturro, Patsy Kensit, Bruce Davison
Opened September 13, 1996

Kicked in the Head
(De Fina-Cappa)
87 minutes
Director: Matthew Harrison
Screenplay: Kevin Corrigan, Matthew Harrison
Cinematography: Howard Krupa, John Thomas
Executive producer: Martin Scorsese
Producer: Barbara De Fina
Line producer: Ann Ruark
Cast: Kevin Corrigan, Linda Fiorentino, Michael Rapaport, Lili Taylor, James Woods, Burt Young, Olek Krupa
Opened September 26, 1997

The Hi-Lo Country
(De Fina-Cappa/Polygram Filmed Entertainment/
Working Title Films)
114 minutes
Director: Stephen Frears
Screenplay: Walon Green
Cinematography: Oliver Stapleton
Executive producer: Rudd Simmons
Producers: Tim Bevan, Barbara De Fina, Eric Fellner, Martin Scorsese
Co-producer: Liza Chasin
Cast: Billy Crudup, Woody Harrelson, Patricia Arquette, Cole Hauser, Sam Elliott
Opened January 22, 1999

Smiling Fish & Goat on Fire
(One Sock Productions/Parabellum Productions/
Red Horse Films/Smiling Fish and Goat on Fire LLC)
90 minutes
Director: Kevin Jordan
Screenplay: Derick Martini, Steven Martini
Cinematography: Frederick Iannone
Executive producers: Richard Abramowitz, Sheilah Goldman, Tommy Lynch, Michael Silberman, Ronna B. Wallace, Martin Scorsese
Producers: Kevin Jordan, Derick Martini, Steven Martini
Co-producers: Kristen Dolan, Phillip Pennestri, Mark Poggi, Ryan Rothmaier, Brittany Taylor
Cast: Derick Martini, Amy Hathaway, Steven Martini, Heather Moudy, Wesley Thompson
First shown September 16, 1999 (Toronto International Film Festival)

You Can Count on Me
(Hart-Sharp Entertainment/Cappa Productions/
Crush Entertainment/Shooting Gallery)
111 minutes
Director: Kenneth Lonergan
Screenplay: Kenneth Lonergan
Cinematography: Stephen Kazmierski
Executive producers: Steve Carlis, Donald C. Carter, Martin Scorsese, Morton Swinsky
Producers: Barbara De Fina, John Hart, Larry Meistrich, Jeffrey Sharp
Co-producers: Keith Abell, Julian Iragorri
Associate producers: Robert Kravis, Rachel Peters
Line producer: Jill Footlick
Cast: Laura Linney, Mark Ruffalo, Matthew Broderick, Jon Tenney, Rory Culkin, Kenneth Lonergan
First shown January 21, 2000 (Sundance Film Festival)

Rain
(Antena 3 Televisión/Cappa Films/Kinowelt Filmproduktion/
Lolafilms/Via Digital)
97 minutes
Director: Katherine Lindberg
Screenplay: Katherine Lindberg
Cinematography: Vanja Cernjul
Executive producers: Andrés Vicente Gómez, Rainer Kölmel,

Martin Scorsese
Producer: Jordi Ros
Associate producers: Gretchen Campbell, Grant Gilmore, Nadine Luque, Tim Pearce
Line producer: Víctor Albarrán
Cast: Melora Walters, Kris Park, Jamey Sheridan, Diane Ladd, Jo Anderson
First shown September 2001 (Venice Film Festival)

Deuces Wild
(CineWild/Cinerenta Medienbeteiligungs KG/Eternity
Pictures/Presto Productions/The Antonia Company/
Unity Productions)
96 minutes
Director: Scott Kalvert
Screenplay: Paul Kimatian, Christopher Gambale
Cinematography: John A. Alonzo
Executive producers: Eberhard Kayser, Mario Ohoven, Marc Sferrazza, Martin Scorsese
Producers: Willi Baer, Fred C. Caruso, Michael Cerenzie, Paul Kimatian
Co-producers: Melissa Barrett, Charlie Loventhal, Scott Valentine, David E. Ornston, Richard Salvatore
Associate producer: Shira Levin
Line producer: Robert Rothbard
Cast: Stephen Dorff, Brad Renfro, Fairuza Balk, Norman Reedus, Max Perlich
Opened May 3, 2002

Frankenstein
(Television feature film)
(Flame TV/Flame Ventures/L.I.F.T. Production/
USA Cable Network)
88 minutes
Director: Marcus Nispel
Screenplay: John Shiban
Cinematography: Daniel Pearl
Executive producers: Tony Krantz, Martin Scorsese, John Shiban
Co-executive producers: Nina R. Lederman, Kim Moses, Malcolm Petal, Ian Sander
Supervising producer: Vincent Oster
Producer: Marcus Nispel
Co-producers: John J. Anderson, Kimberly C. Anderson, Ra'uf Glasgow
Line producer: Jacky Lee Morgan
Cast: Parker Posey, Vincent Perez, Thomas Kretschmann, Adam Goldberg, Ivana Milicevic, Michael Madsen
First broadcast October 10, 2004

Brides
Nyfes (original title)
(Alco Films/Cappa DeFina Productions/Eurimages/K.G.
Productions/Alpha TV/CL Productions/Cinegram/FilmNet/
Greek Film Center/Lexicon Factory/Odeon/Eurimages
Council of Europe/Greek Ministry of Culture)
128 minutes
Director: Pantelis Voulgaris
Screenplay: Ioanna Karystiani
Cinematography: Giorgos Arvanitis
Executive producers: Martin Scorsese, Panos Papahadzis
Producers: Barbara De Fina, Terry Dougas, Pantelis Voulgaris
Associate producers: Valerie Gobos, Shira Levin, Despina Mouzaki, Haris Padouvas, Michèle Ray-Gavras
Line producer: Kostas Lambropoulos
Cast: Damian Lewis, Victoria Haralabidou, Andréa Ferréol, Evi Saoulidou, Dimitris Katalifos
Opened October 22, 2004 (Greece)

The Aviator
Executive producers: Chris Brigham, Colin Cotter, Leonardo DiCaprio, Aslan Nadery, Volker Schauz, Rick Schwartz, Bob Weinstein, Harvey Weinstein, Rick Yorn, Martin Scorsese
Producers: Sandy Climan, Matthias Deyle, Charles Evans Jr., Graham King, Michael Mann
Co-producer: Joseph Reidy
Line producers: Dan Maag, Philip Schulz-Deyle

Lymelife
(Bartlett Films/Cappa DeFina Productions/Cappa
Productions/El Dorado Pictures)
95 minutes
Director: Derick Martini
Screenplay: Derick Martini, Steven Martini

Cinematography: Frank Godwin
Executive producers: Leonard Loventhal, Martin Scorsese
Producers: Alec Baldwin, Jon Cornick, Barbara De Fina, Steven Martini, Angela Somerville, Michele Tayler
Co-producers: William Baldwin, Michael G. Jefferson, Tiffany Nishimoto, Jamin O'Brien
Associate producer: Arvind Singh
Cast: Rory Culkin, Alec Baldwin, Jill Hennessy, Emma Roberts, Timothy Hutton, Cynthia Nixon
First shown September 8, 2008 (Toronto International Film Festival)

The Young Victoria
(GK Films)
105 minutes
Director: Jean-Marc Vallée
Screenplay: Julian Fellowes
Cinematography: Hagen Bogdanski
Executive producer: Colin Vaines
Producers: Sarah Ferguson, Tim Headington, Graham King, Martin Scorsese
Co-producers: Denis O'Sullivan, Anita Overland
Line producers: Elisabeth-Ann Gimber, Marie-Hélène Panisset
Cast: Emily Blunt, Rupert Friend, Paul Bettany, Miranda Richardson, Jim Broadbent
Opened March 6, 2009 (UK)

Shutter Island
Executive producers: Chris Brigham, Laeta Kalogridis, Dennis Lehane, Gianni Nunnari, Louis Phillips
Producers: Brad Fischer, Mike Medavoy, Arnold Messer, Martin Scorsese
Co-producers: Amy Herman, Joseph Reidy, Emma Tillinger

Hugo
Executive producers: David Crockett, Barbara De Fina, Christi Dembrowski, Georgia Kacandes, Charles Newirth, Emma Tillinger Koskoff
Producers: Johnny Depp, Tim Headington, Graham King, Martin Scorsese
Line producer: John Bernard

The Family
(EuropaCorp/Relativity Media/TF1 Films Production/
Grive Productions/Malavita/Canal +/TF1)
111 minutes
Director: Luc Besson
Screenplay: Luc Besson, Michael Caleo
Cinematography: Thierry Arbogast
Executive producers: Jason Beckman, Jason Colodne, Martin Scorsese, Tucker Tooley
Co-executive producers: Ron Burkle, Jason Colbeck
Producers: Luc Besson, Ryan Kavanaugh, Virginie Silla
Cast: Robert De Niro, Michelle Pfeiffer, Dianna Agron, John D'Leo, Tommy Lee Jones
Opened September 13, 2013

The Wolf of Wall Street
Executive producers: Danny Dimbort, Georgia Kacandes, Alexandra Milchan, Irwin Winkler
Producers: Riza Aziz, Leonardo DiCaprio, Joey McFarland, Martin Scorsese, Emma Tillinger Koskoff

The Third Side of the River
(Rommel Film/Tresmilmundos Cine/Waterland Film)
90 minutes
Director: Celina Murga
Screenplay: Gabriel Medina, Celina Murga
Executive producer: Martin Scorsese
Producer: Juan Villegas
Co-producers: Alexander Djeranian, Jaime Mateus-Tique, Peter Rommel, Jan van der Zanden
Associate producers: Diego Dubcovsky, Julia Solomonoff
Cast: Alian Devetac, Daniel Veronese
Opened February 20, 2014 (Netherlands)

Revenge of the Green Dragons
(The 7th Floor/Artfire Films/IM Global Octane/Initial A
Entertainment)
95 minutes
Directors: Wai-keung Lau, Andrew Loo
Screenplay: Michael Di Jiacomo, Andrew Loo
Cinematography: Martin Ahlgren
Executive producers: Michael Bassick, Corey Large, Alan Pao,

Martin Scorsese, Art Spigel, Steven Squillante
Producers: Allen Bain, Stuart Ford, Ara Katz, Jesse Scolaro
Associate producer: Charles M. Barsamian
Cast: Justin Chon, Kevin Wu, Harry Shum Jr., Ray Liotta, Shuya Chang
Opened October 24, 2014

The Wannabe
(Electric Entertainment/Traction Media)
90 minutes
Director: Nick Sandow
Screenplay: Nick Sandow
Cinematography: Brett Pawlak
Executive producer: Martin Scorsese
Producers: Michael Gasparro, Lizzie Nastro
Co-producer: Richard J. Bosner
Associate producer: Vince Cupone
Cast: Patricia Arquette, Michael Imperioli, Vincent Piazza, Doug E. Doug, Adriana DeMeo
Opened December 4, 2015

Bleed for This
(Bruce Cohen Productions, Magna Entertainment, Sikelia Productions, The Solution Entertainment Group, Verdi Productions, Younger Than You)
117 minutes
Director: Ben Younger
Screenplay: Ben Younger
Cinematography: Larkin Seiple
Executive producers: David Gendron, Michael Hansen, Myles Nestel, Joshua Sason, Martin Scorsese, Michelle Verdi, Lisa Wilson
Producers: Bruce Cohen, Emma Tillinger Koskoff, Chad A. Verdi, Noah Kraft, Pamela Thur, Ben Younger
Associate producers: Ben Empey, David Gere, Marielle Olentine, Vinny Pazienza, Gino Pereira, Robert Tarini
Cast: Miles Teller, Aaron Eckhart, Katey Sagal, Ciarán Hinds, Ted Levine, Jordan Gelber
Opened November 18, 2016

Silence
Executive producers: Brandt Andersen, Michael Barnes, Lawrence Bender, Len Blavatnik, Paul Breuls, Dale A. Brown, Stuart Ford, Manu Gargi, Aviv Giladi, Wayne Marc Godfrey, Niels Juul, Dan Kao, Ken Kao, Nicholas Kazan, Matthew J. Malek, Gianni Nunnari, Chad A. Verdi, Michelle Verdi, Tyler Zacharia
Co-executive producers: George Furla, Ben Rodriguez, Randall Emmett, Anthony Jabre,
Producers: Vittorio Cecchi Gori, Barbara De Fina, David Lee, Gastón Pavlovich, Martin Scorsese, Emma Tillinger Koskoff, Irwin Winkler
Associate producers: Agustín Coppel, Ruben Coppel, Josh Cowell, Brent Ryan Green, Arnaud Lannic, Christophe Lannic, Cary Brown
Co-producers: Eriko Miyagawa, Diane L. Sabatini, David Webb, Marianne Bower

Free Fire
(Film4 Productions, BFI, Rook Films, Protagonist Pictures)
90 minutes
Director: Ben Wheatley
Screenplay: Amy Jump and Ben Wheatley
Cinematography: Laurie Rose
Executive producers: Reno Antoniades, Lizzie Francke, David Kosse, Sam Lavender, Dan MacRae, Danny Perkins, Ben Roberts, Martin Scorsese, Emma Tillinger Koskoff
Producer: Andrew Starke
Associate producer: Pete Tombs
Cast: Cillian Murphy, Armie Hammer, Brie Larson, Sharlto Copley, Jack Reynor, Babou Ceesay, Enzo Cilenti, Sam Riley, Michael Smiley, Noah Taylor, Patrick Bergin, Tom Davis, Mark Monero
Opened March 31, 2017

Abundant Acreage Available
(Abundant Productions)
80 minutes
Director: Angus MacLachlan
Screenplay: Angus MacLachlan
Cinematography: Andrew Reed
Executive producers: Jeanne Hagerty, Martin Scorsese
Producers: Kate Churchill, Angus MacLachlan

Cast: Amy Ryan, Terry Kinney, Max Gail, Francis Guinan
Opened April 20, 2017

A Ciambra
(Stayblack, RT Features, Rai Cinema, Sikelia Productions)
120 minutes
Director: Jonas Carpignano
Screenplay: Jonas Carpignano
Cinematography: Tim Curtinn
Executive producers: Joel Brandeis, Fernando Fraiha, Alessio Lazzareschi, Sophie Mas, Lourenço Sant' Anna, Martin Scorsese, Dario Suter, Daniela Taplin, Emma Tillinger Koskoff
Producers: Paolo Carpignano, Jon Coplon, Christoph Daniel, Constance Meyer, Gwyn Sannia, Rodrigo Teixeira, Ryan Zacarias
Co-producers: Julie Billy, Tomas Eskilsson, Carole Scotta, Sean Wheelan
Associate producer: Charles M. Barsamian
Cast: Pio Amato, Koudous Seihon, Damiano Amato
Opened August 31, 2017

The Current War
(Bazelevs Company, Film Rites, Thunder Road Pictures)
107 minutes
Director: Alfonso Gomez-Rejon
Screenplay: Michael Mitnick
Cinematography: Chung-hoon Chung
Executive producers: Adam Ackland, Garrett Basch, Benedict Cumberbatch, David Glasser, David Hutkin, Michael Mitnick, Ann Ruark, Martin Scorsese, Adam Sidman, Michele Wolkoff, Bob Yari, Steven Zaillian
Producers: Timur Bekmambetov, Basil Iwanyk
Line producer: Matthew Patnick
Co-producer: Jayne Sullivan
Cast: Benedict Cumberbatch, Michael Shannon, Nicholas Hoult, Katherine Waterston, Tom Holland, Simon Manyonda, Stanley Townsend, Tuppence Middleton, Matthew Macfadyen
Opened October 25, 2019

The Snowman
(Perfect World Pictures, Working Title Films, Another Park Film)
119 minutes
Director: Tomas Alfredson
Screenplay: Hossein Amini, Peter Straughan, Søren Sveistrup
Cinematography: Dion Beebe
Executive producers: Tomas Alfredson, Liza Chasin, Amelia Granger, Martin Scorsese, Emma Tillinger Koskoff
Producers: Tim Bevan, Eric Fellner, Piodor Gustafsson
Co-producers: Richard Hewitt, Alexander O'Neal
Cast: Michael Fassbender, Rebecca Ferguson, Charlotte Gainsbourg, Val Kilmer, J. K. Simmons, Toby Jones, David Dencik, Ronan Vibert, Chloë Sevigny, James D'Arcy
Opened October 13, 2017

Diane
(AgX, Sight Unseen Pictures)
95 minutes
Director: Kent Jones
Screenplay: Kent Jones
Cinematography: Wyatt Garfield
Executive producers: Julia Lebedev, Leonid Lebedev, Martin Scorsese, Eddie Vaisman
Producers: Luca Borghese, Ben Howe, Caroline Kaplan, Oren Moverman
Co-producers: Allison Rose Carter, Jon Read
Associate producer: Gabi Madsen
Cast: Mary Kay Place, Jake Lacy, Deirdre O'Connell, Glynnis O'Connor, Joyce Van Patten, Phyllis Somerville, Andrea Martin, Estelle Parsons
Opened March 29, 2019

Happy as Lazzaro
(Tempesta, Rai Cinema, Amka Films Productions, Ad Vitam Production, KNM, Pola Pandora Filmproduktions, RSI-Radiotelevisione Svizzera, Arte France Cinéma, Zweites Deutsches Fernsehen (ZDF), ARTE)
130 minutes
Director: Alice Rohrwacher
Screenplay: Alice Rohrwacher
Cinematography: Hélène Louvart
Executive producer: Martin Scorsese
Producers: Carlo Cresto-Dina, Gregory Gajos, Arthur

Hallereau, Alexandra Henochsberg, Pierre-François Piet, Tiziana Soudani, Michael Weber
Co-producers: Viola Fügen, Michel Merkt, Olivier Père
Associate producer: Francesca Andreoli, Valeria Jamonte, Alessio Lazzareschi, Manuela Melissano, Meinolf Zurhorst
Cast: Nicoletta Braschi, Adriano Tardiolo, Sergi López
Opened May 31, 2018

Tomorrow
(Futurescope Films, Roaring Mouse Productions, Rodaje a la Carta, Studio 82, Studio DWB)
92 minutes
Director: Martha Pinson
Screenplay: Stuart Brennan, Sebastian Street
Cinematography: Darran Bragg
Executive producer: Jack Binder, Roger Carlsson, Marcel Ducharme, Connor Earley, Jamie Edgerton, Alex Fergusson, David Fleming, Glenn Kinniburgh, Jason Owolabi, Quintin Pomeroy, Martin Scorsese, Mohamed Hasan Tatanaki, Emma Tillinger Koskoff, Tunku Ya'acob
Producer: Stuart Brennan, Christina de la Sala, Sebastian Street, Dean M. Woodford
Co-producer: Ismael Issa
Associate producers: Chris Sandford, Tom Fenwick Smith
Cast: Sebastian Street, Stuart Brennan, Stephen Fry, Sophie Kennedy Clark, James Cosmo, Paul Kaye, Stephanie Leonidas, Joss Stone
Opened September 27, 2019

The Souvenir
(BBC Films, BFI Film Fund, JWH Films, Sikelia Productions)
119 minutes
Director: Joanna Hogg
Screenplay: Joanna Hogg
Cinematography: David Raedeker
Executive producers: Dave Bishop, Lizzie Francke, Rose Garnett, Martin Scorsese, Andrew Starke, Emma Tillinger Koskoff, Michael Wood
Producers: Joanna Hogg, Luke Schiller
Associate producer: Crispin Buxton
Cast: Honor Swinton Byrne, Tom Burke, Tilda Swinton, Richard Ayoade
Opened May 17, 2019

Port Authority
(MUBI, RT Features, Madeline Films, Sikelia Productions)
94 minutes
Director: Danielle Lessovitz
Screenplay: Danielle Lessovitz
Cinematography: Jomo Fray
Executive producers: Bobby Allen, Efe Cakarel, Frédéric de Goldschmidt, Fernando Fraiha, Sophie Mas, Lourenço Sant' Anna, Martin Scorsese, Lawrence Snookie Taylor, Emma Tillinger Koskoff, Celina Torrealba
Producers: Zachary Luke Kislevitz, Virginie Lacombe, Rodrigo Teixeira
Associate producers: Kate Antognini, Damian Bao, Jari Jones, Arnaud Quesada
Cast: Fionn Whitehead, Leyna Bloom, McCaul Lombardi, Devon Carpenter, Eddie Bloom, Louisa Krause
Opened May 18, 2019

The Irishman
Executive producers: Richard Baratta, George Furla, Niels Juul, Nicholas Pileggi, Jai Stefan, Chad A. Verdi, Berry Welsh, Rick York, Tyler Zacharia
Producers: Marianne Bower, Gerald Chamales, Robert De Niro, Randall Emmett, Gabriele Israilovici, Gastón Pavlovich, Jane Rosenthal, Martin Scorsese, Emma Tillinger Koskoff, Irwin Winkler
Co-producer: David Webb

Uncut Gems
(A24, Elara Pictures, IAC Films, Sikelia Productions, Scott Rudin Productions)
135 minutes
Directors: Josh Safdie and Benny Safdie
Screenplay: Ronald Bronstein, Josh Safdie and Benny Safdie
Cinematography: Darius Khondji
Executive producers: Oscar Boyson, Anthony Katagas, David Koplan, Anthony Katagas, David Koplan, Martin Scorsese, Emma Tillinger Koskoff
Producers: Sebastian Bear-McClard, Eli Bush, Irfaan Fredericks,

Scott Rudin
Co-producers: Michael Bartol, Catherine Farrell
Cast: Adam Sandler, Lakeith Stanfield, Julia Fox, Kevin Garnett, Idina Menzel, Eric Bogosian, Judd Hirsch
Opened December 13, 2019

Shirley
(Killer Films, Los Angeles Media Fund)
107 minutes
Director: Josephine Decker
Screenplay: Sarah Gubbins
Cinematography: Sturla Brandth Grøvlen
Executive producers: Allison Rose Carter, Cherilyn Hawrysh, Martin Scorsese, Alisa Tager
Producers: Sarah Gubbins, David Hinojosa, Simon Horsman, Elisabeth Moss, Sue Naegle, Jeffrey Soros, Christine Vachon
Associate producers: Morgan Earnest, Evan Scott Nicholas
Cast: Elisabeth Moss, Michael Stuhlbarg, Odessa Young, Logan Lerman, Victoria Pedretti, Orlagh Cassidy, Robert Wuhl
Opened June 5, 2020

Pieces of a Woman
(Bron Studios, Little Lamb, Creative Wealth Media)
128 minutes
Director: Kornél Mundruczó
Screenplay: Kata Wéber
Cinematography: Benjamin Loeb
Executive producers: Jason Cloth, Aaron L. Gilbert, Sam Levinson, Stuart Manashil, Suraj Maraboyina, Richard McConnell, Rolf Pedersen, Viktória Petrányi, Martin Scorsese, Steven Thibault
Co-executive producers: Cheryl, Harrison Kreiss, Cheryl Leib, Adam Somer, Andria Spring, Katia Washington
Producers: Ashley Levinson, Aaron Ryder, Kevin Turen
Cast: Vanessa Kirby, Shia LaBeouf, Ellen Burstyn, Molly Parker, Sarah Snook, Iliza Shlesinger, Benny Safdie, Jimmie Fails, Domenic Di Rosa
Opened December 30, 2020

Documentaries

We Have Come for Your Daughters
Medicine Ball Caravan (original title)
(France Opera Film/PECF)
88 minutes
Director: François Reichenbach
Screenplay: Christian Haren (story concept)
Cinematography: Christian Odasso, Jean-Michel Surel, Serge Halsdorf
Producer: Tom Donahue
Associate producer: Martin Scorsese
Opened August 25, 1971

A Personal Journey with Martin Scorsese Through American Movies
Executive producer: Bob Last, Colin MacCabe
Producers: Florence Dauman, Martin Scorsese
Associate producer: Raffaele Donato
Line producer: Dale Ann Stieber

Eric Clapton: Nothing But the Blues:
An *In the Spotlight* **Special**
(PBS)
Executive producers: John Beug, David Horn, Martin Scorsese
Producers: Ken Ehrlich, Stephen Weintraub
First broadcast June 19, 1995

Lady by the Sea: The Statue of Liberty
Producer: Martin Scorsese
Co-producer: Rachel Reichman
Associate producer: Edwin Schlossberg

Lightning in a Bottle
(Vulcan Productions/Jigsaw Productions)
103 minutes
Director: Antoine Fuqua
Cinematography: Greg Andracke, Lisa Rinzler
Executive producers: Jody Patton, Paul G. Allen, Martin Scorsese
Producers: Margaret Bodde, Alex Gibney, Jack Gulick
Co-producers: Richard Hutton, Susan Motamed
First shown February 12, 2004 (Berlin International Film Festival)

Something to Believe in
(Snapdragon Films)
Director: Bonnie Palef
Screenplay: Bonnie Palef
Executive producer: Martin Scorsese
Producer: Bonnie Palef
First shown 2004

Val Lewton: The Man in the Shadows
(Turner Classic Movies/Turner Entertainment/Sikelia Productions)
77 minutes
Director: Kent Jones
Screenplay: Kent Jones
Cinematography: Bobby Shepard
Executive producers: Tom Brown, Emma Tillinger
Producers: Margaret Bodde, Martin Scorsese
Line producer: Mikaela Beardsley
First shown September 2, 2007 (Telluride Film Festival, Colorado)

Picasso and Braque Go to the Movies
(Cubists)
60 minutes
Director: Arne Glimcher
Cinematography: Petr Hlinomaz
Executive producer: Bonnie Hlinomaz
Producers: Arne Glimcher, Robert Greenhut, Martin Scorsese
Associate producer: Bernice Rose
First shown September 7, 2008 (Toronto International Film Festival)

No Direction Home: Bob Dylan
Executive producers: Jody Patton, Paul G. Allen, Barbara De Fina, Susan Lacy, Jeff Rosen, Nigel Sinclair, Anthony Wall
Co-executive producers: Guy East, Gub Neal, Justin Thomson-Glover
Producers: Martin Scorsese, Susan Lacy, Jeff Rosen, Nigel Sinclair, Anthony Wall
Co-producer: Margaret Bodde
Associate producer: Chelsea Hoffman
Line producers: Jessica Cohen, Tia Lessin

A Letter to Elia
Executive producers: Stone Douglass, Taylor Materne
Consulting producer: Diane Kolyer
Producers: Martin Scorsese, Emma Tillinger
Co-producer: Rachel Reichman

Public Speaking
Executive producers: Ted Griffin, John Hayes
Supervising producer: Jenny Carchman
Producers: Margaret Bodde, Graydon Carter, Fran Lebowitz, Martin Scorsese, Emma Tillinger Koskoff
Associate producers: Erin Edeiken, Chris Garrett

George Harrison: Living in the Material World
Executive producers: Margaret Bodde, Scott Pascucci, Emma Tillinger Koskoff
Supervising producer: Blair Foster
Consulting producer: Tia Lessin
Producers: Olivia Harrison, Martin Scorsese, Nigel Sinclair
Associate producers: Rachel Cooper, Erin Edeiken

Surviving Progress
(Big Picture Media Corporation/Cinémaginaire/National Film Board of Canada)
86 minutes
Directors: Harold Crooks, Mathieu Roy
Screenplay: Harold Crooks, Mathieu Roy
Cinematography: Mario Janelle
Executive producers: Mark Achbar, Silva Basmajian, Betsy Carson, Martin Scorsese, Emma Tillinger Koskoff
Producers: Gerry Flahive, Daniel Louis, Denise Robert
Associate producer: François Girard
First shown September 11, 2011 (Toronto International Film Festival)

Glickman
(Blind Date Productions/Sikelia Productions)
84 minutes
Director: James L. Freedman
Screenplay: James L. Freedman
Cinematography: Lon Magdich, Marc Miller, Zvonimir Vidusin

Executive producers: Martin Scorsese, Emma Tillinger Koskoff, Rick Yorn
Producer: James L. Freedman
Associate producers: Frank Laughlin, Stu Lisson, Keith Robinson
First broadcast August 26, 2013

Life Itself
(Film Rites/Kartemquin Films)
115 minutes
Director: Steve James
Cinematography: Dana Kupper
Executive producers: Mark Mitten, Justine Nagan, Gordon Quinn, Martin Scorsese, Kat White, Steven Zaillian
Producers: Garrett Basch, Steve James, Zak Piper
First shown January 19, 2014 (Sundance Film Festival, Utah)

The New York Review of Books: A 50 Year Argument
Executive producers: Anthony Wall, Kayo Washio
Producers: Margaret Bodde, Martin Scorsese, David Tedeschi

Before the Flood
(Appian Way, RatPac Documentary Films, Insurgent Docs, Mandarin Film Productions)
96 minutes
Director: Fisher Stevens
Written by: Mark Monroe
Cinematography: Antonio Rossi
Executive producers: Adam Bardach, Zara Duffy, Stanislas Graziani, Jennifer Hile, Mark Monroe, Martin Scorsese
Producers: Trevor Davidoski, Jennifer Davisson, Leonardo DiCaprio, James Packer, Brett Ratner, Fisher Stevens
Co-producers: Marie Therese Guirgis, Marco Krapels, Associate producers: Marjorie Crowley, Jeffrey Dye, Rachel Guest, Max Tromba
Consulting producers: Phillip Watson Henry Joost, Julie Nives, Ariel Schulman
Narrated by: Leonardo DiCaprio
Opened October 21, 2016

Long Strange Trip
(Double E Pictures, AOMA Sunshine Films, Sikelia Productions)
238 minutes
Director: Amir Bar-Lev
Executive producers: Bernie Cahill, Andrew Heller, Sanford Heller, Thomas J. Mangan IV, Alicia Sams, Martin Scorsese, Emma Tillinger Koskoff, Rick Yorn
Producers: Alex Blavatnik, Ken Dornstein, Eric Eisner, Nick Koskoff, Justin Kreutzmann
Co-producer: Ezekiel Morgan
Associate producers: Evan Lesser, Ross O'Connor, Austin Short
Supervising/archival producers: Jenny Carchman, Stuart Macphee, Jim McDonnell, Annie Salsich
Cast: Grateful Dead
Opened January 23, 2017

Once Were Brothers: Robbie Robertson and the Band
(Bell Media Studios, Imagine Documentaries, White Pine Pictures)
98 minutes
Director: Daniel Roher
Cinematography: Kiarash Sadigh
Executive producers: Sara Bernstein, Corrie Coe, Brian Grazer, Dave Harris, Ron Howard, Randy Lennox, Jared Levine, Michael Levine, Steve Ord, Peter Raymont, Jeffrey Remedios, Michael Rosenberg, Martin Scorsese, Randi Wilens, Justin Wilkes
Co-executive producers: Paul Crowder, Meredith Kaulfers, Mark Monroe
Producer: Andrew Munger, Lana Belle Mauro, Stephen Paniccia, Sam Sutherland
Archival producers: Andre Coutu, David Daniloff, Jessica Joy Wise, Larry Yelen
Opened September 5, 2019

Television series

The Blues
(TV documentary series with films directed by Martin Scorsese, Wim Wenders, Richard Pearce, Charles Burnett, Marc Levin, Mike Figgis, and Clint Eastwood)
(Road Movies Filmproduktion/Vulcan Productions)

Screenplays: Charles Burnett, Robert Gordon, Peter Guralnick, Wim Wenders
Cinematography: John L. Demps Jr., Barry Ackroyd, Mark Benjamin, Mike Eley, Richard Pearce
Series producer: Alex Gibney
Executive producers: Jody Allen, Paul G. Allen, Ulrich Felsberg, Martin Scorsese
Supervising producers: Mikaela Beardsley, Susan Motamed
Consulting producer: Lisa Day
Producers: Margaret Bodde, Robert Kenner, Samuel D. Pollard, Samson Mucke
Co-producers: Richard Hutton, Wesley Jones, Melissa Robledo
Associate producers: Salimah El-Amin, Agnes Chu, Belinda Clasen, Robert Gordon, Belinda Morrison, Jeff Scheftel
Line producer: Daphne McWilliams
First broadcast September 28, 2003

Boardwalk Empire
(HBO/Leverage Management/Closest to the Hole Productions/Sikelia Productions/Cold Front Productions)
TV series, each episode 60 minutes
Series directors: Timothy Van Patten, Allen Coulter, Jeremy Podeswa, Ed Bianchi, Brad Anderson, Alik Sakharov, Simon Cellan Jones, Brian Kirk, Martin Scorsese, Alan Taylor, David Petrarca, Susanna White, Kari Skogland, Jake Paltrow
Series writers: Nelson Johnson, Terence Winter, Howard Korder, Bathsheba Doran, Itamar Moses, Meg Jackson, Steve Kornacki, Lawrence Konner, David Flebotte, David Matthews, Margaret Nagle, Paul Simms, Timothy Van Patten, Diane Frolov, Chris Haddock, Rolin Jones, Andrew Schneider, David Stenn, Jennifer Ames, Cristine Chambers, Dennis Lehane, Eric Overmyer, Steve Turner
Executive producers: Stephen Levinson, Martin Scorsese, Timothy Van Patten, Mark Wahlberg, Terence Winter, Howard Korder
Co-executive producers: Gene Kelly, Diane Frolov, Chris Haddock, Andrew Schneider
Supervising producers: David Stenn, Margaret Nagle
Consulting producer: Dennis Lehane
Producers: David Coatsworth, Rick Yorn
Co-producers: Joseph E. Iberti, Steve Kornacki, Pepper O'Brien, Brad Carpenter
Associate producers: Jennifer Ames, Cristine Chambers, John Flavin, Emma Tillinger Koskoff
Line producers: Joseph E. Iberti, Dana J. Kuznetzkoff
Cast: Steve Buscemi, Kelly Macdonald, Michael Shannon, Shea Whigham, Michael Stuhlbarg
First episode broadcast September 19, 2010

AS ACTOR

For films that Scorsese directed or produced and acted in, only acting details are listed here.

Feature films

Who's That Knocking at My Door
Scorsese as Gangster (uncredited)

Boxcar Bertha
Scorsese as Brothel Client (uncredited)

Mean Streets
Scorsese as Jimmy Shorts (uncredited)

Taxi Driver
Scorsese as Passenger Watching Silhouette

Cannonball!
(Cross Country/Harbor Productions/New World Pictures/Shaw Brothers)
93 minutes
Director: Paul Bartel
Screenplay: Paul Bartel, Don Simpson
Cinematography: Tak Fujimoto
Scorsese as Mafioso
Opened July 6, 1976

Il pap'occhio
(Eidoscope S.r.l./Radiotelevisione Italiana)
110 minutes
Director: Renzo Arbore

Screenplay: Luciano De Crescenzo
Cinematography: Luciano Tovoli
Scorsese as TV Director
Opened September 19, 1980 (Italy)

Raging Bull
Scorsese as Barbizon Stagehand

The King of Comedy
Scorsese as TV Director

Pavlova: A Woman for All Time
(Poseidon Productions/Mosfilm/Sovinfilm/Cosmos Film/Deutsche Film/Instituto Cubano del Arte e Industrias Cinematográficos/Lenfilm Studio/Poseidon Film Distributors)
113 minutes
Director: Emil Loteanu
Screenplay: Emil Loteanu
Cinematography: Yevgeni Guslinsky, Vladimir Nakhabtsev
Scorsese as Gatti-Cassaza
Opened December 2, 1983 (Finland)

After Hours
Scorsese as Club Berlin Searchlight Operator (uncredited)

'Round Midnight
(Little Bear/PECF)
133 minutes
Director: Bertrand Tavernier
Screenplay: David Rayfiel, Bertrand Tavernier
Cinematography: Bruno de Keyzer
Scorsese as Goodley
Opened October 3, 1986

The Color of Money
Scorsese speaks opening voiceover (uncredited)

New York Stories
Segment "Life Lessons"
Scorsese as Man Having Picture Taken with Lionel Dobie (uncredited)

Dreams
(Warner Bros./Akira Kurosawa USA)
119 minutes
Director: Akira Kurosawa
Screenplay: Akira Kurosawa
Cinematography: Takao Saitô, Shôji Ueda
Scorsese as Vincent Van Gogh
Opened August 24, 1990

The Grifters
Scorsese speaks opening voiceover (uncredited)

Guilty by Suspicion
(Warner Bros.)
105 minutes
Director: Irwin Winkler
Screenplay: Irwin Winkler
Cinematography: Michael Ballhaus
Scorsese as Joe Lesser
Opened March 15, 1991

The Age of Innocence
Scorsese as Photographer (uncredited)

Quiz Show
(Baltimore Pictures/Hollywood Pictures/Wildwood Enterprises)
133 minutes
Director: Robert Redford
Screenplay: Paul Attanasio
Cinematography: Michael Ballhaus
Scorsese as Martin Rittenhome
Opened September 14, 1994

Search and Destroy
Scorsese as The Accountant

The Muse
(October Films)
97 minutes
Director: Albert Brooks
Screenplay: Albert Brooks, Monica Mcgowan Johnson

Cinematography: Thomas E. Ackerman
Scorsese as Himself
Opened August 27, 1999

Bringing Out the Dead
Scorsese as Dispatcher (voice)

Gangs of New York
Scorsese as Wealthy Homeowner (uncredited)

Shark Tale
(DreamWorks Animation/DreamWorks SKG/Pacific Data Images)
90 minutes
Directors: Bibo Bergeron, Vicky Jenson, Rob Letterman
Screenplay: Michael J. Wilson, Rob Letterman
Scorsese as voice of Sykes
Opened October 1, 2004

The Aviator
Scorsese as Hell's Angels Projectionist and voice of Man on Red Carpet (uncredited)

Hugo
Scorsese as Photographer (uncredited)

Television episodes

Curb Your Enthusiasm
Episode "The Special Section"
(HBO)
30 minutes
Director: Bryan Gordon
Screenplay: Larry David (uncredited)
Cinematography: Bill Sheehy
Scorsese as Himself
First broadcast October 20, 2002

Curb Your Enthusiasm
Episode "Krazee-Eyez Killa"
(HBO)
30 minutes
Director: Robert B. Weide
Screenplay: Larry David (uncredited)
Cinematography: Bill Sheehy
Scorsese as Himself
First broadcast November 3, 2002

Entourage
Episode "Return to Queens Blvd"
(HBO/Leverage Management)
30 minutes
Director: Mark Mylod
Screenplay: Doug Ellin, Ally Musika
Cinematography: Rob Sweeney
Scorsese as Himself
First broadcast November 23, 2008

30 Rock
Episode "Audition Day"
(Broadway Video/Little Stranger/Universal Media Studios)
30 minutes
Director: Beth McCarthy-Miller
Screenplay: Tina Fey, Matt Hubbard
Cinematography: Matthew Clark
Scorsese as Himself (voice)
First broadcast November 5, 2009

AS WRITER

See pages 279–284 for details of films that Scorsese wrote and directed/produced.

Feature films

Bezeten: Het gat in de muur
(Scorpio Film Productions)
90 minutes
Director: Pim de la Parra
Screenplay: Martin Scorsese, Wim Verstappen, Pim de la Parra
Cinematography: Frans Bromet, Hubertus Hagen
Cast: Alexandra Stewart, Dieter Geissler, Tom van Beek, Marijke Boonstra, Donald Jones
Opened August 15, 1969 (West Germany)

Select Bibliography

Books

Biskind, Peter. *Easy Riders, Raging Bulls*. New York: Simon & Schuster, 1998.

Brunette, Peter, ed. *Martin Scorsese: Interviews*. Jackson: University Press of Mississippi, 1999.

Christie, Ian., and David Thompson, eds. *Scorsese on Scorsese*. London: Faber & Faber, 2003.

Dougan, Andy. *Martin Scorsese Close-Up: The Making of His Movies*. London: Orion, 1997.

Ebert, Roger. *Scorsese by Ebert*. Chicago: University of Chicago Press, 2008.

Ehrenstein, David. *The Scorsese Picture: The Art and Life of Martin Scorsese*. New York: Birch Lane, 1992.

Farber, Manny. *Farber on Film*. New York: Library of America, 2009.

Friedman, Lawrence S. *The Cinema of Martin Scorsese*. Oxford: Roundhouse, 1997.

Kael, Pauline. *When the Lights Go Down: Complete Reviews 1975–1980*. New York: Henry Holt & Co., 1980.

Kael, Pauline. *Movie Love: Complete Reviews 1988–1991*. New York: Plume, 1991.

Kagan, Jeremy, ed. *Directors Close Up 2: Interviews with Directors Nominated for Best Film by the Directors Guild of America 2006–2012*. New York: Rowman & Littlefield, 2013.

Kelly, Mary Pat. *Martin Scorsese: A Journey*. Rev. ed. New York: Thunder's Mouth Press, 1996.

Lane, Anthony. *Nobody's Perfect*. New York: Pan Macmillan, 2003.

Said, Edward. *On Late Style*. New York: Vintage, 2007.

Sangster, Jim. *Scorsese*. London: Virgin, 2002.

Schickel, Richard. *Conversations with Scorsese*. New York: Alfred A. Knopf, 2011.

Stern, Lesley. *The Scorsese Connection*. Bloomington: Indiana University Press, 1995.

Thomson, David, ed. *The New Biographical Dictionary of Film*. Rev. ed. New York: Little, Brown, 2003.

Thomson, David. *"Have You Seen?": A Personal Introduction to 1,000 Films*. New York: Alfred Knopf, 2008.

Wilson, Michael Henry. *Scorsese on Scorsese*. Rev. ed. Paris: Cahiers du Cinéma, 2011.

Woods, Paul A., ed. *Scorsese: A Journey Through the American Psyche*. London: Plexus, 2005.

Features and interviews

Bennett, Tara. "Martin Scorsese, Leonardo DiCaprio, Ben Kingsley, and the *Shutter Island* Writers Descend into Darkness." www.fandango.com, February 17, 2010.

Billen, Andrew. "I Get the Church and the Movies Confused." *London Evening Standard*, March 25, 1998.

Biskind, Peter. "The Resurrection." *Independent on Sunday*, December 22, 1991.

Brown, Mick. "Martin Scorsese Interview for *Shutter Island*." *Telegraph*, March 7, 2010.

Calhoun, Dave. "Martin Scorsese Talks *Shutter Island*." *Time Out*, March 2010.

Christie, Ian. "Martin Scorsese's Testament." *Sight & Sound*, January 1996.

Daly, Steve. "*Casino's* Big Gamble." *Entertainment Weekly*, October 6, 1995.

Dougary, Ginny. "Original Sinner." *Times Magazine*, February 2, 1996.

Flatley, Guy. "Martin Scorsese's Gamble." *New York Times*, February 8, 1976.

Fleming, Mike. "Martin Scorsese on *Wolf of Wall Street*." *Deadline Hollywood*, January 6, 2014.

Foundas, Scott. "Andrew Garfield to Star in Martin Scorsese's *Silence*." *Variety*, May 7, 2013.

Galloway, Stephen. "Martin Scorsese, Leonardo DiCaprio Finally Open up About *Wolf of Wall Street*." *Hollywood Reporter*, December 4, 2013.

Gilbey, Ryan. "Blood, Sweat and Tears." *Guardian*, July 31, 2007.

Goldstein, Patrick. "Graham King on *Hugo's* Box-Office Woes: 'It's Been Painful." *Los Angeles Times*, February 6, 2012.

GQ staff. "Getting Made the Scorsese Way." *GQ*, October 2010.

Hardie, Giles. "Cinema Lovers Cinema." *Sydney Morning Herald*, June 24, 2012.

Hill, Logan. "Martin Scorsese, Leonardo DiCaprio, and Jonah Hill Discuss *The Wolf of Wall Street*." *Wall Street Journal*, October 13, 2013.

Hirschberg, Lynn. "Michael Ovitz Is on the Line." *New York Times*, May 9, 2009.

Hiscock, John. "Scorsese: This Is My Last Big Movie." *Telegraph*, December 10, 2004.

Hiscock, John. "The Day Mad Jack Drew a Gun on Set." *Telegraph*, September 22, 2006.

Hoberman, J. "Metaphysical Therapy." *Village Voice*, November 2, 1999.

Hodenfield, Chris. "A Personal Journey with Martin Scorsese through American Movies." *American Film*, March 1989.

Jagernauth, Kevin. "Martin Scorsese Says *Sinatra* Is 'Still Going Strong,' Explains Why He Thinks *Italianamerican* Is His Best Film." blogs.indiewire.com, December 4, 2013.

Kermode, Mark. "Martin Scorsese: '3D Is Liberating. Every Shot Is Rethinking Cinema.'" *Observer*, November 21, 2010.

Kiang, Jessica. "Marrakech Q&A ..." blogs.indiewire.com, December 9, 2013.

Lane, Anthony. "Not Fade Away: *Shine a Light*." *New Yorker*, April 14, 2008.

Leach, Jim. "The Art of Martin Scorsese." *Humanities*, July/August 2013.

Levy, Emanuel. "*Shutter Island*: Interview with Director Scorsese." Emanuel Levy Cinema 24/7 (www.emanuellevy.com), January 29, 2010.

Luck, Richard. "You Talkin' to Me? Scorsese, De Niro, Keitel, and Foster on the Making of *Taxi Driver*." *Sabotage Times*, October 19, 2013.

Lyman, Rick. "In Little Italy with Martin Scorsese." *New York Times*, February 13, 1998.

Macnab, Geoffrey. "I Was in a Bad Place." *Guardian*, July 6, 2006.

McAfee, Annalena. "No More Mr Nasty Guy." *Financial Times Weekend*, March 7–8, 1998.

McLean, Craig. "And We're Rolling." *Observer*, August 12, 2007.

Moline, Karen. "The Good Fella from New York's Mean Streets." *Sunday Times*, September 30, 1990.

Moyes, Jojo. "I've Been Lucky Not to Win an Oscar, Says Scorsese." *Independent*, June 28, 1997.

Murray, Rebecca. "Director Martin Scorsese Discusses *The Departed*." movies.about.com, September 30, 2006.

Nepales, Ruben V. "How Scorsese Avoided NC-17 Rating for *Wolf of Wall Street*." *Philippine Daily Inquirer*, December 14, 2013.

Palmer, Martin. "Back on the Streets." *Times Metro*, January 15–21, 2000.

Pond, Steve. "Martin Scorsese on *Wolf of Wall Street*: I Wanted It Big and Ferocious." *The Wrap*, December 23, 2013.

Pressburger, Angela. "The Making of *Kundun* 1." *Shambhala Sun*, January 1998.

Rafferty, Terence. "Talking Pictures." *DGA Quarterly*, Winter 2007/2008.

Rafferty, Terence. "Cue the Director's Adrenaline." *New York Times*, February 5, 2010.

Rapkin, Mickey. "A Conversation with Martin Scorsese." *Details*, April 6, 2012.

Salamon, Julie. "A Character with Phobias? Scorsese Can Relate." *New York Times*, December 16, 2004.

Schickel, Richard. "Brutal Attraction: The Making of *Raging Bull*." *Vanity Fair*, March 2010.

Schilling, Mary Kaye. "Leonardo DiCaprio and Martin Scorsese Explore the Funny Side of Depravity in *The Wolf of Wall Street*." www.vulture.com, August 26, 2013.

Scorsese, Martin. "The Persisting Vision: Reading the Language of Cinema." *New York Review of Books*, August 15, 2013.

Scorsese, Martin. "A Letter to My Daughter." *L'Espresso*, January 2, 2014.

Shelley, Jim. "Down these Mean Streets Many Men Have Gone." *Times Saturday Review*, February 20, 1993.

Smith, Gavin. "Martin Scorsese Interviewed." *Film Comment*, January/February 1998.

Taubin, Amy. "Dread and Desire." *Sight & Sound*, December 1993.

Tetzelli, Rick. "Martin Scorsese on Vision in Hollywood." *Fast Company Magazine*, December 2011.

Theroux, Paul. "The Sixth Beatle?" *Newsweek*, October 3, 2011.

Updike, John. "Late Works." *New Yorker*, August 7, 2006.

Williams, Alex. "Passion Play." *New York*, December 16, 2002.

Williams, Alex. "'Are We Ever Going to Make This Picture?'" *Guardian*, January 3, 2003.

Wise, Damon. "Martin Scorsese Exclusive *Uncut* Interview!" *Uncut*, April 2008.

Wolcott, James. "The Executioners." *Vanity Fair*, April 2002.

"Martin Scorsese Interviewed." http://www.industrycentral.net/director_interviews/MS01.HTM

"Martin Scorsese on *Shutter Island*." http://www.film4.com/special-features/interviews/martin-scorsese-on-shutter-island

"Scorsese and DiCaprio on Exploring *Shutter Island*." http://www.fearnet.com/news/interview/scorsese-and-dicaprio-exploring-'shutter-island

"Scorsese: Gangster Style." http://www.creativeplanetnetwork.com/dcp/news/exclusive-scorsese-gangster-style/15592

Picture Credits

Acknowledgments

Every effort has been made to trace and acknowledge the copyright holders. We apologize in advance for any unintentional omissions and would be pleased, if any such case should arise, to add appropriate acknowledgment in any future edition of the book.

T: top; B: bottom; L: left; R: right

Corbis: 1 (Lynn Goldsmith); 2 (Fabrice Dall'Anese/Tuxedo by Giorgio Armani/Corbis Outline); 6–7 (Columbia/Bureau L.A. Collection); 8 (Catherine Cabrol/Kipa); 14–15 (Didier Olivré); 17 (Ken Schles/Corbis Outline); 71, 74, 75, 82 L, 82–83, 84–85 (Columbia/Steve Schapiro); 88 R (Bettmann); 91, 107 (United Artists/Sunset Boulevard); 110 R (20th Century Fox/Steve Schapiro); 133 (Universal/Sunset Boulevard); 191 (Michael O'Neill/Corbis Outline); 255 (SWAP/Splash News); **Martin Scorsese Collection:** 20 L & R, 21, 22, 23 T & B, 24, 25, 27, 28, 29, 30 T & B (early photography); 10 (Columbia); 11, 13 (United Artists); 36–37, 37 R (Tri-Mod); 65 (Warner Bros.); 129 (Buena Vista); 238 T (Paramount); 267 (National Communications Foundation); **M. H. Wilson collection:** 90 (United Artists); 78 T (Columbia); **Photofest:** 12, 102, 106, 269 T (United Artists); 38, 52, 55, 58 T & B, 59, 60, 61, 67, 121, 266 R (Warner Bros.); 42 L (American International Pictures); 72 R, 73 R, 81 R, 162, 165 T (Columbia); 124 L, 124–125 (Buena Vista); 132 L, 174 L (Universal); 205 B (Miramax/Dimension Films/Mario Tursi); 236, 239 (Paramount); 268 (New Empire Films); **Alamy:** 16, 204, 200–201 (Miramax/AF Archive); 42 R (American International Pictures/United Archives/IFTN Cinema Collection); 49 L, 216 (Warner Bros./AF Archive); 50, 218–219 (Warner Bros./United Archives GmbH); 72 L (Columbia/AF Archive); 113 T (20th Century Fox/AF Archive); 123, 127 (Buena Vista/AF Archive); 136 (Universal/Pictorial Press); 138, 174 R (Universal/Moviestore Collection); 141 (Warner Bros./Pictorial Press); 157, 159 (Universal/AF Archive); 183 L (Buena Vista/Pictorial Press); 190 R (Touchstone/Paramount/Phillip V. Caruso/United Archives GmbH/IFTN Cinema Collection); 217 (Warner Bros./Moviestore Collection); 225 B (Warner Bros./Andrew Cooper/AF Archive); © **Ferdinando Scianna/Magnum Photos:** Front cover, 18–19; **Getty Images:** 31 (Elliot Landy); 46–47, 48 (Jack Manning/New York Times Co.); 100–101 (United Artists/Brian Hamill); 114–115 (Olivia Morris); 120 B (Ron Galella); 186 B (Matt Campbell/Hulton Archive); 256 T (Bobby Bank/Wire Image); 269 B (AFP); 276–277 (Jeff Vespa/Wire Image); 278 (Kevin Winter); **Photo12.com:** 34–35, 36, 39 (Tri-Mod/Archives du 7e Art); 64 L, 116 L, 145 T, 213, 215 B (Warner Bros./Archives du 7e Art); 98 R (United Artists/Collection Cinéma); 110 L (20th Century Fox/Archives du 7e Art); 113 B (20th Century Fox/Collection Cinéma); 137 (Universal/Archives du 7e Art); 175 (Universal/Collection Cinéma); 225 T (Warner Bros./Andrew Cooper/Archives du 7e Art); 234 (Paramount/Archives du 7e Art); 242–243, 244 R, 245, 246, 246 T & B, 247, 248, 249, 250, 251 (GK Films/Archives du 7e Art); **Ronald Grant:** 40–41, 45 T (American International Pictures); 63, 211 (Warner Bros.); 116 R (Geffen Company); 132 R, 173 T; 155, 158 L (Amblin Entertainment/Cappa Films/Tribeca Productions/Universal); 186 T (Touchstone/Capra/De Fina/Mario Tursi); 266 L (Wadleigh-Maurice); **Rex Features:** 43 R (Universal/Everett); 64 R, 143, 144, 148, 210–211, 212 (Warner Bros./Everett); 73 L (Columbia/Everett); 88 L (United Artists/Everett); 190 L (Paramount/Everett); 205 T (Miramax/Dimension Films/Everett); **mptvimages.com:** 43 L & 44–45 (American International Pictures); 76–77, 79 (Columbia/Steve Schapiro); 86–87, 96–97, 99, 105 (United Artists);

92–93, 95 (United Artists/Photo by Bruce McBroom); 170–171, 173 B, 176 (Universal); **The Kobal Collection:** 45 B (American International Pictures); 49 R, 51, 53, 56–57 (Taplin-Perry-Scorsese); 69 B, 117, 118, 119, 120 T, 142, 146, 149, 151, 208–209, 214, 215 T, 219 (Warner Bros.); 80 L, 80–81 (Columbia); 92 L, 98 L, 104 (United Artists); 112 (20th Century Fox); 126 (Touchstone); 154 L, 156, 170 T, 177 B (Universal); 162–163, 165 B (Columbia/Phillip V. Caruso); 180, 182 (Touchstone/Capra/De Fina); 195 (Touchstone/Paramount/Phillip V. Caruso); 198 (Miramax/Dimension Films); 220–221, 222 L, 222 R, 226 L, 226–227, 229 (Warner Bros./Andrew Cooper); 232–233, 235, 237, 238 B (Paramount); 240–241, 244 L (GK Films); 252–253, 254, 256 B, 256–257, 258–259, 261 T & B, 262 T & B, 263 (Red Granite Pictures); 265, 272 (Concert Promotions International/Brigitte Lacombe); **British Film Institute Stills, Posters and Designs, London:** 54, 66, 68 (Warner Bros.); 111 (20th Century Fox); 125 (Buena Vista); 134 B, 170 B (Universal); 192 B, 194 (Touchstone/Paramount/Phillip V. Caruso); **akg-images:** 69 T (Warner Bros./Mondadori Portfolio); 223 (Warner Bros./Album); **Photoshot:** 78 B (Columbia/LFI); 94 (United Artists); 128 (Buena Vista); 135, 154–155, 168–169 (Universal/LFI); 147 (Warner Bros./CBS); 183 R (Touchstone/Capra/De Fina/Mario Tursi); 188–189, 193 (Touchstone/Paramount); 273 (HBO/Retna); **Globe Photos, Inc.:** 89; **S. Karin Epstein:** 109 (20th Century Fox); © **Mario Tursi Photo:** 131, 134 T, 138–139 (Universal); 178–179, 181, 184–185, 187 (Touchstone/Capra/De Fina); 196–197, 199, 202–203, 206, 207 (Miramax/Dimension Films); © **David Leonard:** 145 B (Warner Bros.); **Mary Evans Picture Library:** 150 (Warner Bros./Rue des Archives/RDA); **Phillip V. Caruso:** 152, 158 R, 177 T (Universal); 160–161, 163 R, 164, 166, 167 (Columbia); 192 T (Touchstone/Paramount); **Warner Bros/Andrew Cooper:** 228, 230 L, 230–231, 231 R; © **Barry Feinstein Photography, Inc.:** 270–271; **Michael Grecco/michaelgrecco.com:** 275; © **Patrick Swirc/modds:** 288. **Alamy:** 266, 270l (AI-Film/Cappa Defina Prod/Cecchi Gori Pictures/SharpSword Films/Sikelia Prod/Waypoint Ent); 292 (Astrid Stawiarz/Netflix); 274l (BFA); 267, 269r, 270r (Kerry Brown/Paramount Pictures/Everett Collection); 277 (Netflix/Landmark Media); 278, 279lb, 279r (Netflix/TCD/Prod.DB); 275, 276, 279lt (Niko Tavernise/Netflix/TCD/Prod.DB); 268t, 269l (Paramount Pictures/Entertainment Pictures/ZumaPress); 268b, 271 (Paramount Pictures/Moviestore Collection); 272 (STX Entertainment/Album); 264 (TCD/Prod.DB)

We would like to give special thanks to Marianne Bower, archivist at Sikelia Productions, for her help in sourcing images from Mr. Scorsese's archive.

First and foremost, I'd like to thank Martin Scorsese, who has been very generous with his time over the years and whose office was so helpful in the compilation of material for this book. I also owe a huge debt to Richard Schickel, who has written many superb things about the director over the years, including his book *Conversations with Scorsese*, and whose advice I sought out as soon as I started researching this book. Other works I found useful include *Scorsese on Scorsese* by Michael Henry Wilson, *Easy Riders, Raging Bulls* by Peter Biskind, *Scorsese on Scorsese* ed. by Ian Christie and David Thompson, and *Martin Scorsese: Interviews* ed. by Peter Brunette. Finally, I'd like to thank my wife, Kate, without whom very little of worth in my life would be possible.

Tom Shone

Palazzo Editions thanks Chloe Pew Latter for compiling the filmography and Matthew Coniam for sourcing of quotes.

Overleaf: Portrait by Patrick Swirc, 2005.

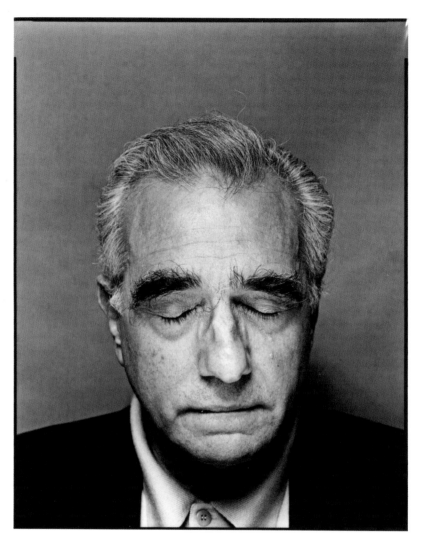

"Look, let's face it, the cinema—the classical cinema—is gone.
It's over. The cinema as we know it, up to now, is disappearing."